THE

PUBLICATIONS

OF THE

Lincoln Record Society

FOUNDED IN THE YEAR

1910

VOLUME 70

FOR THE YEAR ENDING 31st AUGUST 1975

Rowland Winn, 1st Lord St. Oswald

Letters and Papers
concerning the establishment of the
Trent, Ancholme and Grimsby Railway, 1860—1862

EDITED BY

FRANK HENTHORN, PH.D.

PRINTED FOR
THE LINCOLN RECORD SOCIETY
BY
J. W. RUDDOCK & SONS LIMITED, LINCOLN
1975

First published 1975
Unaltered reprint 2005

ISBN 0 901503 73 8

A Lincoln Record Society Publication
Published by The Boydell Press
an imprint of Boydell & Brewer Ltd
PO Box 9, Woodbridge, Suffolk IP12 3DF, UK
and of Boydell & Brewer Inc.
668 Mt. Hope Avenue, Rochester, NY 14620, USA
web site: www.boydellandbrewer.com

A catalogue record for this book is available
from the British Library

The first edition of this volume was produced
with the assistance of grants from
The British Academy
Lincolnshire and Humberside Arts
and
the former Council of
the borough of Scunthorpe

The blocks for the illustrations have been provided by
Dr Henthorn

This publication is printed on acid-free paper

Printed in Great Britain by
Antony Rowe Ltd, Eastbourne

PREFACE AND ACKNOWLEDGEMENTS

Transcripts of Crown-Copyright Records in the Public Record Office appear by permission of the Controller of Her Majesty's Stationery Office. Permission to quote from the documents in their care has also kindly been granted by the Public Record Office (B.T.H.R.), the House of Lords Record Office, the Sheffield Central Library and the Scunthorpe Museum. My thanks are due to the staffs of these institutions, of the Cusworth Hall Museum, Doncaster and of the Mayor of Scunthorpe for the research facilities they have provided. I am especially grateful to Mr. H. S. Cobb of the House of Lords Record Office and the Librarian of the Guildhall, City of London, for information provided by them; from the staff of the Lincolnshire Archives I have received much kindness over a number of years.

I must acknowledge also the kindness of Lord St. Oswald in providing a portrait of the first Lord St. Oswald, and Mr George Dow, the Scunthorpe Museum and Art Gallery, and the Scunthorpe Area Library (Humberside C.C. Leisure Services Dept.), who allowed me to reproduce photographs and maps in their own collections. I must thank Mr. Dow too for his helpful advice.

Acknowledgement must also be made of some help given by the Lincolnshire Association (now the Lincolnshire and Humberside Arts) and of a generous grant by the Leverhulme Trust for research for this volume.

Finally I must express my gratitude to Dr. Kathleen Major for her help and encouragement.

F.H.

CONTENTS

ILLUSTRATIONS

All these illustrations follow p. lv.

ABBREVIATIONS

B.R. & Co.	Baxter, Rose & Co.
C.J.	*Commons Journals*
C. W.	Charles Winn
D. & Co.	Dyson & Co.
G.D.	George Dawes
Herepath	*Herepath's Railway Journal*
H.L.R.O.	House of Lords Record Office
J.H.	John Hett
J.R.	John Roseby
J.W.L.	J. W. Lancaster
L.A.O.	Lincolnshire Archives Office
Lith. & G.P.O.	Lithographic & General Printing Offices
L.J.	*Lords Journals*
L.R.S.M.	*Lincoln, Rutland & Stamford Mercury*
M. & E. Ironworks ..	Milton & Elsecar Ironworks
M.S.L.	Manchester, Sheffield & Lincolnshire Railway
N.H.F.	Nicholson, Hett, & Freer
O.H..	Old Hummums
P.R.O.	Public Record Office (except on p. xl)
P.R.O. (B.T.H.R.).. ..	Public Record Office (British Transport Historical Records)
R.W.	Rowland Winn
S.Y.	South Yorkshire Railway
S.Y. (K.E.)	South Yorkshire Railway (Keadby Extension)
T.A.G.	Trent, Ancholme & Grimsby Railway
T.C.	Thomas Coates
T.F.	Thomas Freer

INTRODUCTION

It was remarked by G. R. Walshaw and C. A. J. Behrendt[1] and by Harold Dudley[2] that the existence of iron in the Scunthorpe area was known and exploited in prehistoric times, but it was not until 1859 that it came to modern notice. In that year, according to Edward Watkin, speaking at a luncheon ("an elegant champagne lunch in the beautiful Town-hall of Grimsby") on 14th May 1864, Mr. Rowland Winn and his brother "observed it as they were shooting in the district", though no one had suspected its presence until then.[3] The discovery was to make a considerable difference to the appearance and life of the district.

The main line railways of the early period had been created in response to a commercial and industrial demand. In rural areas railways were sometimes spoken of as landowner railways, built to suit the convenience of landowners and their tenants along the chosen routes. The railway which was to spring up through the newly-discovered ironfield was to be both an industrial line and one to suit the needs of a landowner. The landowner was Rowland Winn of Appleby, and his tenants were not farmers but ironmasters—principally W. H. & G. Dawes.

Until the re-discovery of iron in North Lincolnshire was made, little hope of new railway building there could be sustained. The truth of this was shown by the failure of two schemes in the 1850s —the one for a Barton, Blyton, and Gainsborough line[4], and the other for a North Lincolnshire railway[5]. Both projected lines would have cut through Frodingham. But both schemes were dropped despite the support of local landowners and even of the M.S.L. Railway.[6] It is true that the 1850s were a bad time for promoters of railways,[7] partly because of the reaction after the excesses of the railway speculators of the '40s, partly because of the competition afforded by new outlets for capital.[8] Nevertheless it proved possible for the new Scunthorpe ironfield railway to be promoted at the end of the '50s and for the line to be in operation by the middle '60s.

[1] *History of Appleby Frodingham* (1950), p. 6.

[2] *Early Days in North-West Lincolnshire* (1949), p. 8.

[3] *L.R.S.M.*, 20 May 1864, a good, but not the whole, story.

[4] L. A. O. Stubbs 7/31.

[5] Advertised in the *Hull Advertiser*, 20 Dec. 1856, as "the South Yorkshire and North Lincolnshire Junction Railway Company".

[6] L. A. O. Stubbs 7/31.

[7] It should be added, though, that, as George Dow's *Great Central* (1959) I, p. 262 points out, the early 1860s were also a bad time for railway building because of the American Civil War. *Herepath's Railway Journal* for 1861, p. 711, states, after reporting the passing of the Acts for the T.A.G. and S.Y. railways, that "unfortunate disputes in the [U.S.A.] have led to a great stagnation of trade and corresponding loss of revenue" to the M.S.L. company.

[8] See M. C. Reed, *Railways in the Victorian Economy* (1969), p. 215.

Yet it cannot have been iron alone which ensured success for the railway scheme. Scunthorpe was only one tiny village in a wide area containing ironstone, and the landowners in other nearby places where there already existed a railway were confident for a while that a development of railways and industry was bound to come. A correspondent in the *L.R.S.M.*[1], writing from Kirton Lindsey[2], spoke of an important impetus now to be added to Kirton's trade "in the wonderful and extensive business of mining. On the estate of T. M. Richardson, Esq., a most wonderful bed of the richest iron ore has been discovered, which will yield many hundreds a year to that gentleman, and which will further enhance the value of his lands by the necessity for building numerous cottages for the miners who are to be introduced by the lessees, Messrs. Roseby and Oxley, men qualified in every respect to carry out the operations of mining, and who have already made every arrangement for carrying on the works on a most extensive scale, commensurate with the facilities afforded them by the [M.S.L.] Company, who, unfortunately for the 'body of shareholders', do not meet the lessees with that spirit of energy calculated to ensure a large dividend. Surely in this instance, however, they will not be blind to their own interests, but will give every assistance . . . to carry out the arrangements of the lessees without extortion. Then will Kirton in a few years rival not only the humble towns of Brigg and Gainsboro', but perhaps Birmingham."

A few weeks later[3] a paragraph concerning Kirton appeared, remarking on the "very surprising rumours . . . being circulated in regard to the Lindsey iron works speedily to be established at this place". The writer was cautious but thought work would soon be provided there for 500 workers—"a boon to Kirton, notoriously desolate, dreary, and dead". And despite the efforts of a more knowledgeable correspondent[4] to moderate the swelling transports of delight, it was reported[5] that work at the ironstone mines of Kirton had begun "in good earnest". It was admitted that the lack of sidings was a drawback, but that was said to be partly owing to the weather; confidence still abounded: "at 'Clay-lane' bridge (over the railway) the embankment has been cut on each side, the embrasure disclosing under a surface of about 2 feet very valuable beds of the mineral, in thickness about 5 feet, and extending, it is believed, several miles. At this spot too, other operations are going on with a view to the discovery of coal, which it is confidently stated will soon be found".[6] Even though by the summer it was clear that the iron-

[1] 11 Nov. 1859.

[2] The M.S.L. Railway from Retford to Grimsby and New Holland ran through Kirton Lindsey.

[3] *L.R.S.M.*, 9 Dec. 1859.

[4] *L.R.S.M.*, 16 Dec. 1859.

[5] *L.R.S.M.*, 20 Jan. 1860.

[6] *L.R.S.M.*, 17 Feb. 1860

stone enterprise "was not so briskly followed up [at Kirton] as was expected", hopes endured as new ground had been opened[1]. They had not died three years later[2], when it was stated that the ironstone operations there were "steadily progressing, to the satisfaction, we understand, of the company". But by 1864 defeat had been conceded[3]: ironstone had now become "ironstone speculation", and the works were "permanently closed"; "these diggings, it appears, will not pay". Kirton was not fated to steal the future from Scunthorpe.

If Kirton, already provided with a railway, could not build an iron industry, what hopes had places like Caistor, long feeling itself deprived of a line, and the long railway-less gap between Keadby and Lincoln? Each had iron and each had hopes for a bright future. At Caistor it was jubilantly reported[4] that "our indefatigable townsman, Mr. J. T. Chant", had explored the surrounding countryside, testing "the iron ore found there both chemically and magnetically"; more, he had also discovered the essential limestone. It was, however, not enough to enable Caistor to get either a railway or an industry, in spite of the representations made by Mr. Owston of Brigg to the M.S.L. Directors.[5] The other area where it was proposed to build a line was "along the foot of an escarpment of the Oolites extending northwards from Lincoln to one mile north of Kirton when it crosses the lias to the terminus at Althorpe".[6] It was shown that ironstone was to be found at Burton, North and South Carlton, Brattleby, Cammeringham, Fillingham, Blyborough, Cleatham and northward to the existing railway. Important landowners, including the Earl of Scarborough, Sir Thomas Whichcote, Sir Digby Cayley, Mr. Luard, were concerned.[7] With influential backing it was possible to get an Act of Parliament authorizing construction of the Althorpe to Lincoln Railway in July 1865. It seemed as if the possession of iron and adequately strong support from the local landowners sufficed to ensure the creation of a railway and an industry. But what had really been decisive was the backing given by the M.S.L. Railway. A power struggle was going on (one is tempted to add, as usual at that time) in the railway world, involving the Great Eastern, the Lancashire and Yorkshire, and the M.S.L. railways[8]. The 1865 Act helped Watkin of the M.S.L. win his battle. Once that had been achieved, the new railway scheme simply faded away, and the Act was repealed in 1868 as a result of joint action by the Great Northern and M.S.L. railways.

Clearly at least three factors were needed to produce a railway

[1] *L.R.S.M.*, 13 July 1860.
[2] *L.R.S.M.*, 19 June 1863.
[3] *L.R.S.M.*, 26 Feb. 1864.
[4] *L.R.S.M.*, 22 June 1860. Mr. Chant was described a few weeks later as "chemist of this place [Caistor]."
[5] P.R.O. (B.T.H.R.) MSL/1/5 (28 Sept. 1860).
[6] L. A. O. Stubbs 7/37/1.
[7] L. A. O. Stubbs 7/37/50. Lord Monson's name should be added to the list.
[8] See Dow, *op. cit.* II, pp. 7, 11 and 12.

running through a newly discovered ironfield. Support from landowners in the area was vital; hardly less important was an established firm of iron-masters; and, perhaps most essential of all, there must be either goodwill from neighbouring railways, or at least an absence of enmity. Rowland Winn and Scunthorpe were fortunate in being able to enlist the help of the M.S.L. and the S.Y. railways.

Although the M.S.L. Railway had been reproached for its lack of vigour in helping to establish an infant iron industry at Kirton, the Directors were alive to the importance of developments in the north of Lincolnshire. They refused to build a branch line to Caistor in September 1860, but the following month (12 October) they reviewed a report by John Hedley on the ironstone deposits in North Lincolnshire.[1] This report was enthusiastic about the possibilities. It began by stating that there were three beds of ore there: an upper bed "too lean in iron" to be worked; a second, or Kirton bed, about four feet thick; and a lower bed at Scunthorpe eight to nine feet thick and about forty yards below the Kirton bed. The Kirton bed would yield 400,000 to 500,000 tons of ore, but, when the outcrop was worked out, the ore would have to be got by mining, which would add 2s. 6d. per ton to the cost of production; and "extensive outcrops of the lower bed will exclude from the market the ore that requires mining at Kirton". Although this Kirton bed was "unlimited, as it exists under many square miles of Country to the east and north of Kirton", Mr. Hedley had the opinion of several ironmasters that, with a high percentage of "silicious matter", only 22% or 23% of inferior iron would be yielded. "I do not think there will be a demand for this ore." One senses that it was at this moment that Kirton's future was decided.

The lower, or third, bed, however, was a different matter: it lay under Rowland Winn's property about eight miles north of Kirton station, and there were to be found easily worked deposits from which would come about 5,000,000 tons of good ore. The open work or outcrop exhausted, there would still remain ten square miles where ore could be obtained at a depth of fifty yards from the surface; and at the depth of 100 yards, over ten square miles "there is an unlimited supply of this bed". From this (Scunthorpe) area the yield of iron would be 35%. There would be a demand for Scunthorpe iron ore in South Staffordshire, Derbyshire, Shropshire, and North Staffordshire, owing to a scarcity of mining labourers in these areas. Furthermore, both South Wales and South Staffordshire had to import a considerable proportion of the ironstone they used. Ore could be obtained from Northamptonshire, but it could not be delivered in South Staffordshire for less than 13s. to 14s. per ton. When a branch line was laid to Scunthorpe, Lincolnshire ore could be delivered in South Staffordshire at 11s. per ton. A market could be expected in Manchester, at that time drawing a part of its sup-

[1] P.R.O. (B.T.H.R.) MSL/1/5.

plies of iron from Derbyshire. As "native ironstones" of Derbyshire cost 9s. to 11s. per ton, and yielded only about 33% of iron, Lincolnshire would have a clear advantage with the cost at 8s. per ton and a 35% yield. Mr. Hedley does not appear to have foreseen much iron manufacture in North Lincolnshire because he thought the iron made from Lincolnshire ore alone "would not suit the general market", although he knew Dawes contemplated "erecting Furnaces on the banks of the Trent". However, he was also aware that Dawes was investigating "some Shireoaks Ironstone" which seemed likely to be cheap and of excellent quality. Taking all these things together, the M.S.L. Directors must have felt that they were on to a good thing. They lost no time in deciding to come to an agreement with Rowland Winn.[1] But they would naturally drive a bargain.

The agreement would not have been made but for Winn's enterprise. It is certainly true[2] that the railway would have been made anyhow, but it might have taken a little longer. It was Rowland Winn[3] who produced the drive and business sense. His father, Charles Winn, lived at Nostell Priory, near Wakefield, and appears not at this time to have taken much interest in North Lincolnshire developments, though, as a landowner he was, of course, concerned[4]. In Rowland Winn's correspondence in the course of obtaining the Act of Parliament for the railway, it is clear that his father wished to

[1] P.R.O. (B.T.H.R.) MSL/1/5 (9 Nov. 1860).

[2] See John Parker's evidence before the Commons Select Committee on Private Bills (H.L.R.O. Commons Evidence 1861, S.Y. (K.E.) Railway, Vol. 72, S8, 22 April, p. 8).

[3] Rowland Winn, born 1820, died 1893, was the eldest son of Charles Winn of Nostell Priory. (C. W. d. 1874 aged 79). Charles Winn was the nephew of Sir Rowland Winn, 6th baronet; his brother and he successively inherited Sir Rowland's estates at Nostell, when Sir Rowland died in 1805. The two brothers—John and Charles Williamson—changed their surname to Winn on inheritance. The Winn family had a long connection with Lincolnshire. Edmund Winn (born 1583) was "of Thornton Curteis"; his grandsons and a great-grandson all married Pelhams of Brocklesby. (Burke's *Peerage* (1956), pp. 1074, 1928, 1929). Abraham de la Pryme's Diary (Surtees Society, Vol. 54, pp. 124-5) gives no enthusiastic picture of the Winn family. After recording that George Winn had bought Appleby from Stephen Anderson of Manby, he goes on to say: "George Win, in King James the First's days, was but a country gentleman, but reckon'd very rich by the gripeing methods that he used . . . The next of the name was Edmund Win, who was knighted . . . (or pretended to be so). He marryed to his second wife his maid servant, who was the daughter of one Jackson, a baker in Gainsbur . . . His first son, Sr Rowland . . . owns Appleby . . . and Nostell . . . He is a mighty mad, proud, spark, exceeding gripeing and penurious, and a great oppressour of the poor".

[4] John Bateman, *The Great Landowners of Great Britain and Ireland* (1883) shows Rowland Winn (he having succeeded his father at Nostell and Appleby by that time) as having 5,522 acres in Lincolnshire, and 2,461 acres in Yorkshire. He was thus one of the larger landowners of North Lincolnshire. The holdings of other landowners there are given as follows: Lord Yarborough 56,795 acres in Lincolnshire; Sir John Astley (inheriting through his wife T. G. Corbett's Elsham estate) 10,000 acres; V. D. H. Cary Elwes 9,171 acres; Sir Robert Sheffield 9,370 acres; R. N. Sutton Nelthorpe 7,263 acres; Miss Boucherett (of Willingham) 5,826 acres; G. B. Shipworth (of Moortown) 5,300 acres; the Duke of St. Albans 5,255 acres; M. H. Dalison (of Greetwell Hall) 3,800 acres; H. J. Hope Barton (of Saxby), 3,404 acres; R. J. H. Parkinson (of Ravendale) 2,500 acres; Sir Charles H. J. Anderson (of Lea Hall) 2,153 acres. Earl Beauchamp had only 2,878 acres in Lincolnshire.

avoid any personal involvement (9/1/42; 9/1/53; 9/1/57; 9/1/127). Charles Winn could not keep altogether clear of the affair because the property at Frodingham and near the Trent was in his name (9/1/48).

Rowland Winn, however, lived at Appleby Hall; he was awake to the possibilities opening up in the middle of the century, and, as a youngish, vigorous man, well able to take a leading part in them. He had been active in the attempt to promote the Barton, Blyton, and Gainsborough Railway. Both he and his father were named as Directors on the prospectus issued in that year, but it was Rowland Winn who showed the interest and willingness to work for success,[1] In the Memorandum of Association Charles Winn was down for 100 £20 shares, and Rowland Winn for 80. Only Lord Yarborough, with 200 shares, was investing more deeply in the concern[2]. There does not seem much doubt that Charles Winn's proposed investment was to be on the advice of his son who was living at Appleby then (his letters in 1856 were written from Appleby). At this stage of his life he was apparently driven more by commercial than by political ambition; certainly in his correspondence over the arrangements with Dawes, 1860-61, he showed a marked business sense (9/1/76). Even later he retained a personal interest in the iron-working on his estates, as the papers in the Scunthorpe Museum (Normanby Hall) reveal[3]. By 1868 he had become Member of Parliament for North Lincolnshire, and he became a Lord of the Treasury in Disraeli's 1874-80 administration[4]; after he became Lord St. Oswald in 1885, presumably he took a less active part in politics and could once more devote his time to his estates and iron. But in 1858 he was free to give all his attention to business and the idea of industrial development. He made contact with the Dawes brothers, who, as an experienced firm of iron-masters, represented the third of the essential factors.

George Dawes—"Mr. Dawes, from Staffordshire"[5]—had in 1850 been about to become Earl Fitzwilliam's tenant at the Milton Iron-

[1] L. A. O. Stubbs 7/32/1; 7/32/9; 7/32/12; 7/32/27; 7/32/29; 7/32/33.

[2] L. A. O. Stubbs 7/32/38. Lord Yarborough (succeeded 1846, died 1862) was also interested in iron ore mining. James Tolson White told the Commons Committee in 1861 that he was a mineral engineer and agent to Lord Yarborough, who, he said, had leased land for iron working. (H.L.R.O. Commons Minutes of Evidence 1861, S.Y. (K.E.) Railway, Vol. 72 S8, 22 April, p. 75.)

[3] See St. Oswald Papers, packet 12.

[4] He claimed in 1879 that he had not found his parliamentary duties uncomfortably onerous as a mere M.P.; but since he had taken office he had to work 14 hours a day (presumably on official business) for four days in the week. (*L.R.S.M.*, 31 Oct. 1879).

[5] A. K. Clayton, *The Story of the Elsecar and the Milton Iron Works from the opening until the year* 1848 Cusworth Hall Museum Publication No. 9 (1973), p. 52. A letter from Mary G. Dawes, 18 April 1924, to G. R. Walshaw, stated that her father, W. H. Dawes, George's brother, "was known as the 'gentleman Ironmaster' and was not asked to sign any document buying thousands of tons of coke, etc., as he always kept his word, and gave thousands away anonymously to Hospitals, etc." (Scunthorpe Museum, file of letters, notes, and cuttings relating to local railways).

works; these works, together with the Elsecar works[1] about one mile away, had been operated by Henry Hartop from 1821 to 1829, and by William and Robert Graham from 1829 to 1848; times were bad then and the Milton works appear to have been closed down from 1848 to 1851. George Dawes seems to have taken up residence at Skiers Spring Lodge in 1850 and to have opened the works in 1851. If he came from John Dawes and Sons in Staffordshire, he came from a first-class iron-making background. Even in the bad years, 1841 and 1842, the Dawes firm was making comparatively large quantities of iron: in the first six months of 1841[2] they made 3,500 tons, and 3,560 tons from two furnaces in the first six months of 1842. In the first six months of 1842, Yorkshire produced only 23,471 tons from thirty-one furnaces. George Dawes came to Lincolnshire, however, not to set up a new works but simply to obtain cheap ore and limestone.[3] But whether ironstone or iron was to be produced, a railway was necessary to carry the output away. The Dawes firm[4] wanted it carried to their works at Milton and Elsecar. Rowland Winn agreed to provide the land, Dawes the labour and the means of working (7/36). Rowland Winn stated that on 22 April 1861[5] he had leased about 900 acres to the Dawes firm, and about 100 to Samuel Beale & Co. of Parkgate Works. There seems to be some doubt about the accuracy of the second figure, as Beale, speaking before the same committee on the same day,[6] said he had taken land from the Winns, though not the 500 acres which Denison suggested in his examination of Beale before the committee: "It is not quite so large as that" was Beale's remark.

A notice appeared in June 1860[7]: "To Railway Contractors . . . W. H. & G. Dawes . . . will be glad to receive tenders for constructing a portion of the intended railway, from the Trent Side, nearly opposite the Terminus of the [S.Y.] Railway at Keadby, to a certain point on the Scunthorpe Flat . . . upon the estate of Charles Winn Esq. . . . the length being about 4¼ Miles. Plans and Specifications of the Works may be seen on or after the 18th day of June, 1860, and every necessary information may be obtained at the Offices of

[1] Described (L. A. O. Stubbs 9/4 Addresses of distant owners) as "near Barnsley"; said by James Henderson ("Notes on the Early History of the Iron Making Industry of North Lincolnshire" in "Proceedings of the Lincolnshire Iron and Steel Institute", I, p. 121) to be near Rotherham; and asserted by Clayton (*op. cit.*) to be in Hoyland.

[2] Clayton, *op. cit.*, p. 64.

[3] Walshaw and Behrendt, *op, cit.*, p. 36.

[4] The firm was W. H. & G. Dawes (of what was later known as the Trent Iron Works); but it appears that George Dawes alone was taking an active part in Lincolnshire by 1860: see 9/1/47, 50, 55). W. H. Dawes writes from "Mosely Hall" (9/1/59). Samuel Beale & Co. too had a lease from Rowland Winn, allowing them to mine ore, but their intention was to mine ore only for their own use at the Parkgate Ironworks (P.R.O. (B.T.H.R.) MSL/1/5).

[5] H.L.R.O. Commons Minutes of Evidence 1861, S.Y. (K.E.) Railway, Vol 72, S8, 22 April, pp. 25-6.

[6] *Ibid.*, pp. 67-9.

[7] *L.R.S.M.*, 8 and 15 June 1860.

Mr. John Roseby,[1] Mining Engineer, Brigg . . . " The notice added that Roseby would attend "at the house of Mr. Bowskin of Burringham Ferry" at 10 a.m. on the 21 June to give information. The line that was to be constructed was to be completed from the Ancholme to the "Roman road" by summer, 1860 (9/1/76); the line sufficed to carry ore from the workings to the Trent, where it was loaded into barges at a wharf.[2]

The rails may have been laid from Frodingham to the river Trent by the autumn of 1860. Mr. A. Woodley stated[3] that his father accepted a situation with George Dawes in October 1860. His job was to "take charge of the two tank Locos" at the Trent Iron Works "then being built at Manning Wardle & Co., Leeds". From October 1860 the ore was "carted to the top of the hill and filled into wagons run down on the railway by rope to the bottom and then by Loco to boats for Elsecar at Gunness Wharf". Then in December of the same year "the other Loco arrived and was put to work at the top to work the stone from the Mine instead of carting it to the hill". G. R. Walshaw, however,[4] asserted that the stone—first dug in the field near Dawes Lane and "the present station yard"—was carted "across the Mill Field in Scunthorpe, through Old Frodingham to the top of the hill in Brumby Wood Lane. From there it was taken by small trucks and a wire rope down the hill" to the river "by means of small tubs on rails drawn by a rope, the full tubs running down the hill drawing up the empty ones". And he added a note "from Mr. Outram": "First load . . . [was] carted to a wharf on the Trent near Flixboro' on the 21st June 1860" and then to Elsecar. "For six years [the note continued] the Ironstone . . . was . . . conveyed by a Gin road (an endless rope) to the Trent until 1866 when the river was bridged". This assertion cannot be true of the whole period mentioned in view of the engine-driver's recollections recorded above; but both methods—"gin road" and locomotive—may well have been operated at the same time. In any case there can be no doubt that the mode of operating must have been slow and a cause of "great expense".[5]

The evidence given before the House of Commons Select Committee in April 1861[6] revealed the urgency of the need for a proper railway. Rowland Winn said: "We are working a certain amount of [the ore] and sending it to Newcastle and Middlesbro". The ore was being

[1] John Roseby was said to have come with George Dawes to test the newly-discovered ironstone in 1859, and to have remained as Rowland Winn's mining agent (Dudley, *The History and Antiquities of the Scunthorpe and Frodingham District*, p. 139).

[2] Chatterton's Wharf (Henderson, *loc. cit.*).

[3] Letter to G. R. Walshaw, 31 March 1924 (Scunthorpe Museum, file of letters, notes, and cuttings relating to local railways).

[4] Scunthorpe Museum, *loc. cit.*

[5] William Read, *History of the Isle of Axholme*, ed. Thomas C. Fletcher, 1859 (though the date 1864 occurs on p. 382), p. 383.

[6] H.L.R.O. Commons Evidence 1861, S.Y. (K.E.) Railway, Vol. S8, 22 April, pp. 23-8.

taken from the surface; there was no "sinking to it at present"; the amount available for shipment immediately was, therefore, the greater. He added that there had been a great dearth of ships—why, he could not say,—but they had contracted to send a thousand tons of ore a week and found they were unable to deliver because of the inadequate transport facilities. Furthermore the coal that would be needed if furnaces were constructed on the ironfield must come from Yorkshire. At that time coal was coming into Lincolnshire by way of the Keadby Canal, but that mode was inconvenient as it entailed loading on to and off river vessels. Clearly a railway was the answer to the problem—a railway to and across the Trent. Either this step must be taken by the Winns and Dawes, or the S.Y. railway must be persuaded to bridge the river.

That George Dawes now had in mind the erection of blast furnaces at Scunthorpe is beyond doubt; construction, in fact, began in 1862[1]; and it seems clear (from L.A.O. Stubbs 7/36 "Instructions to settle Draft Clause" 18 April 1861) that Winn had in 1861 known of, and possibly encouraged, this new development. At any rate he was ready to commit himself to carry at a fixed rate for 99 years iron ore and the iron made therefrom. His letter to John Hett on 14 Jan. 1861 (9/1/76) reveals that he had also for some time had in mind the extension of the new line westward to reach Grimsby.

As far as getting the co-operation of the S.Y. company was concerned, the way seemed open, since that railway had decided in 1858 to extend its line from Thorne to Keadby on the west bank of the Trent. They had consulted counsel (J. H. Lloyd) and been told that they would not exceed their powers if they proceeded (without obtaining Parliament's sanction) to construct the line to Keadby along the banks of the "Navigation" (the Stainforth and Keadby Canal)[2]. What the company's plans were after that work had been done was probably uncertain then.

The Chairman of the company, John Parker, admitted in April 1861[3] that the discovery of iron ore at Scunthorpe had been "a very agreeable surprise" to the company "about a year or two ago . . . so much so that we then immediately took into consideration this question of a bridge over the Trent which of course would have been desirable on other accounts but it is not a thing which the company with which I am connected could have entertained for some years to come had it not been for the discovery of this ironfield". This statement is in conflict with what he had said at the S.Y. half-yearly meeting at Doncaster on 27 February 1861[4]: he agreed then that at the previous Shareholders' Meeting (in 1860), when the matter of

[1] Dudley, *The History and Antiquities of the Scunthorpe and Frodingham District*, p. 141.

[2] P.R.O. (B.T.H.R.) SYD/1/6, 14 August 1858.

[3] H.L.R.O. Commons Evidence 1861, S.Y. (K.E.) Railway, Vol. 72, 72, S8, 22 April, p. 8.

[4] *The Railway Times* 1861, p. 295.

bridging the Trent was raised, it had been categorically affirmed that the Directors had no intention of going over the Trent; "and indeed there was then no idea of doing so". This claim was probably the truth. What decided the S.Y. to proceed with the bridge was the request of the Winn brothers that the railway should be extended to Barnsley for the accommodation of the coal needs of the ironstone industry; "and thus it became more than ever necessary to go over the Trent"; the Board felt there was no other course to pursue. Rowland and Edmund[1] Winn met the S.Y. Directors at Doncaster on 27 October 1860[2]; the minutes record that the discussion then concerned the linking of the S.Y. line across the Trent with the Winn-Dawes line. Such action would undoubtedly require Parliamentary authority. So would the extension of Winn's line westward as it must pass over the land of other owners to get to a junction with the M.S.L.

At this stage Rowland Winn had to bring into the process his solicitors in Brigg, the firm still known in 1860 as Nicholson, Hett, and Freer, though John Nicholson had died in 1840. It was an old-established firm with a sound reputation. John Nicholson had been spoken of as "well known and esteemed . . . for his uncompromising rectitude".[3] John Hett had come to Brigg from Lincoln about 1829 to join the firm, possibly as managing clerk.[4] He married his employer's daughter in 1833 and took his father-in-law's place as head of the firm[5] in 1840. For the next thirty years nearly he controlled the business, a sound practical lawyer and a hard-working one. His probity has been questioned[6] over the purchase of the Humber Ferries for the M.S.L. Railway, in which transaction he took a relatively minor part; but his somewhat austere nature, his strong Evangelical religious convictions, as well as the general esteem in which he seems locally to have been held, do not accord at all with the suggested picture of a sharp, loose-principled lawyer and business man. The third member in the firm was Thomas Freer, from a different background, but as good a lawyer as the other two. When he died in 1893 it was recalled that none of the decisions of the Brigg bench of magistrates had been reversed by a higher court while he had been its clerk.[7] Born at Market Rasen of poor parents, he had come to Brigg in 1836 to complete his articles. He had previously been employed in a lawyer's office at Market Rasen as a writing clerk, though, if his handwriting was then as atrocious as it appears in these railway papers, either he must have grossly deceived his employer as to his talents or he soon lost his early mastery of the pen.

[1] Edmund J. Winn was also involved in these railway matters, and also in the "Barnsley Coal Railway" (9/1/21, 23, 127, 171, 188, 188a).

[2] P.R.O. (B.T.H.R.) SYD/1/8.

[3] *L.R.S.M.*, 30 Oct. 1840.

[4] M. J. F. Hett, *A Family History* (1934), p. 37.

[5] *Ibid.*, p. 77.

[6] Alun A. D'Orley, *The Humber Ferries*, 1968, p. 39.

[7] *L.R.S.M.*, 16 June 1893.

He evidently worked diligently at Brigg, like the legendary apprentice, marrying, however, not the daughter but the niece of his principal. His end was as remarkable as his beginning: he died at the age of 81, having become senior partner in 1878; he had been active in his profession until a few months before his death.

John Nicholson died before the new railway era affected Brigg; but John Hett had much to do locally with the coming of the railway to and through Brigg.[1] He and his partner, Thomas Freer, must both have been acquainted with the routine which had to be followed in the obtaining of an Act of Parliament authorizing the construction of a railway, having been concerned also with the abortive railway scheme of 1856.[2] They seem, it is true, to have had to renew their acquaintance in the matter of legal costs (9/4 Letter from William F. Clark).

The correspondence in 9/1 starts with a letter from Rowland Winn dated 5 November 1860, but the first item on N.H.F.'s bill (9/6/1) has the date 26 October 1860. In between those two dates the wheels were set in motion for the obtaining of an Act of Parliament to create the T.A.G. Railway Company, and also for the taking of a part—more passively—in the obtaining of the S.Y. (K.E.) Act; these two schemes formed a twin operation, since neither company could operate successfully without the other. John Hett's first important step was to give notice, in the *London Gazette*, in a London paper, a Manchester paper, and a Doncaster paper, as well as in a Lincolnshire paper, of the intention to apply for an Act (9/1/8 and 9/6). At the same time the land to be traversed by the railway had to be surveyed and an accurate map made (9/1/2); plans and sections had to be drawn with equal accuracy. Inaccuracy might rule out any chance of the Bill's success. When, for instance, a few years earlier, a bill had been promoted for the formation of an Isle of Axholme, Gainsborough, and Goole Railway, the engineer, Birkenshaw, giving evidence before the Parliamentary Railway Committee in the Lords, 7 July 1846, had had to admit to an error of seven feet in the section, "the section showing the line on a level with the ground at Epworth, whilst in fact an embankment of seven feet would be required". He proposed what seemed an entirely satisfactory way of remedying the error, but the opposing counsel had no difficulty in disposing of the scheme; the railway, he said, would not be consistent with the "Railway Acts, and if the promoters were allowed to get away with this they would be enabled to make the railway with any gradient they chose without the control of the Legislature".[3] The Bill was thrown out, in spite of strong support for it locally. In the T.A.G. project two surveyors are spoken of (9/1/2); one was John Lee, whose address in 1861 was Bishop Auckland (9/1/179), and the

[1] L. A. O. Stubbs 7/18-20.
[2] L. A. O. Stubbs 7/30-33.
[3] Report in *L.R.S.M.*, 10 July 1846.

other appears to have been W. C. Atkinson, "civil engineer, land surveyor, and contractor"[1], of Brigg (Bridge Street); and Atkinson speaks (9/1/6) of having "just completed the plotting of the Survey", adding that the junction would be about five furlongs south-west of the Barnetby station. In the N.F.H. bill also (9/6 f. 2) he is called "the Surveyor". John Roseby signs himself (9/7 Draft Estimate of Expense) as Engineer,[2] but the part he played in the preparations is not clear. He acted in valuing the land which was to be taken from the Trent to the Ancholme for the railway (9/1/46); but he acted in a very general capacity on behalf of Rowland Winn (9/1/82); it cannot have been very convenient for him, however, from his office in Bridge Street, Brigg. He moved later to Appleby.

There is no map of the line included in the Stubbs Deposit, but the Lindsey authority has deposited one (L.A.O. Lindsey Dep. Plans 1/76), and the House of Lords Record Office possesses one.[3] The map is Major Colby's 1824 O.S. one inch map, with the T.A.G. line marked on it in red ink. This line was evidently drawn as far as possible with the aid of a ruler and does not coincide exactly with that of the O.S. map "printed from an Electrotype taken in 1890. Railways inserted to 1891" (though perhaps too much should not be made of that; a tracing of this line would not lie with any snugness on a tracing of the line on a modern one inch map).

The course of the line from the Trent to the eastern boundary of Scunthorpe township could have been plotted almost anywhere within the boundaries of Scunthorpe and Frodingham, so much of the land there being in the ownership of Charles Winn as Lord of the Manor. Much of this land had been awarded to him at the enclosure of 1833.[4] Right through "Gunhouse" Ings and Carrs, Frodingham Moors, Frodingham West Common to "Cliffe Closes", Charles Winn held land awarded to him in lieu of tithes, or land he had gained at the time of the enclosure by exchange with Henry Healey or the Rev. John Posthumous Parkinson; some he had purchased from John Fowler. Other land was old enclosure and probably already in Charles Winn's possession, though this is not certain. West of Frodingham Clay Field, which was part of the Winn estate, a barrier had existed in 1833: William Stow Clark owned land through which the railway was to go, but this land was evidently acquired by the Winns in good time. The Book of Reference shows it as in their possession (L.A.O. Stubbs 9/6). In Frodingham village there was a good deal of old enclosure, and here again the Winns must already have bought out the owners to make way for the line (L.A.O. Stubbs

[1] White's *Lincolnshire* (1856), p. 682.

[2] Roseby was not to be the engineer in charge of the construction of the line. Charles Bartholomew began as engineer in September 1861 (P.R.O. (B.T.H.R.) TAG/1/1, p. 1). Bartholomew is shown (TAG/1/1, p. 182) as having deposited the plans. And see N. H. F. bill (9/6, f. 38).

[3] H.L.R.O. 1861, T2.

[4] Scunthorpe and Frodingham Inclosure map in the care of the Town Clerk of Scunthorpe.

9/6, Book of Reference). The only owners here in the Book of Reference are Charles Winn, the Rev. E. M. Weigall, and the Surveyors of the Highways of Frodingham. Beyond the road there referred to (the road from Ashby—Oswald Road) only the Rev. J. P. Parkinson and Earl Beauchamp owned land which the railway needed to cross; and even here the map seems to show that with a little alteration the line could have avoided Earl Beauchamp's property. On the east side of Scunthorpe, in Scunthorpe East Common, a considerable area had been divided into allotments held by eleven occupiers. This area might have proved a difficulty had not Charles Winn merely let the allotments while retaining the ownership. So all that was necessary was to compensate the eleven for loss of tenancy.

When the plans and sections were made the names of owners, lessees and occupiers of the land required for the railway had to be provided, together with the name of the parish in which their land was situated. This job required a good deal of effort, time, and local knowledge. As John Hett had to hold himself in readiness to be called up to London to consult with the Parliamentary Agents for the Bill (Dyson and Co., 6 Victoria Street, Westminster), much of the work fell on Thomas Freer (9/1/2, 40, 41), though Freer himself was called to London on occasion (9/1/81). Once the information was gathered (to be made into a Book of Reference (L.A.O. Stubbs 9/6)[1] to accompany the plans and sections of the line), notices had to be served. The account of expenses (9/6 ff. 5-14) gives an idea of the size of this task. The plans, sections, and book of reference had also to be deposited at the Parliamentary Offices, at the Board of Trade, with the Clerk of the Peace at Spilsby, and with the Clerks of all the parishes affected (9/6, ff. 15, 16, 18-20).

It had to be ensured before the plans were so deposited that they conformed with Standing Orders as drawn up by the Lords and Commons. Those of the Lords, besides imposing the conditions mentioned above, demanded that notices to owners and occupiers must be served before the 15 December of the year before that in which the Act was to be sought, that they should be served by personal delivery at the person's residence between 8 a.m. and 8 p.m., and not on a Sunday; if he lived away, delivery must be by registered post despatched on or before 12 December at a chief Post Office in one of the big towns (fortunately Lincoln ranked as such). Standing Orders also required lists of owners, occupiers, and lessees to be drawn up, showing whether they were in favour of, against the application, or "neuter". Order No. 183 stated that plans must be drawn to a scale not less than four inches to a mile; the limits of

[1] There is only a manuscript book of reference in the Stubbs collection of papers. It is in Thomas Freer's writing and is full of alterations. There is a manuscript fair copy in the deposit made by Lindsey (L.A.O. 1/76) and another in the Cusworth Museum, Doncaster. The H.L.R.O. has a printed copy (1861, T2).

deviation of the proposed line[1] must be marked; buildings, yards, gardens in the line or within the limits of deviation must be shown on an enlarged plan ($\frac{1}{4}$ inch to 100 feet). The radius of every curve not exceeding one mile in length must be noted on the plan in furlongs, roods, and chains; and where tunnelling was to be used instead of an open cutting, a dotted line was to indicate it. Sections must be drawn to the same horizontal scale as the plan, and a vertical scale of not less than one inch to 100 feet must show the surface of the ground marked on the plan; the section must show the intended level of the proposed work, the height of every embankment, and the depth of every cutting. A datum horizontal line—the same throughout the whole length must be given, referred to some fixed point stated in writing on the section, near some portion of the work, or near either terminus. Where the line of railway crossed a road or river, the height of the railway over, or the depth under, the surface was required, and the height and span of every arch of all bridges or viaducts must be marked at every crossing. Where crossings were on the level, that must be clear on the section.

N.H.F. received notice of these requirements from Dyson and Co.[2] Most of the notices—that application might be made to purchase land[3]—were served by hand. A few had to be posted to "distant owners".[4] These were Charles Winn, John Parkinson, Francis Wells (Dunstall near Gainsborough), W. H. and G. Dawes, Samuel Beale & Co. (Park Gate Iron Works, Rotherham), the Rev. J. P. Parkinson (East Ravendale), Wm. Fk. Webb (Northallerton), Lord Yarborough, C. C. Elwes (Ryde, I. of W.), W. B. S. Rackham (Lincolns Inn Fields), Clare College, Cambridge, M.S.L. (Manchester), William Parkinson (Dinnington near Rotherham), Earl Beauchamp (Madresfield Court, Great Malvern). With only one of these (John Parkinson) was there any difficulty: it was uncertain whether his address was Gainsborough or "Gunhouse". Thomas Freer made himself responsible for posting notices to all these owners, posting thirteen of them at Lincoln on 11 December (including notices to T. Kirkby and J. Taylor (not on the list) of Cuxwold near Caistor); two others were posted on 13 December. John Parkinson was stated, on enquiry, to live neither at Gainsborough nor Gunness, but at Carlton near Worksop. (His name, it appeared also, was William, not John,)

[1] The wording of the notice to be sent to all proprietors of land which the railway might need (L. A. O. Stubbs 9/8) says that land might be required "to the extent of 100 yards on either side of the [central] line" shown on the plan. This wording, and, in particular, the reference to 100 yards, does not appear in the form actually sent out.

[2] L. A. O. Stubbs 9/4 Instructions as to Proof . . .

[3] The notice was a formal one of intention to apply for an Act of Parliament. The land in which the recipient of the notice was understood to be "interested" was described, and it was stated whether the land was required for the railway or was merely within the limits of deviation. The person receiving the notice was told where he could see plans, sections, and book of reference, and was asked to send in on the form provided his "assent, dissent, or neutrality".

[4] L. A. O Stubbs 9/4 Addresses . . .

His notice never reached him. It is marked[1] "Not Carlton on Trent", "Try Carlton/Newark"; postmarked "Newark De 14 60", "Newark De 20 60", "London De 21 60", "Worksop De 22 60", also "Lincoln De 11 60". Evidently all concerned at least tried to deliver the message. N.H.F.'s office staff had to perform the delivery by hand where that method was possible, as it was for the majority of notices. Six were delivered by John Roland Hett (the fourth son of John Hett and articled to his father)[2] in Appleby and Frodingham. Sixty-three notices were taken by George Wright, forty by William Henry Tinkler. Stephen Upton was responsible for others. (The entries in N.H.F.'s bill—9/6—reflect these journeys). All these men were described in the affidavits which had to be sworn at the end of January 1861[3] as "Attorney's Clerk", as was also Thomas Wilson,[4] who, with J. R. Hett, had had to deposit copies of plans, sections, and book of reference.

Some notices were served personally; all that was required was that there should be "a personal delivery" at the residence of the recipient, but the method and time of delivery had to be stated and affirmed. Thus W. H. Tinkler recorded that he had served a copy personally on John Mundey the younger "about 6 in the afternoon". Counting duplicates which had to be served, 85 notices were delivered by hand to the person concerned, and 50 were left at the dwelling-house, usually with the man's wife or daughter (the Christian names being specified) or with the servant.[5] Notices were served in duplicate when patron and incumbent were involved, or where an incumbent and his wife were considered to be joint occupiers—e.g., the Rev. William and Mrs. Winifred Ann Keys. Where notices to Surveyors of Highways were concerned, each Surveyor had to be identified and his address discovered.

The notices stated whether the land mentioned thereon was merely within the limits of deviation of the line (and hence unlikely to be required) or whether it was actually in the line of the proposed railway, and whether it would need to be embanked or cut into. Clearly owners and occupiers might be less enthusiastic about a railway which required either of these operations since the work must inevitably affect and perhaps temporarily at least spoil the neighbouring land. The owners who received notice that their land was in the direct line and needed to be cut or embanked were Charles Winn, the Rev. J. R. West, T. G. Corbett, C. C. Elwes, Lord Yarborough, W. Abraham, J. Chesman, W. F. Webb, T. West, T. Kirkby, and G. Taylor, though, as was inevitable, the Ancholme Commis-

[1] L. A. O. Stubbs 9/7 Envelope of Notice . . .

[2] John Roland Hett went to Canada in 1870 and stayed there to practise law until his death in 1891. He became Attorney-General of British Columbia in 1882. (M. J. F. Hett, *op. cit.*, pp. 80, 102, 119).

[3] L. A. O. Stubbs 9/7 Affidavits . . . notices . . .

[4] Thomas Wilson died in 1893; he was with the firm of N. H. F. in Brigg for fifty-five years "as cashier". (*L.R.S.M.*, 3 Feb. 1893).

[5] L. A. O. Stubbs 9/3 List of people served . . .

sioners and the Surveyors of Highways which had to be crossed were also affected by the railway works. As far as can be ascertained 35 occupiers were also likely to be disturbed; and others (occupiers) responsible for drains and occupation roads were concerned.

Altogether there were 130 owners, lessees, and occupiers entitled to receive notices; 120 replies were sent in (113 if three wives, one of the Dawes brothers, the Trustees of C. C. Elwes, and Clare College, in association with the Rev. J. R. West, are excluded): 66 senders said they were in favour of the railway, 35 were against it, and 17 were neuter, while two simply sent acknowledgements (L. A. O. Stubbs 7/34 Replies by . . . ; 9/7 List . . .[1]). Of the seven lessees (effectively six as both Dawes brothers voted) four were opposed; of the 33 owners (again only 27 in effect) only twelve (eleven if a wife is excluded) declared themselves in favour—effectively just over 40%; 51 occupiers (nearly 57% of the full 90) approved of the line, and only 30% were prepared to say they did not want it.[2]

The fact that only 40% of the owners positively wanted a railway if it was going to affect their property might have seemed a real threat to the scheme. But there were really only twenty owners involved, apart from Charles Winn, the Surveyors of Highways, the M.S.L., the Turnpike Trustees, and the Ancholme Commissioners. The clerk to the latter was John Hett, who, provided it was not to the detriment of the Trustees, would urge them to vote for the line. The M.S.L., as has already been suggested, were likely to support it as long as their interests were safeguarded. Of the twenty owners, one was the Vicar of Frodingham, owning the land (fields, garden, and cottage) with "C. Winn, Patron". By far the biggest owner was Charles Winn; the land he owned, as the plans and sections (L. A. O. Stubbs III 102-6) and book of reference (Stubbs 9/6) show, provided a convenient route for the railway Rowland Winn had in mind. The latter had come to a tentative arrangement early with T. G. Corbett, the owner of the Elsham estate (L. A. O. Stubbs 9/4 Letters 10 and 12 Nov. 1860). T. G. Corbett[3] was apparently as anxious as Rowland Winn to make available to the world the iron of North Lincolnshire, though he intended not to be too disinterested. He was willing that a railway should go through his property if a station were provided on the turnpike road from Brigg to Barton (i.e. at the level crossing where

[1] The notice—the "Schedule" delivered to each interested person—made it clear that the "property in the line of the proposed Work as at present laid out" included "property any part of which is within eleven yards or thereabouts of the centre line of such proposed Work, as delineated upon the Plan". Any other property mentioned in the Schedule was "within the limits of Deviation".

[2] Five Wrawby occupiers first declared themselves in favour of the railway, then altered their declaration to one of dissent, having apparently yielded to pressure or persuasion.

[3] " . . . a Justice of the Peace, and a terror to all poachers, pedlars, vagrants, and vagabonds in these parts." (*Barton, Brigg, Caistor, and Winterton News*, 9 Dec. 1858).

it now is), with "a convenient siding" to any point he chose for the conveyance of any iron ore discovered on his land. Rowland Winn had no objection. Corbett seems to have been in some doubt at the end of 1860, even though an agreement had been reached and put on paper (9/1/59). In the end (see L. A. O. Stubbs 9/7 List of owners..) the name of Corbett appears among those making no reply to the question—assent or dissent.

Cary Charles Elwes (9/4) and the M.S.L. (9/7) both decided to petition against the Bill (9/6/f. 7). C. C. Elwes (and his trustee, the Rev. C. J. Barnard, Rector of Bigby) maintained that the Elwes estate would suffer "by severance and otherwise". As it turned out, the petition never reached Parliament (9/1/125). Nevertheless John Hett had consulted with W. C. Atkinson as to the best way of dealing with the Elwes objection, should it be proceeded with (N.H.F.'s bill, 6 April 1861—9/6). The M.S.L. was not so easily shrugged off. A firm agreement over rates had to be made first; and there the S.Y. was involved. At the S.Y. Directors' meeting on 26 Oct. 1860[1], which Rowland and Edmund Winn had attended, a proposed agreement had been drawn up in outline for consideration by the Winns. It seemed unacceptable: after the Winns had withdrawn from the meeting, the Solicitor (Baxter) was authorized to give the necessary Parliamentary notices, not only for a bridge over the Trent, but, in case the Winns refused the terms proposed to them, also for a S.Y. branch to the ironstone field—the threatened opposition mentioned in N.H.F's. bill (9/6/f. 7). The decision was taken to have the necessary surveys for a line through to Brigg, since Rowland Winn did reject the S.Y. terms.[2] The M.S.L. came to an agreement to allow Rowland Winn to make a railway joining its line[3] "at some point to be agreed between Barnetby and Brigg", the M.S.L. giving through rates and giving "proper facilities" for conveyance of ironstone and coal traffic, on condition that the junction with the M.S.L. was made to the satisfaction of the M.S.L. engineer, and provided the M.S.L. was granted running powers for its traffic over the line as far as the Trent. The M.S.L. agreed to pay a toll to Winn and his railway company of 60% of the mileage receipts of the traffic. All the same the M.S.L. petition was still a threat even in March 1861 (9/1/105).

Though the M.S.L. and the S.Y. were separate companies, they had worked together for some time,[4] and the M.S.L.'s involvement in the railway tribal warfare at this moment[5] (the Great Northern, the London and North-Western, and the Midland companies were all concerned) drove it further towards co-operation (ending in the

[1] P.R.O. (B.T.H.R.) SYD/1/8.
[2] P.R.O. (B.T.H.R.) SYD/1/11, 17 Nov. 1860.
[3] P.R.O. (B.T.H.R.) MSL/1/5, 9 Nov. 1860.
[4] C. H. Grinling, *The History of the Great Northern Railway*, 1845-1922 (1898/1966), p. 186; Dow, *op. cit.*, I, p. 246.
[5] Grinling, *op. cit.*, pp. 184-7; Dow, *op. cit.*, I, p. 200.

leasing of the S.Y. to the M.S.L. in 1864[1]). One result was that Rowland Winn got support from both M.S.L. and S.Y. for his line. At the S.Y. Directors' meeting on 9 November 1860[2], R. Baxter announced the terms of the agreement reached: "In consideration of the [S.Y.] withdrawing their project for a Railway from the Trent to Barnetby It is agreed that the Company as well as the [M.S.L.] shall have power to run over and fix rates and that the proprietors of the line between the Trent and Barnetby shall receive their mileage proportion of such rates less 40 per cent for working expenses. Provided always that the minimum sum to be received by such Proprietors as toll shall in no case be less than 6d. per ton upon Ironstone and 4d. per ton upon Coal". The agreement was also accepted by the M.S.L.[3] on 30 November 1860. (One comment on this situation was that the M.S.L. was now in a state of "phenomenal amity with its various neighbours . . . a somewhat remarkable position . . . one in which [it] has rarely if ever been placed"[4].) There were to be difficulties over the agreement, but not until 1861.

Amongst the objectors to the new line, as exhibited in the return made (9/7 List of Owners . . . distinguishing . . .), there was a solid phalanx from Wrawby and Bigby, plainly reflecting the declared objection of the Elwes family. But in Wrawby this objection seems to have been reinforced by the vicar, the Rev. John Rowland West, a saintly man but not prepared to lose part of his small stipend as he feared he might as a result of this scheme (9/1/59). He was evidently reassured on this point. And though it was some years before he got all that was due to him, he received for 5 acres 1 rood 33 perches, together with another 1125 square yards, £556 14s.[5] The objections of the Wrawby and Bigby occupiers remained on record but did not affect the success of the measure.

Apart from the Vicar of Wrawby only two of the landowners who objected to the coming of the railway actually lost any land. One was a small landowner in Worlaby—Thomas West, and the amount he had to concede was not great. The T.A.G. took from him 1 rood 11 perches; for this he received as "price and compensation" in June 1864 £210.[6] The extent of the Elwes loss of land was somewhat greater: in Wrawby and Bigby four parcels of land, 13 acres 3 roods 25½ perches, 2 roods 29 perches, 1 acre 3 roods 34 perches, and 3 roods 15½ perches respectively, were taken. And for this land,

[1] At the Directors' meeting of the M.S.L., 1 Feb. 1861, Watkin, reporting on the discussions with the S.Y. concerning the joint construction of the Keadby-Barnetby railway, said that it appeared to him and to the representatives of the S.Y. that the most beneficial mode of avoiding future dissension was for the two companies to revert to the proposition for a fusion of interests—one made at various times since 1851. (P.R.O. (B.T.H.R.) MSL/1/5).

[2] P.R.O. (B.T.H.R.) SYD/1/8.

[3] P.R.O. (B.T.H.R.) MSL/1/5.

[4] *The Railway Times*, 1861, p. 260.

[5] Sheffield Central Library Archives, Baxter Papers 60959.

[6] *Ibid.*

altogether just under 17½ acres, the price and compensation paid came to nearly £2,500.

The leaseholders who objected—the Mundeys (lessees for 21 years under Clare College) and Edward Twigg (lessee for 14 years under the Vicar of Wrawby) lost 1 acre and 24 perches and 3 acres 1 rood 5½ perches respectively. As compensation the Mundeys were paid £54 12s. 5d. in January 1862, and Twigg got £155 3s. 2d. in the same month.[1] James Burrell is returned in the official list (7/34 Replies by . . . and H.L.R.O. 1861, T2, T.A.G. Railway, Plan, etc.) as an occupier (but in the Baxter papers[2] he is stated to have been a lessee for 14 years under the Vicar of Wrawby); for the 1 acre 1 rood 13½ perches he lost he received in compensation £20.

The objecting occupiers were also compensated: Charles Wharton received £67 4s. 8d., James Dawson £32 12s. 5d., John Nelson £12, Thomas Moorhead £17 3s. 3d., Henry Bilton £9 12s., W. E. Hobson £12 12s. 4d. The following, described as cottagers, received £2 10s. each; M. Wilson, T. Moorhead, M. Hudson, R. Kitching, T. Girdham, G. Taylor, P. Pennythorne, W. and Ann Good. W. Twigg got only 12s. 6d.[3] Whether these Wrawby people were satisfied it is difficult to say; but they can have received little benefit from the railway.[4]

The cost of constructing the line was estimated by John Roseby (9/1/54) to be £117,335 15s., which sum was rounded up by D. and Co. to £120,000; of this £37,247 10s. had already been spent if the value of the land was taken into account (9/1/54). Parliamentary regulations required £6,400 of the remaining £80,000 to be deposited.[5] It was estimated (9/1/56) that about 30 acres of land would be required for the railway from the Ancholme to Barnetby; the cost of the land would be £3,000, the deposit on which (and the share to be borne by the Winns) would be £240. That meant Messrs. Dawes would have to pay £6,160 very soon. Unfortunately, George Dawes had to confess on 12 January 1861 that he could not find the money, having, he said (9/1/72), had an unexpected demand for £4,000 on top of "the heavy pull to the Earl [Fitzwilliam] last March". Rowland Winn's attitude was business-like rather than accommodating (9/1/74), though he seems (9/1/76) to have thought his posture not illiberal. But the money had to be paid by the middle of January. D. and Co. were agitated, though reassuring on the whole (9/1/77), when the money had still not been paid by the evening of the 14 January. Their account of expenses shows (9/4 15-17 Jan. 1861)

[1] Sheffield Central Library Archives, Baxter Papers 60959.

[2] *Ibid.*

[3] *Ibid.*

[4] It should, however, be noted that the Wrawby farmers felt they needed railway accommodation; see their Memorial (signed by 25 owners and occupiers) to the M.S.L. 1860 (L. A. O. Stubbs 9/4).

[5] House of Lords Standing Order CLXXXIV required 8% of the "Amount of the Estimate of Expense" of a railway to be deposited with the Court of Chancery "previously to the Fifteenth Day of January".

that the money was paid in by Mr. Baxter (of the S.Y.)[1] on condition that the Bill should be withdrawn "at his request" if the money were not repaid to him by 5 February. Robert Baxter had in fact no doubt that the scheme was sound, would go through, and therefore that the loan was safe.

The matter was resolved by the agreement between the M.S.L., the S.Y., and Rowland Winn[2]; the three were to make themselves responsible for the construction of the line and its financing (including the payment of the deposit); the cost was to be borne by each interest equally, Rowland Winn's contribution to include the value of the land and the outlay already made by the Dawes; both Winn and Dawes were to take shares in the undertaking at par to the amount of their outlay, and Winn's share was to be liable to purchase by the M.S.L. at their option at a 10% premium. Each of the interests was to have running powers over the line, paying 60% of the mileage receipts of any of them; a special toll was to be agreed on for coal and ironstone. Baxter (who, it was agreed, was to act for them all, superintending the passing of the Bill in Parliament) introduced a discordant note when it was proposed that the M.S.L. should now have entry into the S.Y.'s coal district, by asserting categorically that the S.Y. would never grant that. But by 27 February 1861 all was smoothed out when the leasing of the S.Y. to the M.S.L. was agreed on.[3]

A new agreement now became necessary. Rowland Winn had covenanted with Dawes to "carry for a term of 99 years . . . minerals and Iron made therefrom . . . at a fixed rate of 6d. per ton", Dawes having also covenanted with him to "carry the Minerals from Mr. Winn's Estate whether belonging to Mr. Winn or to his other Lessees".[4] So Winn now wanted the M.S.L. to take over his covenant. As he pointed out, the lessees would hold him to the agreed stipulation; and therefore he wanted the fixed rates and the period of time to be written into the Act of Parliament (9/1/83). Edward Watkin,[5] however, would have none of it. He told the M.S.L. Directors[6] that Winn had entered into some "improvident arrangements" to do with

[1] Robert Baxter was at this time the senior partner of the legal firm of Baxter, Rose, and Norton, in London; he also had a practice in Doncaster, looked after by his younger brother Edmund. He was also Solicitor to the S.Y. railway. For many years he was a power in the railway world, having been associated with Edmund Denison in the 1830s in schemes for linking Yorkshire with London by rail. He died 8 Oct. 1889, aged 87. (*Doncaster Gazette*, 24 Jan. 1935. I owe this reference to Mr. Leslie Smith of Doncaster.) His son, Robert Dudley Baxter, was a member of the London firm; he had a considerable reputation as an economist and statistician. His essay "Railway Extension and Its Results" appeared in the *Journal of the Statistical Society* and is reprinted in *Essays in Economic History*, Vol. III (1962), ed. E. M. Carus-Wilson.

[2] P.R.O. (B.T.H.R.) MSL/1/5, 23 Jan. 1861.

[3] *Ibid.*, 27 Feb. 1861.

[4] L. A. O. Stubbs 7/36. Suggestions for agreement.

[5] General Manager of the M.S.L. 1854-61; Chairman 1864-9 (Dow, *op. cit.*, I, p. 281.

[6] P.R.O. (B.T.H.R.) MSL/1/5, 1 March 1861.

the conveying of ironstone and there might be some difficulty in getting rid of these obligations. Rowland Winn was also told (9/1/112) by D. and Co. that his "embarrassments [were] of [his] own producing", and reminded that he had had to go cap in hand to the companies. He was unwilling to accept this reproof; he struggled, but unavailingly (7/36 Letters R. W. and Baxter Feb. 1861). He sought counsel's opinion—John Bullar in Feb 1861,[1] and J. H. Lloyd's in April 1861.[2] Both these men pointed out the difficulty of making an agreement such as Winn wanted binding on the companies; and when the Bill received the Royal Assent on 22 July 1861, Winn had not got his way. The Act[3] stated that it should be lawful for the company "to contract from time to time with . . . Charles Winn, his heirs . . . with respect to the conveyance of mineral and other traffic . . . and with respect to the payments to be made . . . "

An agreement was drawn up during the passing of the Bill, and signed afterwards (7/36 Agreement 2 Aug. 1861) which expressly stated that "the arrangements as to Tolls shall rest in the Agreement of the parties and not be inserted in the Bill". As Baxter pointed out (7/36 14 Feb, 1861) Rowland Winn was in no position to dictate terms as the M.S.L. were coming to his assistance; the company did not need his help nearly as much as he needed theirs.

Another matter which had to be settled and could not be settled except by insertion in the Act arose from the nature of the country through which the railway was to run. Near the western end of the line the old and new Ancholme rivers had to be crossed, and here the rights of the Ancholme Commissioners were involved. At the other end the line crossed land whose agricultural value depended on the custom of warping; and the drainage of the land between the iron area and the Trent valley—a large district—was of vital importance. The Commissioners of Sewers in the wapentakes of Manley, Corringham, and Aslacoe were in charge of the drainage of this area. Rowland Winn, as the owner (in effect) of much of the land towards the Trent, was anxious to preserve rights of warping.

In the "First Proof" of the draft T.A.G. Bill (it is printed, and dated 13 Dec. 1860[4]) there is no mention of drainage, warping, or Ancholme; these matters appear to have been temporarily overlooked (this draft ran to 51 clauses, compared with the 63 of the Act). D. and Co's bill (9/4) speaks of "making Fair Copy of Draft Bill for Printer", 14 Dec. 1860; and a week later introduces the subject of drainage and warping clauses. But N.H.F.'s bill (9/6/f. 16 5 Dec. 1860) mentions the consideration of the clauses affecting the Ancholme Commissioners—presumably connected with the meeting of the Commisioners on 7 Dec. 1860 (9/7).

[1] L. A. O. Stubbs 7/36. Suggestions . . . agreement, 13 May 1861.
[2] L. A. O. Stubbs 7/36. Instructions . . . 18 April 1861.
[3] 24 and 25 Victoria 1861, c. clvi, clauses xxx-xxxii.
[4] L. A. O. Stubbs 9/4. A Bill to authorize . . .

And at the time of the airing of the S.Y.(K.E.) project the question of protection for drainage was first raised. The alert Archdeacon Stonehouse had (9/6 11 Dec. 1860) apparently reminded John Hett of the possibility of a dispute here; but the Sewers Commissioners themselves brought the matter more noticeably to the fore with their petition against the S.Y.(K.E.) Bill (referred to in 9/6/101). The fears of the Commissioners were dispelled by the inclusion in the Acts (T.A.G. and S.Y.(K.E.)) of safeguarding clauses. Nothing in the Acts was to be construed as authorizing any interference with any "river, stream, cut, drain, or water-course within the limits of the levels" without the Commissioners' consent; anything done or to be done during the construction of the railway must be done or altered to the satisfaction of the Commissioners' surveyor. Further, any lands in the levels taken were to be (as far as drainage went) subject to the control of the Commissioners and were to be liable to the same drainage rates as other lands in the levels, except that they should be rated only on their agricultural value. It was also laid down that "in carrying the Railway over the Ings Drain . . . in . . . Frodingham, numbered 9a in the . . . plans . . . there shall be made under the said Railway a clear opening of the width of twelve feet, and the bottom of the said opening shall be on a level with the top of the sill of the sluice of the Brumby sewer . . . near the . . . Trent"; and "in carrying the Railway over the Bottesford Beck . . . in Scunthorpe, and numbered 42 . . . , and partly in Appleby, and numbered 1 . . . there shall be made under the Railway a clear opening of the width of ten feet, and the bottom of the said opening shall be not less than five feet below the natural surface of the land at such opening". Any damage to the drainage or the "defences" of the levels as a result at any time of the railway's construction or working must be made good by the railway company and compensation paid where necessary—not only to the Commissioners but to any person who sustained damage or injury to his land.

Similarly the warping[1] along the Trent was protected. Rowland Winn himself appears to have understood the working of the system and to have given instructions to John Hett (9/1/119). The clause[2] in the Act said that it might be desirable that Charles Winn, who "is or claims to be the owner of a warping-drain . . . in Frodingham near to and on the north side of the Railway, with works connected therewith" might wish to use the drain for the purpose of warping "certain lands . . . lying on the south side of the Railway"; therefore the T.A.G. must on request from the owner, "make and maintain

[1] Read, *op. cit.*, pp. 30-1, describes the artificial flooding of the Trent-side land periodically by means of specially-cut drains, these carrying the river water over the land and depositing alluvial soil, thus producing a very rich earth.

"*Brumby Moors*—Passengers along the Trent and Ancholme railway may observe to the south of the line between the Frodingham ironworks and the river Trent a large tract of land containing several hundred acres now in process of warping . . . (*L.R.S.M.*, 12 July 1867).

[2] 24 and 25 Vict. 1861, c. clvi, clause xlii.

two openings underneath the Railway, each of the width at the bottom thereof of fifty-five feet, and to be formed with a slope or batter of one foot and a half horizontal to one foot perpendicular. . . such bottom to be on a level with the sill of the sluice of the . . . . warping-drain near the . . . Trent" so that land on the south side of the railway might be warped. A similar clause was to be inserted in the S.Y.(K.E.) Bill (9/1/126).[1]

The meeting of the Ancholme Commissioners' Committee on Railways on 7 December 1860 (9/7) tried to lay down the conditions which it was hoped would be imposed by the Act. The two matters to be watched were the drainage works and rates and the crossing of drains and river by the railway. There was no problem in the matter of drainage: the Act[2] recognised the rights and jurisdiction of the Ancholme Commissioners as it had those of the Sewers Commissioners. No damage must be done to the works of drainage without compensation being paid by the company to the Commissioners and to any person whose land was injured; no interference with the works was allowed except for the purpose of bridge repairing. Adam Smith, the engineer of the Commissioners, had made recommendations as to the bridges the railway was building (9/7 Minutes of Committee, 7 Dec 1860). It is difficult to see much connection between his remarks and the wording of the Act, though there is some relationship between the latter and the entry in 9/6/f. 9 (N.H.F.'s bill). The clauses in the Act simply provide for the height and width of the bridge over the River Ancholme and its construction. It was to be "a good substantial bridge of stone, brick, iron, or wood". Its foundations, "or the piles or pillars" on which it was to be placed must "be perpendicular, and the abutments of [the] bridge be parallel with the . . . river, and the clear height of the arch . . . for the width of fifteen feet in the centre of the river shall be not less than fifteen feet six inches above the top of the waste weir of the sluice . . . in . . . South Ferriby . . . ; there shall be but one arch or opening over the . . . river and the towing-path or cess on the east side of the same, and the span of the same shall be such as to leave thereunder a clear space free from obstructions of the breadth of at least ninety-four feet measured at right angles with the . . . river, in which a clear waterway of not less than eighty-two feet, and a towing-path or cess of the breadth of not less than twelve feet shall be preserved, and the clear height of the arch of such bridge for a width of six at the least in the centre of such . . . cess, shall be not less than ten feet above the surface level of the . . . cess; and there shall be another arch or opening over the . . . cess on the west side

[1] When, however, John Hett had submitted to D. and Co. the proposed "Clauses to be inserted in the Bill on behalf . . . Sewers" 1860 (L. A. O. Stubbs 9/7) Thomas Coates had noted on the manuscript: "I can understand the drainage of the district to be paramount—warping is another matter", and "If the Railway obstructs drainage this [restriction on the company] is right but not for warping".

[2] 24 and 25 Vict. 1861, c. clvi, clauses xxxiii-xli.

of the . . . river, and the span of the same shall be such as to leave thereunder a clear space free from . . . of at least seven feet measured at right angles with the . . . river, and of the height of not less than ten feet above the surface-level of the . . . cess, such height to extend for a width of six feet at the least in the centre of . . . [the] cess; the surface level of the . . . cess . . . shall be not more than three feet three inches above the top of the waste weir of the . . . sluice in . . . South Ferriby".

It was further ordered that during the building or repair of the bridge—or any future bridge "in lieu of such Bridge"—an uninterrupted navigable waterway must be left (where the bridge crossed the river) "of not less breadth than forty feet, and of not less height than ten feet six inches from the surface of . . . the . . . river, for a space of fifteen feet in the centre of the River, and the period . . . during which such contraction . . . shall continue . . . shall in no case exceed fifty-six consecutive days". If, owing to the building or to the bad state of repair of the bridge, the river or towing-path were obstructed, thus preventing boats or horses passing, for as much as two hours in any one day; or if the waterway were contracted to a width less than here specified for the same period of time; or if the contraction of the waterway to 40 feet lasted longer than 56 consecutive days, then the Commissioners could claim from the company £10 for every day the offence continued. Moreover the Commissioners were empowered to make good any injury at the expense of the company.

There were the usual clauses forbidding the company to interfere with or weaken the works of the navigation except for the purpose of constructing the bridge, and requiring the making good of any damage done. The whole of the works done in the Ancholme level by the company were to be done under the supervision of the Commissioners' engineer. The company were to be responsible, in addition, for seeing that the flow of water was not obstructed by any of their works, and they must remove any ice found against these works in any of the waterways in the level. Any failure to obey these regulations and any failure to keep in repair their bridges in the same area rendered the company liable to the payment of compensation for any resulting damage to the Commissioners' works and defences.

The T.A.G. Bill proceeded through Parliament fairly easily during the first six months of 1861, being unopposed in both Houses. The Board of Trade, with which D. and Co. had deposited a copy of the draft Bill on 22 December 1860 (D. and Co. bill 22 Dec. 1860) reported[1] that the proposal was for acquiring and completing a railway 14 miles 1 chain in length "now in course of construction", from the Trent to Barnetby, to be completed within four years, adding that the company was authorized to enter into agreements

[1] *Accounts and Papers* (23) 1861, LVI, p. 545.

with the M.S.L. It was stated that, under Section 9, the exercise of borrowing powers was to be deferred until the whole of the sum of £80,000 remaining to be spent on the construction of the line should have been subscribed for. The Board of Trade's suggestion here was that it might be proper, "in accordance with the usual practice", to require that the whole of the capital of £120,000 should have been subscribed for, including therein the portion of the share capital to be allowed to Winn and Dawes, before borrowing powers were exercised. Attention was drawn, too, to the fact that the amount of the shares to be allotted to Winn and Dawes would not be ascertained until after the passing of the Bill. One other comment made was that the part of Section 9 which said borrowing powers should not come into force until half the total capital of £120,000 should also have been expended, went beyond the second rule of the 126th Standing Order of the House of Commons which merely required that previous to the exercise of borrowing powers, 50% of the whole of the capital should have been paid up. These suggestions appear to have had no significant effect on the wording of the Bill. More serious was the Board of Trade's objection to the level crossings proposed in the Bill. But Mr. Massey, reporting later from the Commons committee[1] said that evidence had been given before the committee that the roads were little frequented and that the landowners and inhabitants of the district would be less inconvenienced by level crossings than by bridges over the railway; the committee therefore recommended that the crossings Nos. 2, 7 and 32 should be allowed (9/1/145). The only alteration made concerning the capital was that there should be inserted a recital that the estimated expense of completing the railway was £80,000.

The stages through which the Bill passed between the drawing up of the Board of Trade's report and the report stage in the Commons are to be followed in the correspondence and in D. and Co's account of expenses (9/1/80, 87, 93, 94, 109, 117, 122, 141, 143 and 9/4 from 19 February to 29 April 1861); that is when Thomas Freer, John Roseby, and W. C. Atkinson gave proofs before the Examiner of compliance with Standing Orders on Friday, 1 February, to when the Bill went to the Lords in the middle of May. (Freer appears to have had no difficulty in convincing the Examiner that the failure to comply[2] with the Orders—i.e., the late payment of the deposit into the Court of Chancery (9/1/93)—was a minor failure and could be overlooked.

The chronology of the Bill's course through the Commons is to be found in the Commons Journals[3]:

[1] *Herepath*, 1861, p. 671.

[2] *L. J.* XCIII 1861, p. 741. The procedure followed in proving compliance with Standing Orders is illustrated in Stubbs 9/7 Statement of Proofs . . . (L.A.O.).

[3] *C. J.* 116, 1861, pp. 9, 12, 62, 63, 67, 76, 183, 203, 211, 347, 362.

6 Feb. 1861	T.A.G. petition was presented, read, and ordered to be referred to the Select Committee on Standing Orders. It was decided that Standing Orders might be dispensed with and the Bill be allowed to proceed.
19 Feb.	The Select Committee's report on the petition was read and leave given for the Bill to be brought in.
20 Feb.	George Hussey Packe and Capt. Jervis introduced the Bill which received its first reading.
25 Feb.	Second reading and committal of the Bill.
3 May	Charles Forster reported from the Committee on the Bill, stating what amendments had been made.
10 May	The amended Bill was considered by the House.
14 May	Third reading; the Bill was sent to the Lords.
11 July	The House considered the Lords' amendments which were read twice and the Bill was sent with amendments to some of the Lords' amendments back to the Lords.
15 July	The Bill was returned to the Commons with no further change.

When the Bill went to the Lords, it was read a first time and referred to the Examiners for Standing Orders on 16 May.[1] On 3 June it was read a second time and committed, and the report was made with amendments on 21 June. The Bill was read a third time with the amendments, passed, and sent back to the Commons on 21 June.[2]

In two respects the Bill had come in for criticism and amendment. Lord Redesdale (on the Lords' Committee) was bound to be an obstacle for the promoters of a Bill for a short length of railway: he was said by *The Railway Times*[3] to have waged "a bitter war" against companies trying to establish the right to impose terminal charges for short distances, with the result that shareholders were subjected to "enormous charges from time to time". A ton or more of merchandise might be sent for loading at one station and unloading at the next one, the whole charge being embodied in the rate per mile at which that particular type of goods had to be carried. But Lord Redesdale seemed now to be moving away from what *The Railway Times* termed the "harsh exclusive policy to which he has been so strangely addicted". After a consultation between railwaymen, their lawyers (like Baxter and Dyson), and the chairmen of committees in June, a concession was made. On 8 June it was reported[4] that the T.A.G. Bill had been revised before Lord Redesdale's Committee during the week; and on 15 June it was announced[5] that the clauses on terminal charges had been agreed to. The Commons,

[1] *L.J.*, XCIII, 1861, p. 741.
[2] *Ibid.*
[3] 1861, p. 734.
[4] *The Railway Times*, 1861, p. 736.
[5] *Ibid.*, p. 763.

however, struck out[1] the clause the Lords had inserted in committee allowing the company to make a terminal charge not exceeding 2s. a ton for goods and 9d. a ton for minerals unless they remained (by the desire or default of the consignor) on the company's premises more than twenty-four hours after notice of their arrival had been given; instead the Commons allowed "a reasonable sum for loading . . . unloading of Goods at any Terminal Station of such Goods . . . performed by the Company", but no station was to be considered a terminal station "in regard to any Goods . . . which have not been received thereat direct from the Consignor or are not directed to be delivered to the Consignee". And that amendment was accepted by the Lords on 12 July.[2]

The other matter on which amendment arose concerned level crossings. As the Bill stood when originally drawn up, there were to be six level crossings: Nos. 2, 59, 84, 23, 32, and 7 on the plan; the first in Brumby, the next two in Frodingham, two in Appleby, and the last in Wrawby. This last one was on the turnpike road from Brigg to Barton. (The list given in 9/7—Roads crossed on the level —does not quite coincide with the list given above). Colonel Yolland, for the Board of Trade, had, on 18 April 1861 (9/7 Report), given reasons for disallowing the second (No. 59), the third (No. 84), the fourth (No. 23), the fifth (No. 32), and the sixth (No. 7). However, in the Lords (17 June),[3] Lord Redesdale's Committee reported that Standing Orders had not been complied with in that the roads were not suitable for the level crossings the company proposed to make, but in two cases the Standing Orders should not be enforced. The crossing at No. 2 (in Brumby) should be allowed because the line would there be on an embankment of five feet and a half, the "country" was low, an underbridge would be impracticable, and an overbridge would require the road to be raised about twenty-three feet. It would also render necessary a bridge over a large warping drain near the line. In Appleby the crossing at No. 32 should stay in the Bill because the road was very little used, "not more than Six Carriages a Day passing over it". The loaded trains would approach this road from the west on a straight line, and would be seen for a distance of half-a-mile. There would be a station here, "chiefly for Agricultural Produce", and an overbridge here would render the station difficult of approach for loaded waggons. But the Lords refused to swallow the arguments for the Elsham crossing (No. 7): they simply ordered No. 7 to be left out.[4] The Bill was then passed and received the Royal Assent on 22 July 1861.[5]

Meanwhile the S.Y. had been pushing on with their own K.E. measure, the object of which was to link up with the M.S.L. at

[1] *L.J.*, XCIII, 1861, p. 503.
[2] *Ibid.*, p. 503.
[3] *Ibid.*, p. 398.
[4] *Ibid.*, p. 398.
[5] *Ibid.*, p. 741.

Barnetby by means of the T.A.G., making a railway from Keadby terminating in the township of Brumby, a total distance of $2\frac{5}{8}$ miles.[1] It was proposed to carry the railway across the Keadby Canal by "by one opening span on the swivel principle", 18 feet wide; and at $1\frac{5}{8}$ miles from its commencement to carry it over the Trent by a bridge of eight spans of 30 feet, three of 50 feet each, and one opening span of 50 feet; the soffit of the viaduct was to be not less than twelve feet above the surface at high water.[2] The Bill had been before the Examiner for the Standing Orders Committee as early as 8 February 1861,[3] but it ran into opposition from the people who used the Trent near Keadby,[4] opposition which had been gathering force right from the beginning of 1861, centring in Gainsborough.

As far back as November 1860 action had been taken by a Gainsborough resident. The *Stamford Mercury* reported[5] he had received from the Admiralty a reply to his letter enquiring if the Lords Commissioners had given their approval to a bridge which was likely to be a great injury to navigation. The reply was that consent had been given for a bridge with an opening span (for the passage of vessels) of 68 feet in width, with a headway of $13\frac{1}{2}$ feet above high water mark. The Gainsborough reader of the *Mercury* called on the inhabitants of Gainsborough and the Isle of Axholme to bestir themselves in the hope that they might induce the Admiralty to reconsider its decision. Although the Pilot Commissioners of the port had met twice to consider the position, no action had been agreed upon. The Port Committee met on 7 December[6] and decided to draw up a memorial to acquaint the Admiralty with the feeling of the local inhabitants.

A town meeting was called next[7] by the Burgess Constable, (F. Gamble[8]) in compliance with "a numerously and influentially signed requisition". At the meeting Mr. Gamble said it behoved the Gainsborough people to lose no time in opposing the railway bridge scheme: "Seamen of all kinds who were accustomed to the navigation of the Trent were of opinion that the erection of a bridge at the place proposed would be exceedingly prejudicial to the interests of this port . . . They were also of opinion that besides impeding the navigation, the erection could prove exceedingly destructive to both life and property". Thomas Howard, who said he had been on the river for forty years, thought Keadby the very worst place for a bridge because that was a part of the river where the tide ran very

[1] *Accounts and Papers* (23), 1861, LVI, p. 187.
[2] *Ibid.*
[3] *L.J.*, XCIII, 1861, p. 735.
[4] *Accounts and Papers* (23), 1861, LVI, p. 187.
[5] *L.R.S.M.*, 7 Dec. 1860.
[6] *L.R.S.M.*, 14 Dec. 1860.
[7] *L.R.S.M.*, 25 Jan. 1861.
[8] Francis Gamble, seed crusher and oil merchant, wine merchant, and ship owner (White's *Lincolnshire* (1856), pp. 184, 185, 187).

fast—a powerful spring tide ran at the rate of eight or nine miles an hour—and at times the river was very shallow. He said the hazard would be all the greater because there was no place in that vicinity where vessels could wait in safety; on account of the nature of the bottom, anchors would not hold. There would be serious difficulties at night: it would be "next to impossible" to go through the bridge then; the lights the bridge might carry would increase rather than diminish the danger and difficulty.

Captain Catley next added his quota of opposition. The bridge would be a great nuisance; even without the bridge there was frequently trouble because of twenty to thirty vessels coming down the Keadby Canal at once; the bridge would increase the difficulty, and, indeed, lives would be lost as all vessels would have to go through the middle arch; with "the tides they had" this would be a problem and many must on occasions "lose a tide". Another speaker, Mr. Hyde, claimed that the bridge would block up the drainage of the land. In addition he raised the point that the bridge would be bound to harm Gainsborough as Keadby would become the port, and Gainsborough would decline in prosperity. Undoubtedly here he touched the nub of the matter.

Eventually J. E. Sandars[1] formulated the objections of the meeting, and when his motion was carried, Mr. Farmer[2] produced another —that a railroad such as was proposed was unnecessary as the ports of Hull and Gainsborough were already adequately connected with Lancashire and the West Riding. Only one voice, it seems, was raised against these proposals. It was that of the Rev. W. Worsley,[3] who thought it would be well not to pass any resolution that would create enemies. A committee was then set up of sixteen (with power to add to their number) who were to meet every Monday, Wednesday, and Friday, and who were to point out the objections to the bridge at the Admiralty and the Board of Trade, at the same time asking for a competent person to be sent down to investigate and report. When the question of expense was raised, Mr Gamble was stated to have said that at least £500 would be required. Immediately Mr. Plaskitt[4] objected that that would be inadequate: a fee of 150 guineas would have to be paid to a senior counsel and 50 guineas to a junior, and 30 guineas would need to be paid afterwards; then twenty to thirty persons would have to spend a month or two in London, the expense of which he would leave the meeting to calculate. Then there would be £300 to pay to a Parliamentary agent, and "other etceteras amounting to a good round sum". W. B.

[1] Corn merchant, Terrace House, Gainsborough (White, *op. cit.*, p. 178).

[2] Possibly T. A. Farmer, a director of Gainsborough United Steam Packet Company (see P.R.O. MT 19/59, letters to the Admiralty).

[3] The Rev. William Worsley of Morton, minister of the Unitarian Chapel, Beaumont Street, Gainsborough (White, *op. cit.*, p. 179).

[4] Presumably Wm. Plaskitt, attorney, Silver Street, Gainsborough (White, *op. cit.*, p. 179).

Heaton,[1] however, thought money could be saved by getting the help of "the Trinity House", the Trent Navigation Company, and "other bodies". He added that he was authorized by the lord of the manor[2] to say he would give £50 to the fund to be raised to fight the bridge scheme. So the committee was set up, headed nominally by H. B. Hickman. This committee co-opted Sir C. H. J. Anderson of Lea Hall to join in a deputation to the Admiralty[3] on 26 January. As a result of this action the Admiralty promised (30 January 1861)[4] to send "a competent person".[5] The *Mercury*, reporting this, added that a steam packet was to be made available for him.

The committee reported at a vestry meeting in the Gainsborough Town Hall on 21 February,[6] and stated that a petition against the Bill was being drawn up, a petition which it was hoped would be supported by the Trent Navigation Company, and the Corporation of Nottingham. A further meeting—the Local Health Board meeting—on 4 March[7] led to a firm decision to draw up a petition from the people of Gainsborough, though Mr. G. Gamble[8] wanted to know by what authority such a petition was to be presented. On being told the authority was that of the representatives of Gainsborough and the hamlets of Morton, Walkerith, and East Stockwith, Mr. Gamble said that was not a satisfactory answer "in a legal point of view" and no petition should be considered until his question had received a satisfactory answer. Only one of the "representatives" supported him, however.

After a letter had been received from the Admiralty to say that there would be no official enquiry until the Commissioners had considered the Bill,[9] the opponents of the bridge took further action by arranging for "Mr. Page, the eminent engineer"[10] to survey the Trent near Keadby. Page's report[11] said the proposed bridge was to have eight arches of 30 feet span, and four arches of 50 feet span, one of

[1] Wm. Barnard Heaton, attorney, Market Place, Gainsborough (White, *op. cit.*, p. 179).

[2] Henry Bacon Hickman of Thonock Hall (White, *op. cit.*, p. 163).

[3] *L.R.S.M.*, 1 Feb. 1861.

[4] *L.R.S.M.*, 8 Feb. 1861.

[5] Sir C. H. J. Anderson, of Lea Hall, had helped by persuading J. Banks Stanhope, M.P. for North Lincolnshire, to write also to the Admiralty in support of the memorial (*L.R.S.M.*, 22 Feb. 1861).

[6] *L.R.S.M.* 1 March 1861.

[7] *L.R.S.M.*, 8 March 1861.

[8] George Gamble was one of the first Directors of the T.A.G., and continued to act until his resignation in February 1863 (P.R.O. (B.T.H.R.) TAG/1/82); he was also a Director of the M.S.L., resigning in January 1863 because he felt the shareholders were opposing his re-election—after thirteen years on the Board (P.R.O. (B.T.H.R.) M.S.L./1/6). At the Commons Select Committee hearing, 22 April 1861, he stated that he lived partly in London and partly in Gainsborough, that he was a Director of the M.S.L. "amongst other things", and that he was engaged "in a very extensive business [in Gainsborough] as a General Merchant". He had also, he said, superintended the construction of the large Grimsby Dock (H.L.R.O. Commons Evidence, 1861, S.Y. (K.E.) Railway, Vol. 72, S8, 22 April, p. 31).

[9] *L.R.S.M.*, 8 March 1861.

[10] *L.R.S.M.*, 15 March 1861.

[11] *L.R.S.M.*, 29 March 1861.

which was to be an opening span. The height from high water mark to the soffit of the girder would be 12 feet. The report compared the proposed Keadby bridge with similar bridges over the Ouse, below Selby; at Torksey; and at Nottingham (58 miles above Keadby), and found the Keadby bridge "totally inadequate". It would obstruct navigation for most vessels passing above Keadby and would tend to injure all the Trent trade above Keadby. Danger must occur as a number of vessels passing up or down the river might arrive when the bridge was occupied by a train and the opening arch could not be used. The report alleged that incidents of engines starting off on the line without a driver were "not infrequent", and any occurrences of this kind might have fatal consequences. It was "not probable that vessels would risk the passage otherwise than by letting go their anchors, swinging by the tide, and then dropping through the opening, a delay which would probably lose a tide, and, if the tides are decreasing, might lose a semi-lunation". Mr. Page thought the traffic could be provided for "by a railway under the Trent or by a floating bridge".

The opposition to the bridge was carried into the House of Commons. The Select Committee on the Bill provided the chance to attack and to defend the scheme on 22 and 23 April 1861. George Gamble, the Gainsborough Director of the M.S.L., was concerned to establish that there had been a steady decline of Gainsborough for years, and hence that it was futile to claim that its prosperity would be destroyed by a Trent bridge: the river traffic was "very much depressed, in fact to an extent that is scarcely describable". He quoted figures to prove his case. The introduction of the "Railway system generally" had led to Gainsborough's decline since 1849; up to then it had been thought well to "make the water carriage as long as you could and the land carriage as short as you could", but once railways had arrived that principle had been reversed. So Gainsborough would continue to decline anyhow, and what mattered was the development of the coal and iron traffic, which, he said, if the bridge was built, would be "fabulous". He regretted the town's decline because most of his income came from Gainsborough property, "I am sorry to say".[1]

Samuel Beale[2] gave evidence in favour of the bridge, all the more effective because he claimed to be disinterested; a railway across the river would, he said, be no use to him: "My Works are on the Water and I can more readily get to them by the Keadby Canal"; others, however, did need the railway.

John Dixon, Collector of Customs at Gainsborough, gave evidence, challenging Gamble's figures, and attempting to prove that Gains-

[1] H.L.R.O. Commons Evidence, 1861, S.Y. (K.E.) Railway, Vol. 72, S8, 22 April 1861, pp. 35-54.

[2] M.P. for Derby, Chairman of the Midland Railway Company, and ironmaster "until recently". (H.L.R.O. Commons Evidence 1861, S.Y. (K.E.) Railway, Vol. 72, S8, 22 April, p. 67).

borough's river trade was increasing; but it was clear that he had not convinced the Committee. The chairman, Michael Dobbyn Hassard, was directed to report the Bill to the House.[1]

By the time the S.Y. (K.E.) Bill reached the Lords for its second reading and being committed on 27 May 1861,[2] the Admiralty, possibly well aware that the opposition came from commercial interests rather than from a lobby for the humanitarian protection of river men, had managed to avoid a local enquiry on the ground that the evidence taken before the committee of the Commons would be the same as that required by the Admiralty and could be made available to their Lordships. This evidence was considered by the Admiralty and the decision was that the Bill should be agreed to, provided, first, that the bridge over the Trent was constructed with two openings of 60 feet span, each on the swivel principle, the headway under the span being 15 feet above the high water mark of ordinary spring tides; second, that all deposits or banks near the east end of the viaduct were removed to the satisfaction of the Admiralty previous to the start of building. The plans for both the Trent and the Keadby Canal bridges must in any case be first submitted to the Admiralty.[3]

The S.Y. (K.E.) Bill received the Royal Assent on 22 July 1861,[4] but all was far from easy travel for the company. At the half-yearly meeting of shareholders at Doncaster on 27 February 1861, the Chairman, John Parker, said that Charles Bartholomew, the company's engineer, had told him the K.E. would not exceed the original estimate (of £40,000),[5] and clearly he expected no problems. The difficulties began to pile up, however, in 1862, and they continued until October 1866. The difficulties were almost entirely to do with the bridge.

Bartholomew was asked to confer with Fairbairn (of the Manchester firm of William Fairbairn & Sons) who was to construct the bridge, and with Edward Watkin[6] on the general principle of the bridge. The interviews took place and tenders were asked for. Fairbairn's tender for a bridge on piles of an average length of 45 feet at a cost of £20,000, exclusive of masonry, was accepted on 10 August 1861.[7] Trouble was reported in May 1862:[8] very high tides had partially removed two "bridge cylinders" on the western side, but (in a fore-shadowing of modern P.R.O. handouts) it was claimed that good engineering would soon set all right, and though there might be difficulties, it was certain they would be surmounted. The

[1] H.L.R.O. Commons Evidence 1861, S.Y. (K.E.) Railway, Vol. 72, S8, 23 April, p. 126.
[2] *L.J.*, XCIII, 1861, p. 741.
[3] *Accounts and Papers* (23), 1861, LVI, p. 187.
[4] *L.J.*, XCIII, 1861, p. 741.
[5] *The Railway Times*, 1861, p. 296.
[6] P.R.O. (B.T.H.R.) SYD/1/8, 1 June 1861.
[7] P.R.O. (B.T.H.R.) SYD/1/8.
[8] *L.R.S.M.*, 23 May 1862.

very next week, however, came the news[1] that the works on the western side had been "thrown backward" by the removal of the second series of cylinders on that side by a coal-laden vessel on 24 May. Not only would the cylinders have to be re-set but fresh piles would need to be driven in. The coal vessel had sunk, but at least there had been no loss of life, either to the crew or to the bridge-builders. Eastward the land was brighter, though it was admitted that even there progress was slow. The cylinders were sunk nearly 30 feet below the bed of the river; unfortunately no solid foundation had yet been reached. However, a "powerful engine" was daily drawing up the water and sand, and hope continued high.

Another collision occurred on 13 July[2]; again it was a coal-laden keel; the vessel had been driven by the force of the tide on the piles which were to protect the "tubes" on which the swivel was intended to work. As the central opening on that day had been 130 feet, it was thought ominous: another set of cylinders had still to be set in the centre of this opening. Not surprisingly, Fairbairn wrote to the Directors[3] on 26 July 1862, suggesting fenders (or dolphins) for the bridge. The Board delayed decision on this until John Fowler[4] had given his opinion on the question of the necessity of the proposed addition to the bridge of the fenders or dolphins so far as the safety of the structure was concerned, and also on the effect such fenders would have on the navigation of the river.[5] It was some time before a decision was reached. On 11 July 1863 it was resolved that the protection recommended should be arranged by Fairbairn, Bartholomew, and Sacré,[6] who were to submit plans and drawings to the Board of Trade.[7] On 15 August, Board of Trade approval was announced.[8] By that time the whole of the cylinder piles were in place.[9] This was in spite of the fact that Lieutenant St. Aubyn had reported on 11 September 1862 that he had, as ordered by the Commodore Controller General on 24 December 1861, inspected the bridge and found that, while no provisions of the Act of Parliament had been broken, "just complaint" was made of the danger to navigation on the river. He considered the "bad position of the Bridge" the cause of the trouble.[10]

And accidents continued in the river. Another keel carrying coal had collided with "the second batch of tubes now in course of being deposited" in November 1862.[11] After an engineer under the Board of

[1] *L.R.S.M.*, 30 May 1862.
[2] *L.R.S.M.*, 18 July 1862.
[3] P.R.O. (B.T.H.R.) SYD/1/9.
[4] M.S.L. Engineer 1847-53 (Dow, *op. cit.*, I, p. 281).
[5] P.R.O. (B.T.H.R.) SYD/1/9, 29 Nov. 1862.
[6] S.Y. Engineer 1861-64 (Dow, *op. cit.*, I, p. 281).
[7] P.R.O. (B.T.H.R.) SYD/1/9.
[8] P.R.O. (B.T.H.R.) SYD/1/9.
[9] *Herepath* 1863, p. 938.
[10] P.R.O. MT 19/59.
[11] *L.R.S.M.*, 28 Nov. 1862.

Admiralty had been sent in December[1] to investigate, and local opinion was hardening that "the site of the bridge is as bad as could have been fixed on", the Directors got Admiralty permission for two pilots to be appointed during the construction of the bridge until "Boatmen are more familiar with the proper mode of passing through it".[2] The Directors, in spite of a spirited letter to the Admiralty on 24 December 1862,[3] claiming that stories of accidents were exaggerated, and any mishaps were the result of "unskilful navigation", were understandably feeling low; the contractors' superintendent told them he did not expect the bridge to be completed in less than eight or nine months from then; so they ordered the Secretary to express "to Mr. Fairbairn the extreme disappointment which such a state of progress occasions to the Board". Fairbairn was to be told that the Board had relied on his professional character, his judgment and fair dealing, and the assurance he had given that the bridge would be ready by May 1862; that time was now long past and great loss was being daily suffered by the company from the want of transit of minerals across the Trent.[4] He was adjured to press on.

Other accidents continued to be reported in 1863: in February two narrow boats towed by a tug, in July a sloop from Grimsby bound for Gainsborough, in September two sloops.[5] An officer of the marine department of the Board of Trade (Captain Sullivan) was reported in the *Mercury*[6] as saying the Keadby bridge affair might be regarded as an instance of unfortunate and hasty decision: the openings of the bridge had been put in the wrong position: the railway did not even dispute that it had been decided on improperly. But despite danger and loss "we have no power to remedy it". By September, however, Fairbairns were able to announce that they had started the "protection works" for the bridge; as, at the same time, they put in a bill for extras[7] the Board's spirits were not cheered, and in October they told Fairbairn how disappointed they were, saying "there is reason to believe that even now [the bridge] might be more expeditiously proceeded with", Fairbairns being "bound for their own credit" to take on extra labour to complete the work.[8]

At the special meeting of S.Y. shareholders on 30 March 1864, the new Chairman, the Hon. W. G. Eden, said the bridge was sufficiently far advanced for him to have crossed it on foot the previous day. At this meeting it was decided to ask the Board of Trade to inspect and approve the line so that traffic could start to

[1] *L.R.S.M.*, 19 Dec. 1862.
[2] P.R.O. (B.T.H.R.) SYD/1/9, 21 Jan. 1863.
[3] P.R.O. MT 19/59.
[4] P.R.O. (B.T.H.R.) SYD/1/9, 21 Jan. 1863.
[5] *L.R.S.M.*, 13 Feb., 17 July, 11 Sept. 1863.
[6] *L.R.S.M.*, 26 June 1863.
[7] P.R.O. (B.T.H.R.) SYD/1/9, 26 Sept. 1863.
[8] *Ibid.* SYD/1/9, 31 Oct. 1863.

pass over it.[1] All that happened as a result of this decision was that a splendid train carrying only those directly interested in the concern—Directors and officials of the company—together with a number of their friends made the journey by train on 14 May 1864 from Liverpool, via Manchester, to Grimsby, stopping at Keadby to inspect the bridge over the Trent. The account of this journey given by the *Mercury*[2] suggests that the train, "consisting of twenty new and handsome first-class carriages", completed the whole distance, including the crossing of the bridge; it speaks of the "good people of Keadby, all of whom were in their holiday attire to witness the arrival and departure of the train". In another part of the same paper (under "Althorpe") a shorter report is given, though here the train has shrunk to fifteen "splendid carriages". But again the impression is given that the train crossed the bridge: it is stated that four of the carriages returned by the same route in the evening from Grimsby, the rest going by way of Retford on the M.S.L. line. A later recollection, that of Mr. A. Woodley[3] in a letter in March 1924 to Mr. G. R. Walshaw, reinforces this interpretation. His father had come to Keadby in October 1860 as locomotive driver; as a possible eye-witness (he was living then at Burringham) he affirmed that the railway and the Trent bridge were opened for passenger traffic on the occasion when Watkin and the M.S.L. Directors went to Grimsby in 1864 (stopping, as the *Mercury* report agreed, at the Trent Works at Scunthorpe to see the furnace tapped). Mr. Woodley's recollection is, however, far from being conclusive proof. A list of dates relating to Great Central matters by "Mr. Taylor of Sheffield"[4] gives: July 1st 1864. Keadby Bridge . . . First opening". And Mr. Dow, the authoritative historian of the Great Central is quite clear that his date—1 July 1864—was the first time Keadby Bridge was crossed by a train.[5]

The bridge was described then[6] as being 475 feet long, 22 feet wide, with about a third of it swinging on a turntable, easily moved, leaving a channel of 60 feet; it was said to be built on cassoons sunk to a depth of 80 feet in the river. The Board of Trade having declined to pass the bridge for traffic, another request for inspection was made on 16 July.[7]

The inspector who was sent down, Capt. F. A. Rich, forwarded his report to the Board of Trade on 27 July[8]: "about 2 miles 56 chns long" and forming a junction with the line to Keadby, about a third of a mile to the south-west of the town of Keadby, and joining the

[1] *Ibid.* SYD/1/9, 30 March 1864.
[2] *L.R.S.M.*, 20 May 1864.
[3] Scunthorpe Museum, file of letters, notes, and cuttings relating to local railways.
[4] Scunthorpe Museum, *loc. cit.*
[5] Dow, *op. cit.*, II, p. 30, and letters (4 and 15 Dec. 1972) to the editor of this volume.
[6] *L.R.S.M.*, 20 May 1864.
[7] P.R.O. MT 6/39/4, (1368R).
[8] *Ibid.*

T.A.G. "about three-quarters of a mile to the east of the river Trent". "I understand that it is proposed to work this single line in connection with the [T.A.G.] on the train staff system, and that the Engines will work thro' to the Elsham Station . . . which is to be a passing Station for the trains, but that the Engines will return from Elsham. Turntables will be required at the terminal Stations to which the Engines work . . .

"A lifting bridge over the Canal of 43 ft. span on the skew. The lifting beams are of Cast Iron and the superstructure and piers are wood.

"A viaduct over the river Trent. The piers are Cast Iron Cylinders, filled in with masonry, concrete and brickwork, and braced above high water. The abutments are Ashlar masonry and the Girders are Wrt Iron. There are four openings of 75 ft. and two of 60 ft. span—the two latter swing on the centre, of the continuous beam, which spans the openings.

"There are four wooden Viaducts, each having three openings, varying from 12 to 27½ ft. in width.

"The Railway is carried over these openings on two baulks 13 in. or 14 in. Square which are not sufficient for spans above 20 ft. wide. Where the spans are above 20 ft. they should be trussed and well strapped or bolted together.

"The present bolts are insufficient and do not fulfil their purpose, being too light and should have iron washers at least 4 in. Square.

"I have not been furnished with drawings of the iron Bridges. They are no doubt strong enough to carry a single line . . . but they are intended to carry two lines of rails.

"The Swinging portions of the Trent Viaduct are not firm when the bridge is closed. It is merely keyed like an ordinary turntable, the ends are not supported firmly when the bridge is closed and the rails to do [*sic*] meet by about 2 in. The ends of the rails on the fixed portion of the Viaduct, next to the swinging parts, are also unsteady.

"I would suggest that the end of the swinging bridge should be brought to a firm bearing by means of a cam and it would be desirable that the same power, which brings the cam into bearing, should work slides at the ends of the rails and form connections between the rails on the fixed parts of the bridge and those on the swinging portion. The Signals should be worked in connection with the swing bridge, so that the latter cannot be opened without the Signals protecting it being at danger. The Dolphins erected to guide vessels through the openings and protect the piers of the bridge, are not of a permanent construction. The wash of the river has already undermined the foundations of one of them, and it has been completely carried away. It would appear desirable, that in addition to strengthening the foundation by filling in with Stones, that the piles should be erected in a stronger manner, and that the portions above low water should be sheeted and perhaps protected from floating ice. Lights are wanted on the dolphins and no provision has yet been made to show vessels approaching whether the bridge is open or shut. The Co. propose to do this, by a high telegraph post on the bridge. Lieut St. Aubyn R.N. who was present at the inspection, consented to this arrangement as an experiment, but his original suggestion, as to the Signal Station at the points above and below the bridge, appears to me the best, particularly if these Signal Stations are worked in connection with the Signal Station on the bridge by the application of the block telegraph system.

"The Swing bridge over the Canal is also defective. It rocks considerably when a train passes over it, and requires some adjusting and some arrangement to make the bearings firm when it is shut and to prevent the Signals being lowered when it is open. A Bridge or flat bottomed rail well bolted down would be preferable to the double-headed rail on all the bridges, but through bolts, fastened into longitudinal timbers are essential, as the ordinary spike driven into a 3-in. plank as now done affords no security." Capt. Rich added that the only station, Althorpe, was incomplete: the platform and the signals were not yet erected. Further there were no houses at the level crossings between Thorne and Keadby; nor were the gradient boards and clocks yet supplied. Not surprisingly this vote of no confidence in Fairbairn's construction ended with the submission that the K.E. could not be opened for passenger traffic without danger to the public.

The carrying away of one of the dolphins was said[1] to have happened on 23 July—two days before Rich visited Keadby. This (southern) wing of timber, "probably weighing 100 tons, floated "up the river" like a large "raff"; but, it was noted, the cylinders, despite the strain on them, "remained immovable as adamant".

The refusal to allow the bridge to be opened encouraged the opposition along the Trent, especially as accidents continued.[2] Meetings were held at Keadby on 11 August 1864 (Lieut. St. Aubyn and C. Bartholomew being present then),[3] and at Gainsborough on 29 August[4], this being attended by people from Lincoln, Nottingham, Mexborough, Newark, Hull and Keadby; at both meetings demands were made that there should be an opening span of 100 feet. The S.Y. Board urged Sacré (brought in since the middle of 1863 when relations between Bartholomew and the Board became less than easy) to speed up operations; he asserted on 7 January[5] that it was only the completion of the "Swing Bridge over the Canal" which was holding up the opening of the line, and that was in the hands, not of Fairbairn, but of Garforth. On 31 August 1865 he reported

[1] *L.R.S.M.*, 29 July 1864.
[2] *L.R.S.M.*, 23 Sept. 1864, 24 March 1865, 31 March 1865, 14 April 1865, 15 Sept. 1865, 20 Oct. 1865.
[3] *L.R.S.M.*, 19 Aug. 1864.
[4] *L.R.S.M.*, 2 Sept. 1864.
[5] P.R.O. (B.T.H.R.) SYD/1/9, 7 Jan. 1865.

the approaching completion of the works.[1] In spite of this reassurance the Board declined[2] to settle Fairbairn's demand for the balance of the account presented in 1864—with good reason.[3] Not until 5 April 1866 did Capt. Rich report that the line was ready to be opened for passage to traffic.[4]

In his report he stated that the line had now been doubled; a wrought iron swing bridge to carry two lines of rails over the canal had been substituted for the cast iron lifting bridge; this new bridge "works easily and well". "The arrangement for supporting the ends when the bridge is closed (which has been adopted with this swing bridge as also with the swing bridge over the Trent) appears to answer very well." The ends were "wedged up by inclined planes, which act on the ends of the swinging parts of the bridge as well as on the ends of the fixed parts, against which the swinging bridge shuts, and they are adjusted by a screw". He went on to say that the cross girders of the Trent bridge were too light to carry the weight of two pairs of driving wheels, but the longitudinal beam carrying the rail was 15 inches square and had been hollowed out above each cross girder so that the rail bore only on the longitudinal timbers between each pair of cross girders, and this distributed the weight on those girders: the strains on them were thus less than five tons to the inch. Nevertheless it would be desirable, he thought, whenever it was necessary to renew the longitudinal baulks, always to adopt some means for distributing the weight of the engine over the cross girders. He had found the swing bridges provided with double signals both at the bridges and at the "Auxiliaries". The closing of the bridges caused one signal arm to lower, but there was also a second, covering arm on each signal post, which the signal man in charge had to lower. The two arms covered "each other" when up or down and looked like one signal; this one signal always remained on till the action of the bridge moved one arm, and the signal man moved the second arm. There were, in addition, auxiliary signals, worked from the bridge, both above and below the bridge, to warn vessels of "the State of the Bridge". All the same, satisfactory as these arrangements seemed to be he suggested that all trains ought to be "brought to a stand" before passing over the swing bridges (i.e., both river and canal). He criticised the locking arrangements at both junctions, the one near the canal, the other near Frodingham on the T.A.G., suggesting that these (particularly when made by "Mr. Stephens") were frequently defective and needed constant watching. The four wooden viaducts had now been taken down, and structures of stone and wrought iron had been put in their place.

[1] *Ibid.* SYD/1/9.
[2] *Ibid.* SYD/1/9, 20 Oct. 1865.
[3] It should be noted that Fairbairns were not responsible for all the works; they had sub-let the making of the cylinders to Butler of Stanningley (*L.R.S.M.*, 20 May 1864).
[4] P.R.O. MT/6/39/4, (885R).

The construction of the line east of the bridge had been relatively simple and elicited less criticism from the Board of Trade inspector: the short stretch of a mile or so presented no engineering problems. The lines of the S.Y. and the T.A.G. converged from points on the Trent about a quarter of a mile apart to a junction just over a mile east of the river. The S.Y. line had, of course, required a plan and book of reference (L. A. O. Stubbs 9/6 Copy of Book of Reference S.Y.).

Official permission to open the K.E. was given on 14 April 1866.[1] The five years allowed by the 1861 Act had nearly all been needed. No wonder Sacré was "glad to inform" his Directors that the bridge might be opened.[2] Delays notwithstanding, however, the building of the bridge was an achievement. It was certainly vital for the development of cross-country traffic.

The T.A.G. was not to open for passenger traffic until 1 October 1866, although Board of Trade sanction had been received in August.[3] The tale of woe had been almost as harrowing as that of the S.Y.—with, however, fewer mitigating factors. The engineer, Charles Bartholomew, seems to have done less than might have been expected of him.

He had been authorized by the S.Y. to proceed with the works on the T.A.G. on 10 August 1861,[4] and at the first of the T.A.G. Directors' meetings, at Doncaster, 28 September 1861,[5] he attended as engineer. Work had already then been started; of the 500,000 cubic yards of earth which, he said, would have to be displaced to reduce the gradient to one in 100, 10,000 had been removed, and he forecast an end to the job within ten months. The Directors (who included Rowland Winn and George Dawes[6]) urged on him the necessity of finishing before the Trent bridge was opened, and he said that "by working night and day" the cutting could be completed by 31 March 1862 at an extra cost of £2,000. Charles Verity, the contractor employed, was authorized to engage the additional labourers needed. Dawes had already completed about seven miles of the railway to Barnetby[7] (and arrangements were now made to have the value of that work assessed so that Dawes's allocation of shares might be known); the remaining part of the line, including the construction of the "girder bridge over the Ancholme", was to be let by contract, tenders to be received by 9 October 1861. At this meeting, too, it was resolved to apply to Parliament for an Act in

[1] P.R.O. MT/6/39/4.
[2] P.R.O. (B.T.H.R.) SYD/1/10, 19 May 1866.
[3] P.R.O. (B.T.H.R.) TAG/1/1, p. 213.
[4] P.R.O. (B.T.H.R.) SYD/1/8.
[5] P.R.O. (B.T.H.R.) TAG/1/1, pp. 1-4.
[6] Dawes resigned at this meeting (P.R.O. (B.T.H.R.) TAG/1/1, p. 7), but was re-elected at the Shareholders' meeting on 28 Dec. 1861 (P.R.O. (B.T.H.R.) TAG/1/1, p. 17). His niece, Mary G. Dawes, claimed that he was made a Life Director (Letter to G. R. Walshaw, 18 April 1944, in file of letters, notes, and cuttings relating to local railways at Scunthorpe Museum).
[7] P.R.O. (B.T.H.R.) TAG/1/1, p. 4.

1862 to allow the T.A.G. to be absorbed into the M.S.L. "on the terms arranged".[1]

At the next meeting on 10 October the contract for the construction of the 3 miles 74 chains to the junction at Barnetby was given to Thos. Waring & Co., subject to modification of prices; otherwise to Skelsey & Micklethwaite.[2] As Waring failed to modify, Skelsey got the contract.[3]

Bartholomew has spoken of working "night and day", but that twenty-four hour system had evidently been discontinued shortly after he spoke, for at the end of November he was reporting that the "Gas Works" would be complete in the course of fourteen days, when night work might be resumed; and by the end of December he was able to state that "the gas works" were completed and the lighting was in operation.[4] He also said at this time that one-third of the cutting was completed at Frodingham Hill. Earlier he had spoken of piers for the viaduct; this was the viaduct 1,017 yards east of Frodingham. On the plans and sections drawn up by Atkinson and Roseby there was to be a tunnel here, but almost immediately after the T.A.G. Act was passed Bartholomew had suggested a viaduct in place of the tunnel, and his suggestion was adopted, as cheaper.[5]

At first all seemed to go well. By 27 February 1862 four miles of railway had been at work for some time, though this had partly been constructed under Dawes's 1860 development. This stretch of line ran down to the Trent from the iron ore workings, a staff of men being employed in working and repairing the line at a cost "for labor and coals" of about £23 a week; the traffic averaged about 200 tons a day, which might "by a little attention" be increased to 300-400 tons a day. The rate paid for the traffic was, as agreed, 6d. a ton, and thus £30 a week was earned. Two engines were at work, one on the level part of the road and one on the incline.[6]

But even as early as 26 April 1862 there were indications of dissatisfaction with the rate of progress. "Greater dispatch" was demanded,[7] "the completion of the line at an early date being of great importance". Bartholomew was ready to promise that the line would be ready for traffic by 1 August. He asserted that 498 men were at work on Frodingham Hill removing 4,000 yards day and night, and there were only 20,000 yards remaining out of 450,000 yards. (His figures are sometimes a little difficult to reconcile with each other, as the Board were soon to think; at one moment he claimed to be doing 4,000 yards a day, at another 10,000 yards a

[1] P.R.O. (B.T.H.R.)TAG/1/1, p. 4.
[2] *Ibid.*, p. 9.
[3] *Ibid.*, p. 10.
[4] *Ibid.*, pp. 12 and 20.
[5] P.R.O. (B.T.H.R.) SYD/1/8, 10 Aug. 1861; TAG/1/1, p. 134. But see D. & Co.' bill, 8 Feb. 1861.
[6] P.R.O. (B.T.H.R.) TAG/1/1, pp. 27-8.
[7] *Ibid.*, p. 39.

week.) The bridge over the Ancholme, he promised, would be finished in a month.[1] Six weeks later there were 70,000 yards remaining to be excavated; apparently in those six weeks the rate of work had been reduced drastically; and the Ancholme bridge was far from complete, though, it was claimed, only ten days' work was needed on that. Another month would see the end of all the work[2]; even though there were still 18,000 yards left to remove in the Wrawby section, "the Gullett" was now "thin", so that would require only three weeks to finish.

After another six weeks it appeared that no progress at all had been made on the bridge over the Ancholme.[3] However, in the Wrawby cutting the contractor had now started ballasting from the land at the east end near Barnetby; that job was not expected to take long as there would be "a locomotive at this work on Monday"; Bartholomew claimed, therefore, that "during the next month" (October) the line would be "immediately available between the Ironstone Field and Grimsby for Mineral Traffic". But at the end of October he had to admit that the Ancholme bridge was still unfinished, and so was the ballasting[4]; at least a month later he could claim a little progress on the arches of the viaduct at the other end of the line: only 17 (out of 94) arches[5] there were incomplete; and the western end of the Frodingham embankment had been joined to the viaduct. At last, too, the Ancholme bridge was completed and rails had been laid across it.

Having been promised on 28 September 1861 that the basic work would take only ten months, and even now being unable to see an end to the operation, the Board may well in November 1862 have felt some alarm, since delay meant extra expense; they therefore called for figures. The figures must have failed to inspirit them.[6]

Bartholomew said Dawes's "Tramway" which had been bought had cost £29,958 5s. 1d.; outlay for new work to October 1862 accounted for £77,532 6s. 5d.; a further outlay of £28,899 18s. 9d. would be called for. To this total of £136,390 10s. 3d. must be added £10,000 for Charles Winn's land, £3,443 9s. 1d. for other land already purchased, while still further land needed to be bought at a cost of £5,300; tenants' claims (for compensation) would come to £247 0s. 7½d., and incidental expenses amounting to £411 14s. 7d. must be reckoned in. Solicitors', engineers', and surveyors' charges had not yet been received. The company had already spent or was committed to spending altogether at least £155,793 4s. 6½d. If the single line then being laid down were to be double there would be another £25,000 to seek. The discrepancy between the original figure of

[1] P.R.O. (B.T.H.R.) TAG/1/1, p. 46.
[2] *Ibid.*, p. 50.
[3] *Ibid.*, p. 56.
[4] *Ibid.*, pp. 61-2.
[5] *Ibid.*, p. 65.
[6] *Ibid.*, pp. 67-8.

£120,000 in the Act and those now revealed must have been discouraging.

The Directors could not be blamed if by this time they felt weary of Bartholomew's excuses. Nearly every meeting they had held had for months been full of them. In June they had been told that wet weather prevented night work and impeded day work[1]; besides that the supply of bricks for the viaduct had "proved very deficient". In September it was a shortage of labour: "Most of the men have gone off harvesting, although the Contractor has been paying 3s. 4d. a day at least. Lodgings are so bad to get that the best men leave, the first chance of other work". Four weeks later it was weather and labour together that were holding up the job. The weather was still unfavourable in October, and though the contractor had now got his bricks, he had failed to get bricklayers "notwithstanding his repeated advertisements and best endeavours". Wet weather had caused soil slips in the Wrawby cutting. Then frost took a hand, Bartholomew was sorry to say, causing further "large slips". To add to his troubles the engine used for ballasting by the contractor "was peremptorily required by its Owner, he having sold it"; but for that the line would have been open at least for "Minor Traffic"; as it was, a broken-down engine which had long been standing at Frodingham was all that could be used.[2] This last complaint seems to have decided the Board upon action. Although they were not ready to go the extent of getting rid of Bartholomew, they asked him to arrange with Charles Sacré to find an efficient engine, and passed a resolution that they had great cause to complain of the slow progress made by the contractor in the works at the Barnetby end and would not make any more payments to him until that part of the line was ready for mineral traffic.[3]

Bartholomew at last on 24 January 1863 reported, after a preliminary—and presumably compulsive—lament about weather, that the line was ready for traffic from the ironstone field to Barnetby[4]; he had ridden over the line himself ("in a Second class carriage")[5]; on 28 March he thought the contractor would reach the embankment at the west end of the Frodingham viaduct within a week; in July he said the bridge at Frodingham was "in progress"; the laying of the line and connecting it with Rowland Winn's line would complete the works; it should not take more than two months.[6] The good news ended two months later, when Bartholomew had to confess he had been too sanguine: harvesting and an accident disabling the engine used in the Frodingham excavation had been too much for him.[7] Not till 30 January 1864 was he able to report that

[1] P.R.O. (B.T.H.R.) TAG/1/1, p. 47.
[2] *Ibid.*, pp. 47, 53, 55, 61, 62, 65, 72-4.
[3] *Ibid.*, pp. 74-5.
[4] *Ibid.*, p. 78.
[5] *Ibid.*, p. 84.
[6] *Ibid.*, p. 97.
[7] *Ibid.*, p. 109.

Verity had completed the contract,[1] eighteen months after the date Bartholomew had originally forecast.

There were still stations, signals, and other equipment to be put in, and it was not until the end of March that the Board of Trade could be asked to inspect and declare the line ready to open to traffic. But the inspector's report, read at the meeting on 10 August 1864, declined to sanction the opening; the reason given was that the works were incomplete.[2] Although no entry was made in the Minutes to indicate the dismissal of Bartholomew, the next Engineer's Report was the work of Sacré, on 25 October 1864. It noted that the cutting at Wrawby had been lowered as the inspector had required, and a five mile stretch of the line which was being doubled was nearly ready for sleepers.[3] Not even a change of engineers produced any miraculous speeding up of the rate of progress. Although Sacré said on 21 February 1865 that the Ancholme embankment was "standing" and no further trouble over subsidence was expected, he was not ready for another inspection until 20 October 1865. The report, drawn up on 4 November 1865, and read on 27 January1866, was damping.

The line, it said, had now been doubled, but junctions were incomplete at Gunness "at the Mineral Sidings where Beale's Sidings, and where Mr. Winn's Siding join the Main Line"; there had been a slip in a deep cutting about a mile from Barnetby; though the long viaduct appeared to be standing well "in spite of the doubtful foundation," cracks and settlements needed pointing (and careful watching); and although the wrought iron girders on the Ancholme viaduct had been strengthened sufficiently to meet Board of Trade requirements for a double line, the inspector refused to pass the line.[4]

The chief reason for this refusal seems to have been the level crossings. Only two had been sanctioned by the 1861 Act, but either the engineer or the Directors (or more likely both) had hoped the Act could be ignored. The Board blandly declared themselves of opinion in October 1862 that level crossings "might be substituted for the several road crossings by bridges with equal advantage to the Railway and the Public", and had asked Baxter to arrange the matter with the Board of Trade[5]; they followed that up in November (when the unpleasant figures above mentioned had been put before them) by asserting that because of the "limited local traffic" (over

[1] P.R.O. (B.T.H.R.) TAG/1/1, p. 127.

[2] *Ibid.*, pp. 142, 153.

[3] The decision to have the line doubled seems to have been taken by 13 August 1863, when, at a half-yearly meeting of shareholders, a resolution was passed authorizing the doubling of the line between the Trent and the Ancholme, and also authorizing the Board to raise an additional loan to pay for it. (*The Railway Times* 1864, p. 1077). Baxter was asked to promote a Bill in 1864 to give the company power to raise another £60,000 in share capital (TAG/1/1, p. 116); but Sacré was still "strongly recommending" the doubling on 28 April 1865 (P.R.O. (B.T.H.R.) TAG/1/1, p. 184). See P.R.O. (B.T.H.R.) TAG/1/1, p. 156, for Sacré's report on the doubling of the line.

[4] P.R.O. (B.T.H.R.) TAG/1/1, pp. 204-6.

[5] *Ibid.*, p. 59.

the turnpike road), and for the convenience of the public, it would be better to have a level crossing than a bridge at Elsham. Baxter was again brought into action, but although he seems at the end of 1862 to have drawn up a memorial with local signatures,[1] the Sectary[2] had to explain on 29 April 1865 that the Board of Trade would require the company to undertake to go to Parliament for permission to regularize the unauthorized level crossings[3]; so evidently Baxter had not been successful. The inspector, Capt. Rich, now, therefore, drew attention to the fact that although a bridge had been constructed in place of one of the unauthorized crossings, No. 23, at 6 miles 49 chains, there were still three unauthorized public crossings: one, No. 59, at 3 miles 21 chains at Frodingham Village; one, No. 84, at 3 miles 75 chains at Frodingham station; and one at Elsham station, at "about the 12 mile post".[4]

However, by February 1868, it emerged that the level crossing at Elsham had received Parliamentary sanction[5]—the Board of Directors' intransigence had been rewarded. There had been local support for the crossing on the ground that a bridge there would be very awkward for vehicles and would entail the making of "very heavy approaches on each side, in consequence of the level nature of the road"; a bridge there could not be made to look "much sightlier than the 'hump' upon a camel's back".[6] In this instance local opinion had prevailed. Baxter had to apply to the Board of Trade for an extension of time to allow the other crossings to be converted, but permission to open the line was received, it was announced, in August 1866.[7] The expenditure had amounted to £265,848 7s. 9d.[8] As John Parker said on 22 April 1861 before the Commons Committee on Railway Bills (Group 5), when asked why, if the cost of the Keadby Bridge was estimated to be only £27,000, it was necessary to apply for permission to raise £100,000, in railway matters there are "always odds and ends".[9]

Long before the completion of the work Bartholomew's connection with the line had ceased. He was a difficult man to get rid of, as the S.Y. had found in 1859.[10] He had been accused then of being too much involved in and preoccupied with his interests in the Yorkshire coal trade. Whether he did then and in the T.A.G. affair fail to give adequate attention to his job as engineer, it is difficult to say,

[1] P.R.O. (B.T.H.R.) TAG/1/1, pp. 71-2.
[2] Edward Ross who had taken the place of C. H. Thiel, 10 Aug. 1864.
[3] P.R.O. (B.T.H.R.) TAG/1/1, p. 185.
[4] *Ibid.*, pp. 204-5.
[5] *Ibid.*, p. 237.
[6] *L.R.S.M.*, 29 March 1867.
[7] P.R.O. (B.T.H.R.) TAG/1/1, p. 213. The Frodingham crossings remained.
[8] *Ibid.*, pp. 216-7.
[9] H.L.R.O. Commons Evidence 1861, S.Y. (K.E.) Railway, Vol. 72, S8, 22 April, p. 16.
[10] See *The Railway Record*, 10 Sept. 1859. He had been driven to resigning—but he was on the Board of Directors within four years. See also P.R.O. (B.T.H.R.) SYD/1/9, Oct. 1863—Oct. 1864.

but there is no doubt that ill feeling built up against him. It was, however, over his accounts that the split came. The dispute began over the question of the accuracy of the contractor's measurements, in September 1863, Bartholomew being, he insisted, unable to say whether the measuring had been done accurately. Accordingly F. C. Blackburn of Oldham was asked to make an independent measurement of the work done; his report was that the value of that work was £69,148 14s. 4d., whereas Bartholomew had given a certificate for £72,825 4s. 3d. William Hutton, a Director, now therefore objected to the payment to Verity of the difference between the two figures, particularly as he said he had met Blackburn, who had admitted that on consideration he realised he had underestimated the difference by £3,400. Asked for an explanation, Bartholomew (producing a mass of figures for the viaduct portion of the line) conceded that on account of a "clerical error in extending an amount in the account" certified for Verity, there could have been an overpayment of £873 7s. 9d.[1] The Board let the matter go then—but also, it seems, let Bartholomew go. He demanded to be summoned to Board meetings. He was told (January 1865) that the Board did not consider him "any longer responsible for the Engineering of the Line". Sacré had, in fact, supplanted him. Always a fighter, Bartholomew then chose to attack Sacré, saying that the latter had alleged to Baxter that the eastern end of the line (for which Bartholomew had been responsible) "was in a regular mess".[2] He failed to get very far with that. In the end he had to acknowledge defeat, but he then submitted his account for £3,573 8s. 7d. On 3 January 1865 it was reported that he had agreed to accept £2,250 in full discharge of all claims, the amount being paid in 5% Debentures issued by the T.A.G.[3]

One other dispute occurred, this time between Rowland Winn and the T.A.G. On 31 August 1865 attention was drawn to the fact that "an impression seemed to exist in the mind of Mr. Winn that the Branch from Gunhouse to the Trent, was his private property". As the company might need this line, it was pointed out, the exact position ought to be ascertained.[4] Eventually Baxter, to whom the matter was referred, reported that Rowland Winn had got a clause inserted in the Act (No. 17) prohibiting the company from deviating from the centre line shown on the plans between the beginning of the railway at the Trent and the spot marked on the plans at the fourth furlong of the second mile. He had thought this provision would leave him the part of the railway from the junction to the Trent already made. But he had overlooked the fact that the Act

[1] P.R.O. (B.T.H.R.) TAG/1/1, pp. 111-6, 132-6. Bartholomew's aim seems to have been to show that whatever the truth concerning the comparatively small sum owed by Verity he (Bartholomew) had saved the company over £20,000 in the construction of the viaduct.

[2] *Ibid.*, pp. 174-5.

[3] *Ibid.*, pp. 187-8.

[4] *Ibid.*, p. 192.

transferred to the company all the railway there made, including the part referred to.[1] Moreover he had received compensation for that part. True, the land had not been conveyed, but as he had made a contract to convey to the railway all the land it required for the railway, that did not affect the matter: the branch belonged to the company and not to Mr. Winn. Unfortunately, Baxter went on, the company had treated this portion as belonging to Mr. Winn and actually sent him a bill for the materials used in constructing it. However, Baxter said, it seemed the branch was of no value to the company since they had under their agreement the right to charge 6d. a ton whether goods were carried to the Trent or to the junction only. So if Mr. Winn had any desire to pay the cost of the line, it would be so much money in the pocket of the company. In strict law, though, the land was the company's.[2] The exact form of the final settlement does not appear in the Minutes, but it seems that Rowland Winn conveyed the land to the company; it had still not been completed, however, on 22 February 1873.[3]

When the Secretary produced figures for the Board in November 1863, he mentioned that tenants' claims to come, on account of land taken by the railway, would amount to £240 0s. 7½d. In fact they were to come to more than that. There had already been paid out as compensation to tenants £1,212 15s. 1d., and another £564 1s. 4d., with an extra £13 7s. for legal costs and valuers' charges, was to be paid between December 1863 and 2 March 1866. Had that been all there was to worry about the Directors might have slept easily. But, in addition to the compensation which had already been paid to owners, amounting to £2,720, £9,844 11s. 3d. was to be paid between December 1863 and December 1875 (£10,064 6s. 3d. if compensation paid to the Frodingham Surveyors of Highways is taken into account); the length of time for which the compensation was delayed meant much interest at 5% had to be added. So the sum of £4,564 13s. 11d. had to be found to provide interest, vendors' costs, surveyors' fees, and valuers' charges, with another £403 5s. 10d. for additional costs. Altogether land and tenant compensation cost £14,561 2s. 8d.; interest and the various types of charges amounted to £5,763 18s. 4d., or nearly 40% of the cost of compensation—spread, of course, over 14 years.[4]

Yet it had been a line which had met little opposition either in Parliament or in North Lincolnshire. It had caused surprisingly little disturbance. Apart from drains and occupation roads, there had been only eight public roads and two turnpike roads to cross, in addition to the old and new Ancholme rivers. Fifty names occur

[1] Winn seems to have wanted to insist that the part of the T.A.G. line between "where the Bridge branch joins and the River" should "be abandoned, as of course two lines to the Bridge are quite unnecessary". (L.A.O., Stubbs 7/36. Copy of letter to R. Baxter, 14 Feb. 1861).

[2] P.R.O. (B.T.H.R.) TAG/1/1, pp. 201-3.

[3] *Ibid.*, p. 24.

[4] Sheffield Central Library Archives, Baxter Papers 60959.

in the list of those tenants and cottagers who received compensation; of these names four occur twice and one three times; so, with another three described as occupiers, we can say there were only 47 tenants disturbed. There were four leaseholders; besides Charles Winn and the representative bodies there were 19 effective owners; ten of them had their land disturbed and were entitled to compensation; only one had to be paid compensation because the line necessitated the removal of buildings; he was the Vicar of Frodingham.[1] Surprisingly, his land was only within the limits of deviation and not in the direct line of the railway.

The T.A.G. had a short life (it was vested in the M.S.L. on 12 July 1882[2]), and it was never really independent. But the main aim of its begetter had never been the creation of an independent railway; he was no railway pioneer or enthusiast. He was the heir to an estate containing ironstone, and all he wanted was the means to exploit the latent wealth there. He was successful and his name was so closely associated with the T.A.G. that it could be called Mr. Winn's line.[3] It is doubtful if he was ever really interested in asserting such a claim; nor did he need to be while ironstone continued to engage his attention and to yield a good profit.[4]

[1] Sheffield Central Library Archives, Baxter Papers 60959

[2] Dow, *op. cit.*, II, p. 33.

[3] John Parker told the Commons committee in April 1861 that the proposed T.A.G. line was actually called "Mr. Winn's line" then. (H.L.R.O. Commons Evidence 1861, S.Y. (K.E.) Railway, Vol. 72, S8, 22 April, p. 10).

[4] That is not to say that his railway was of only temporary value, or that it merely served Rowland Winn's immediate purpose. It was no lame duck that the M.S.L. picked up in 1882: the first ordinary dividend declared by the T.A.G., in February 1869, was $2\frac{1}{2}\%$ for the half-year; but for the whole year in 1881 the dividend was $11\frac{3}{4}\%$, and the final dividend declared (Feb. 1882) was 6%; in between 1869 and 1881 the dividend never fell below $4\frac{1}{2}\%$ for the year. The M.S.L. had paid no ordinary dividend from Dec. 1848 to June 1854; it paid nothing in 1858 and 1862; and its highest dividend for the whole year never rose above $3\frac{1}{2}\%$ from 1872 to 1881. Even with the help of the comparatively prosperous T.A.G. its dividend sank steadily to under 2% from 1883 to 1885. (Dow, *Great Central*, 11, p. 350, P.R.O. (B.T.H.R.) TAG/1/1, pp. 257-272, and 1/2, pp. 3-109).

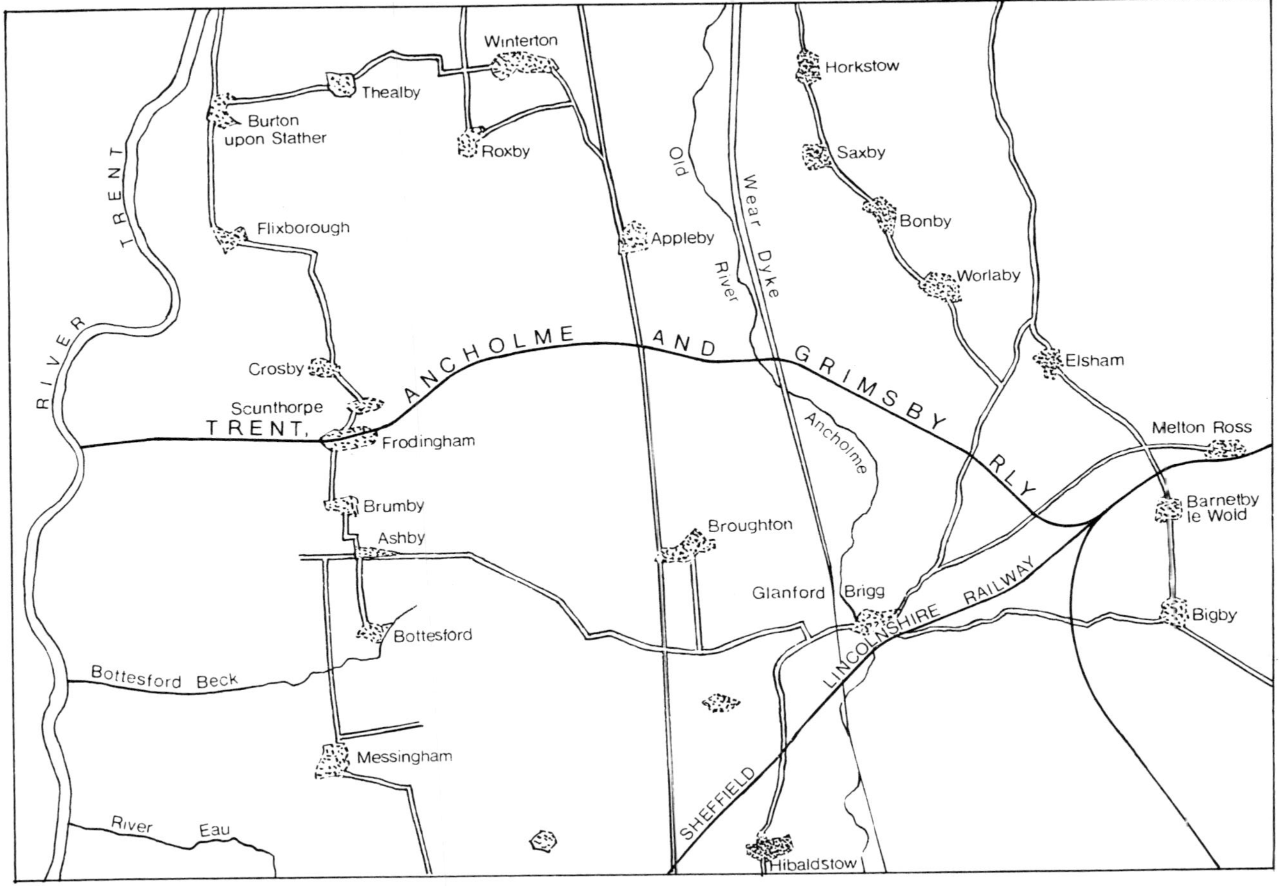

Sketch-map showing the line of the T.A.G. Railway. Drawn by R. Ingamells. Based on the map in L.A.O. (Deposited Plans: Lindsey County Council 1/76) based on the ordnance survey map of 1824.

The first railway swing-bridge at Keadby seen from the Althorpe side. It became dangerous and a new rail bridge with a road attached was erected and opened in 1916 just to the north of the old bridge.

(From *Great Central* Vol. II by George Dow, by kind permission)

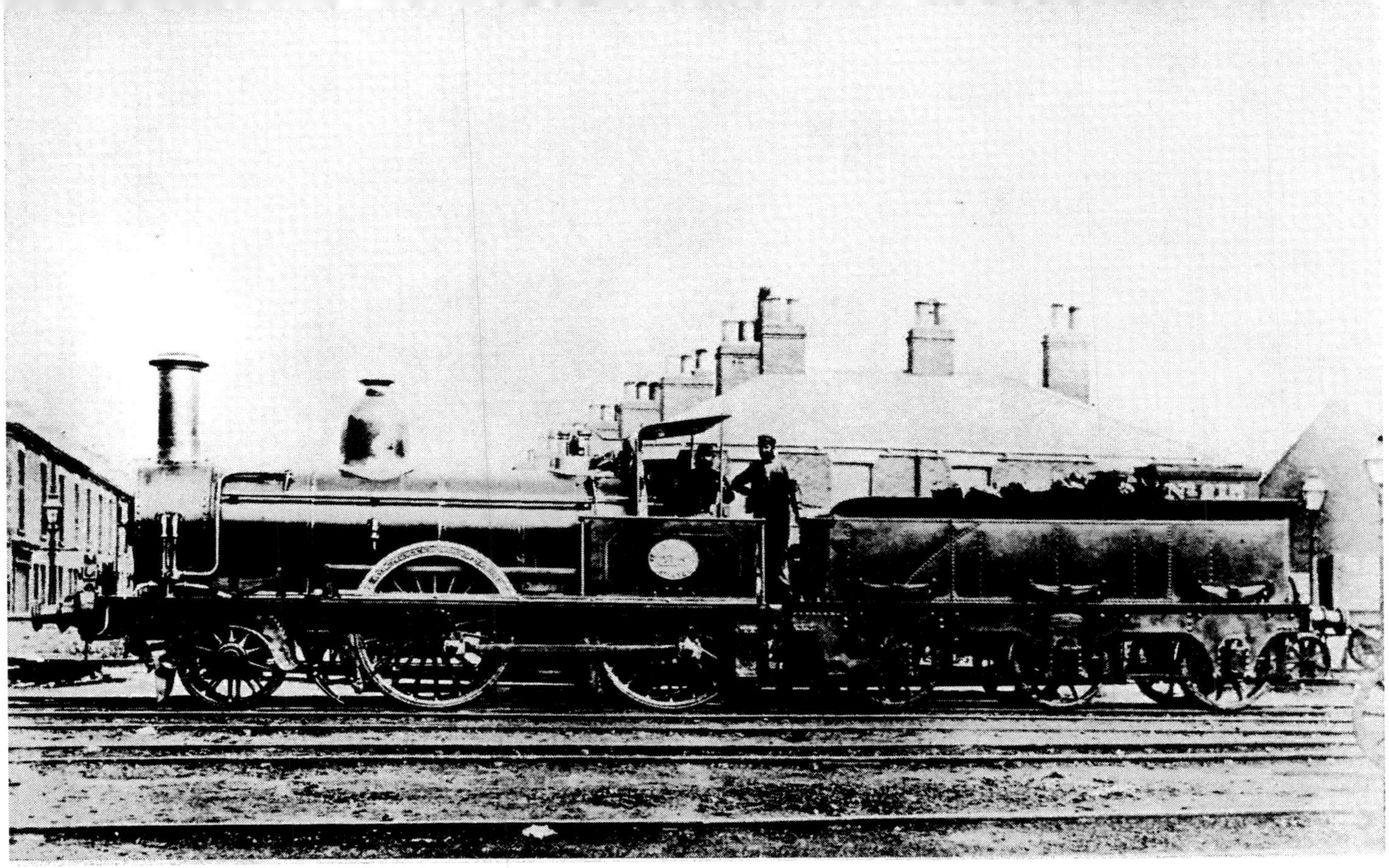

One of the early engines used on the T.A.G. Railway: one of four 2-4-0 engines with 5′ 6″ wheels, built by Beyer Peacock for the Sardinian Railways, but bought by the M.S.L. in 1865. The colour was basically a darkish green but there was a polished brass dome.
(From *Great Central* Vol. II by George Dow, by kind permission)

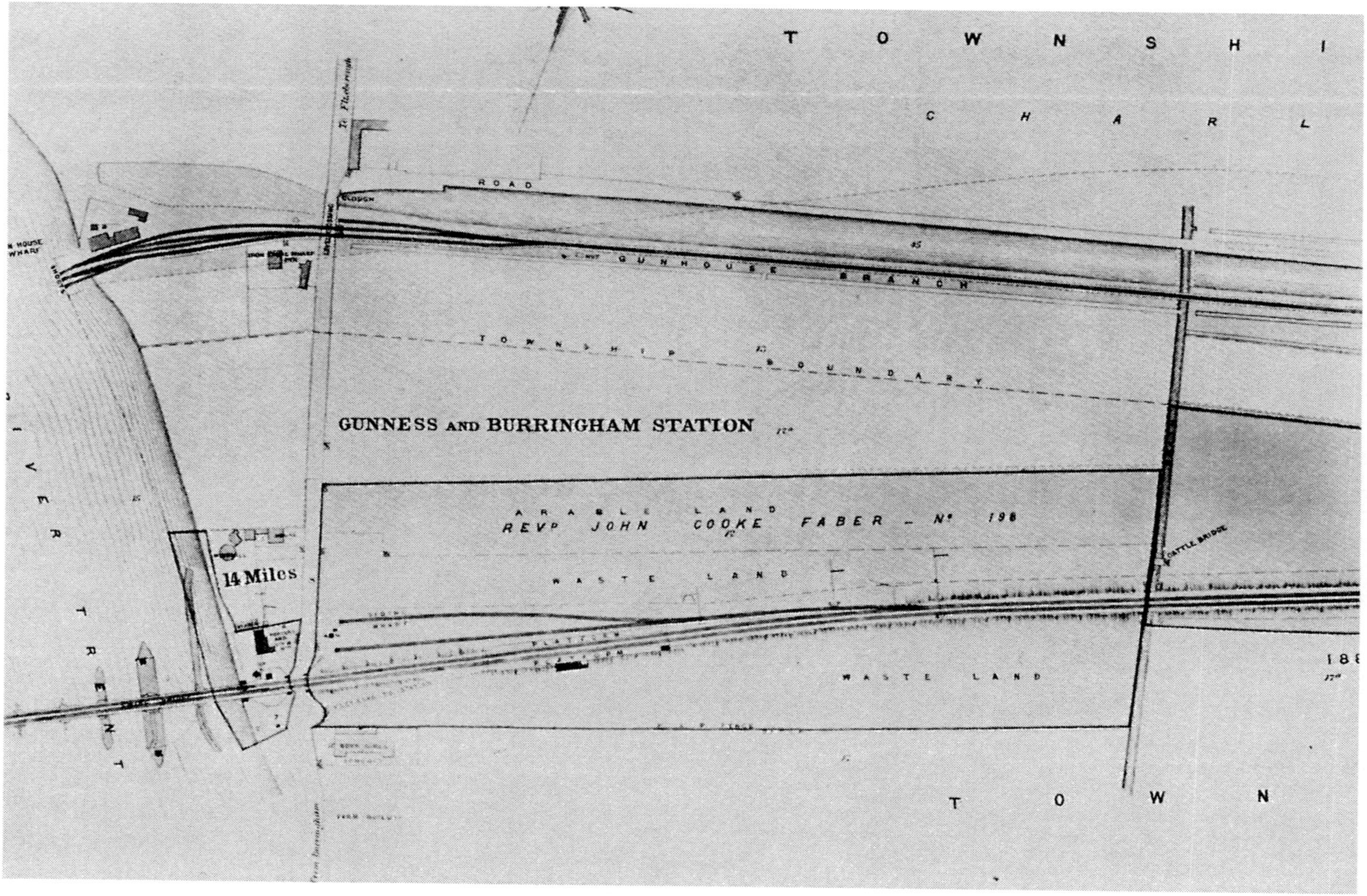

From Sheet 24 of M.S.L. Railway Maps. South Yorkshire Line. Trent and Ancholme from River Trent to Barnetby, *ca.* 1885.
(In Scunthorpe Library)

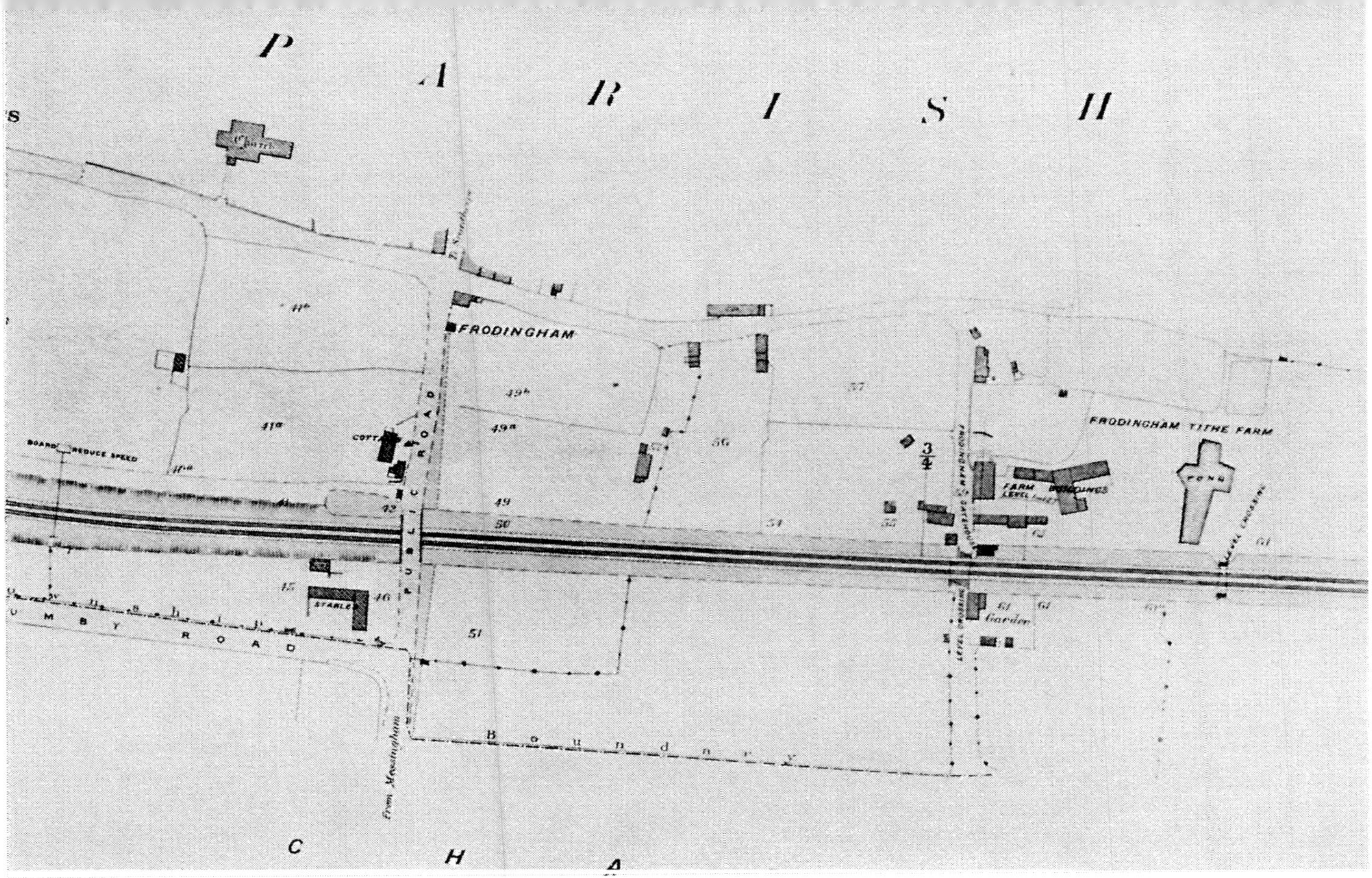

From Sheet 25 of M.S.L. Maps. South Yorkshire Line. Trent and Ancholme from River Trent to Barnetby, *ca.* 1885.
(in Scunthorpe Library)

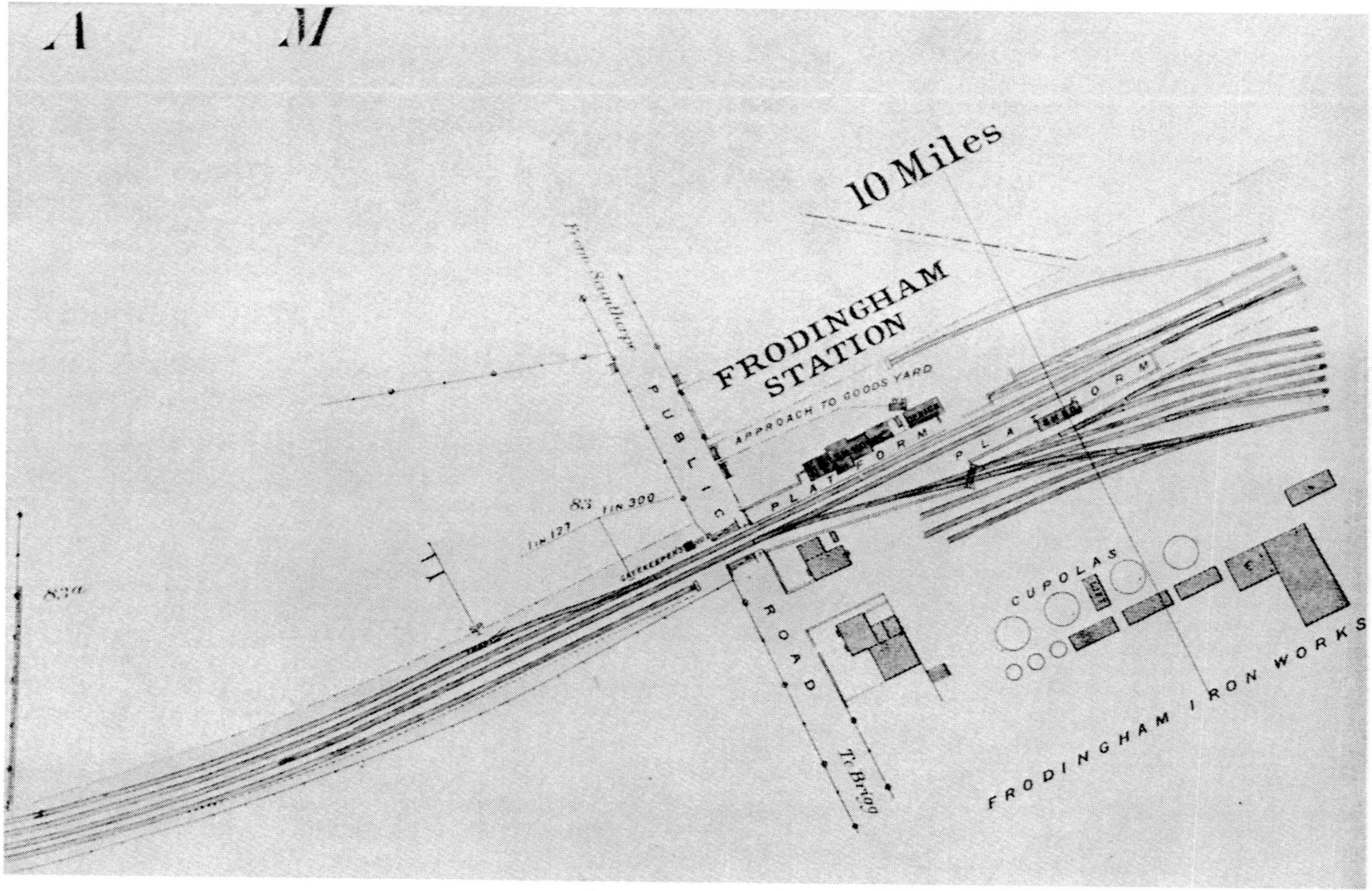

From Sheet 25 of M.S.L. Railway Maps. South Yorkshire Line. Trent and Ancholme from River Trent to Barnetby, *ca.* 1885. (In Scunthorpe Library)

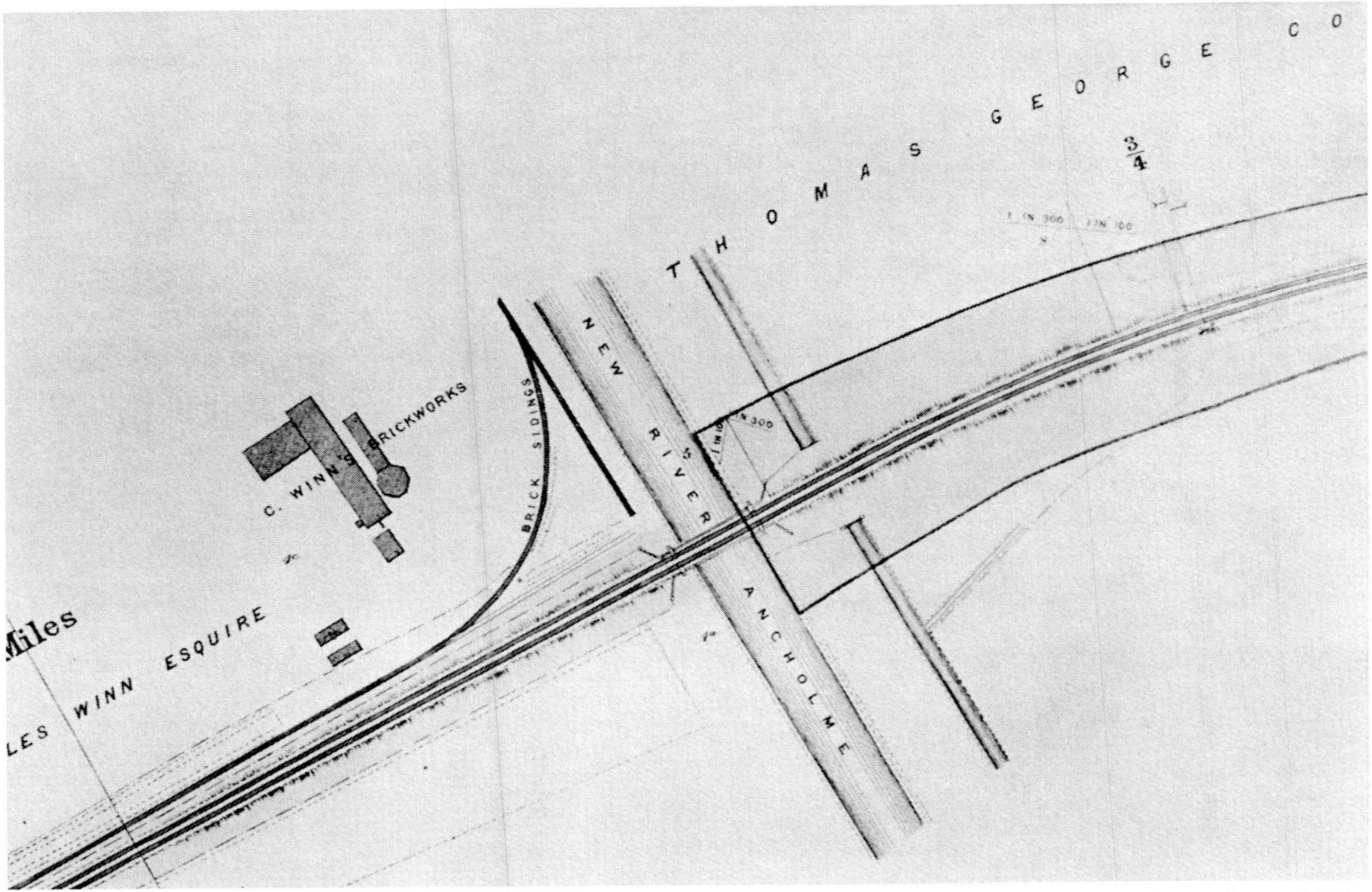

From Sheet 28 of M.S.L. Railway Maps. South Yorkshire Line. Trent and Ancholme Line from River Trent to Barnetby, *ca.* 1885.
(In Scunthorpe Library)

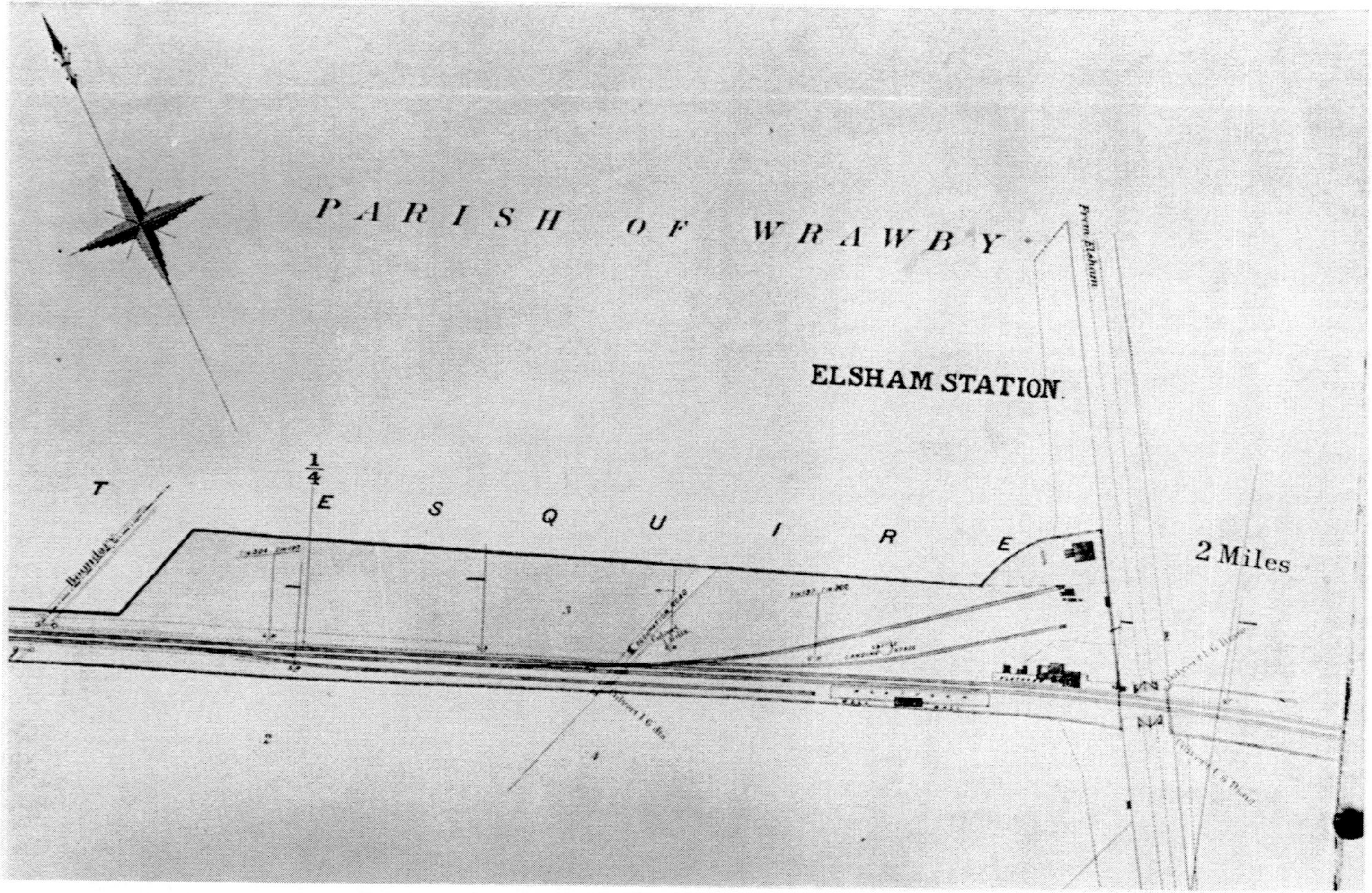

From Sheet 29 of M.S.L. Maps. South Yorkshire Line. Trent and Ancholme from River Trent to Barnetby, *ca.* 1885.
(in Scunthorpe Library)

Part of Frodingham Viaduct (the "Gunhouse incline") near the Scotter Road, between 1900 and 1910, in which latter year most of the viaduct was filled in by an embankment.
(From the Scunthorpe Museum and Art Gallery Railway Papers and Photographs)

I/9/6
Trent, Ancholme, and Grimsby Railway.
(Railway from the Trent, near Keadby, to Barnetby-le-Wold).

Application is intended to be made to Parliament in the next Session thereof for leave to bring in a Bill to incorporate a Company, and to vest in the same Company, upon such pecuniary and other conditions as the said Bill shall define, a Railway now constructing by Charles Winn, Esquire, between the right bank of the River Trent, near Boggard Hall, in the Parts of Lindsey, in Lincolnshire, and the West Side of the new River Ancholme, at a spot called Worlaby Plains, which Railway traverses the following Places, all in the said Parts of Lindsey, namely:—The Township of Brumby, in the Parish of Frodingham; the Township of Gunhouse, in the Parish of Frodingham; the Townships of Frodingham and Scunthorpe, in the said Parish of Frodingham; the Hamlets of Low Santon, High Santon, and Thornham, otherwise Thornholme, in the Parish of Appleby; and the Parishes of Appleby and Worlaby, otherwise Worletby; and to enable the same Company to complete and maintain the same Railway, with all necessary Stations, Approaches, Conveniences, and Works.

To enable the Company to make and maintain an extension of the said Railway, with all necessary Stations, Approaches, Conveniences, and Works, commencing by a junction with the last-named Railway at its termination as aforesaid on the west side of the new River Ancholme, in the said Parish of Worlaby, passing through the same Parish, and the Parishes of Elsham, and Wrawby otherwise Wrawby-cum-Brigg, the Hamlet of Kettleby, otherwise Kettleby-Thorpe, in the Parish of Bigby, and the Parishes of Bigby and Barnetby-le-Wold, all in the said Parts of Lindsey, and terminating in the said Parish of Barnetby-le-Wold, by a junction with the Manchester, Sheffield, and Lincolnshire Railway, near and about five furlongs to the south-west of the Barnetby Station of the same Railway.

The Bill will authorize the Company to purchase lands, houses, and other property, compulsorily, for the purposes of the said Extension and Works, to levy tolls, rates, and charges in respect thereof, and also of the Railway so to be vested in them by the Bill; to cross, alter, and divert roads, tramways, drains, sewers, navigations, rivers, streams, and watercourses, and to maintain any crossings or alterations already made; and to vary and extinguish existing rights and privileges, so far as may be necessary in constructing or maintaining the said Railway and Extension, or any of the Works connected therewith respectively.

The Bill will enable the Company to be thereby incorporated on the one hand, and the Manchester, Sheffield, and Lincolnshire Railway Company, and the South Yorkshire Railway and River Dun Company, or either of them, on the other hand, from time to time to make and carry into effect agreements for and in respect of the working, management, maintenance, and use by either or both of the said Companies of the said Railway and Extension; the supply of rolling stock and machinery, and of Officers and Servants for the conduct of the traffic on the same; the payments to be made and the conditions to be performed with respect to such working, management, maintenance, use, and services; the interchange, accommodation, and conveyance of traffic coming from or destined for the undertakings of the contracting Companies, and the division and apportionment of the revenue arising from that traffic; and the Bill will confirm any agreements already made between or on behalf of the said parties touching the matters aforesaid, and will authorize the appointment of joint committees for carrying into effect any such agreement as aforesaid.

The Bill will incorporate with itself the necessary provisions of "The Railways Clauses Consolidation Act, 1845", "The Companies Clauses Consolidation Act, 1845"," The Lands Clauses Consolidation Act, 1845", and "The Lands Clauses Consolidation Acts Amendment Act, 1860"; and it will amend and enlarge the powers and provisions of the Act 12 and 13 Vict., cap. 81, and of the other Acts relating to the Manchester, Sheffield and Lincolnshire Railway Company, and of the Act 10 and 11 Vict., cap. 291, and the other Acts relating to the South Yorkshire Railway and River Dun Company.

Duplicate Plans and Sections describing the line, situations, and levels of the Railway already constructed or constructing, and of the proposed Extension thereof, and the lands, houses, and other property to be taken for the purposes of the Bill, together with a Book of Reference to the Plans, containing the names of the owners and lessees, or reputed owners and lessees, and of the occupiers of the said lands, houses, and other property; also a published Map with the line of Railway delineated thereon, and a copy of this Notice, will on or before the 30th day of November instant be deposited for public inspection with the Clerk of the Peace for the said Parts of Lindsey, at his Office at Spilsby; and on or before the same day a copy of so much of the said Plans, Sections, and Book of Reference as relates to each of the Parishes in or through which the said Railway and Extension pass, and a copy of this Notice, will be deposited for public inspection with the Parish Clerk, of each such Parish, at his place of abode; and in case of any extra-parochial place, with the Parish Clerk of a Parish immediately adjacent thereto.

Printed copies of the intended Bill will be deposited in the Private Bill Office of the House of Commons before the 23rd day of December next.

Dated this 13th day of November, 1860.

Nicholson, Hett, and Freer
Solicitors for the Bill

[This notice had to be published in November 1860, once in the *London Gazette*, and once in each of three successive weeks in a newspaper published in Lindsey, in a Manchester paper, in a Doncaster paper, and in a London paper.

In the Stubbs Deposit (7/33) the only copies of newspapers carrying the notice were the *Barton, Brigg, Caistor, and Winterton News* for 18 Nov. 1860, and the *Manchester Guardian* for 16, 23 and 28 Nov., 1860.]

I/9/4

Papers relating to the arrangements made by Mr. Winn with Mr. Corbett, 1860.

Letter: T. G. Corbett to N.H. & F.; from Elsham Hall, 10 November 1860:

As the Railway which is now in contemplation from the Ancholme to join the Manchester S. & L. Railway near Barnetby may pass from Mr. Winn's into other hands I think it best to reduce to writing and obtain a written guarantee for the performance of the conditions on which alone I shall give my consent to the Railway crossing my Land which conditions have been already verbally assented to. These conditions are a Station on the Turnpike Road from Barton to Brigg at the spot already indicated—also in case of any Minerals being worked on my Estate a convenient siding to be made at any point of the Railway I may select for their conveyance. A siding to be at once made for the use of the Worlaby Brickyard and a Siding for the use of the tenants at the Worlaby Causeway. The Station and Sidings to be all made both as to purchase of Land and every other outlay and kept in repair at the expense of the Proprietors of the above-mentioned Railway.

Letter: R. W. to T. G. Corbett (copy) 12 November 1860:

My time has been so completely taken up since I saw you at Elsham that I have never had time to write to you as I intended doing. I only got back from London late on Saturday night and found on calling that Evening at Mr. Atkinsons the surveyors house at Brigg that he had nearly completed his survey of the intended line of Railway and I hope the course he has selected for it will be one that is agreeable to you. I shall direct him to see you on the subject immediately and also to hear what are your wishes as to the exact spot where the station is to be especially as to which side of the Turnpike road as it is necessary I am told to show on the plans the site of the intended Station. If there is anything else about which you have any particular wish you may be sure I shall always be most happy to do the best I can to carry it out. It may be satisfactory to you that I should repeat in writing what I conceive to be the arrangement we verbally made the other day—

1st That a station is put up on your Brigg turnpike with a siding.

2nd That you have a siding provided for your Brickyard and another siding if you desire it at the place where the Rail will cross the Worlaby courseway [*sic*] (as I think it is called).

3rd That in the Event of your hereafter finding Ironstone at Elsham and deciding to work it we should make you a siding into our line for such mineral purposes to enable you more easily to work your stone. This siding would of course run across your own Estate only.

This is I think the general arrangements which were made the other day and with which I am quite satisfied. When we come to the Erection of the station I will have the plans submitted to you before the building is commenced as you may very likely wish to see them.

Letter: R. W. to J. H.; from Appleby Hall, 2 March 1861:

I have a note from Mr. Baxter this morning "There will be no manner of difficulty in the companies' taking upon themselves the obligations with Mr. Corbett". This is the whole of his letter. It therefore settles that part of the question.

I have written to Mr. Coates also Mr. Dickson.

I/9/7

Agreement between T.A.G. [?] C. Winn and T. G. Corbett [1860]

Rider A

The said Charles Winn having agreed with Thomas George Corbett Esquire an Owner of Land in the Parish of Worlaby and Elsham across which the said Line is intended to pass to make the undermentioned accommodation Works it is agreed that the Company shall take upon themselves the liability of carrying such Agreement into effect and indemnify the said Charles Winn from all responsibility in respect of the same namely

To construct a Station in the Parish of Wrawby on the West side of the Turnpike Road leading from Brigg to Barton upon Humber upon Land to be purchased by the Company.

To make in a convenient situation on the South side of the said intended Railway in the Parish of Worlaby upon Land to be provided by and to remain the property of the said Thomas George Corbett and also to keep in repair a single line of Railway from the said intended Railway to the Brick Yard of the said Thomas George Corbett in the same Parish with proper points Switches and Cross over Road.

To make in a convenient situation on the North side of the intended Railway in the Parish of Worlaby upon Land to be provided by and to remain the property of the said Thomas George Corbett and also to keep in repair a single line of Railway from the said intended railway to the Worlaby Causeway in the same Parish with proper points Switches and Cross over Road.

To make in a convenient situation on the North side of the said intended Railway in the Parish of Wrawby upon Land to be provided by and to remain the property of the said Thomas George Corbett and to keep in repair proper points Switches and Cross over Road by means of which the said Thomas George Corbett may have access to the intended Railway from a Railway to be constructed by him from any Mines or Quarries of Ironstone which may be found upon his Estate at Elsham.

Rider B

The said intended Company in the event of its incorporation to execute a Deed under its Common Seal ratifying and confirming or adopting this Agreement and undertaking that the same so far as not then performed and so far as relates to acts to be done by or to the intended Company shall and may be done by the said Company as incorporated.

CORRESPONDENCE

I/9/1

1. Rowland Winn to John Hett; from Appleby Hall, 5 November 1860:

I am sending over to Brigg to see if Roseby gets back by the 8.22 train, as for some reason or other he did not return on Saturday. I find he gave instructions to Mr. Lee the surveyor before he left to prepare all the plans for Parliament of this end of the line and I conclude therefore he had instructions from Mr. Dawes to that effect.

I have written a Note to Roseby to beg him to come on here tonight if he returns. I have a letter from Mr. Dawes this morning in reply to my Telegram to say that he is obliged to be the whole of this week in London on an important arbitration case he has with Lord Fitzwilliam. I therefore propose going up tomorrow afternoon, if Roseby returns tonight, and if not on Wednesday morning—to see him and get matters definitely arranged—and if I get things settled with him, as no doubt I shall I will then Telegraph to you to come up and see a Parliamentary agent as to the notices.

I find Mr. Lee has nearly got the plans for the line from the Trent to the Ancholme completed. I have not see[n] them but he informed me so. I have seen this afternoon to the Trent and find the S.Y. Co. are surveying for the Bridge today. In haste . . .

2. John Hett to Rowland Winn (copy); from Brigg, 5 Nov. 1860:

I will hold myself in readiness to go to Town on hearing from you. I want in the meantime a correct enumeration of the Parishes,

Townships, and places through which the line is to pass, and this I have not the means of preparing at present—especially as regards the district between the Trent and the Ancholme. You are aware it is essential to be correct on this point.

Then with regard to the "Reference" to the plan, great care is necessary in preparing it, and a tracing of the line is requisite to enable us to get it up.

The two surveyors should meet to arrange as to the early lithographing of the Plans, etc.

There will be no time to spare to complete everything.

The plans and references must be deposited in the several parishes as well as in the Private Bill Office and with the Clerk of the Peace by the 30th inst.

3. R. W. to J. H.; from Appleby Hall, 6 Nov. 1860:

Roseby not having returned last night, I shall determine to go up to London tomorrow morning from Retford by the York Express getting to London at 4 o'clock. I will write by this post for an appointment with Mr. Dawes, at the Tavistock Hotel, Covent Garden, where he is staying, as soon as I get to London, so as to enable me to Telegraph to you tomorrow Evening. This I hope you would get before Brigg Telegraph Office closes tomorrow Evening (8 o'clock I think) if not you would have it early in the morning, so as to be able to leave for London by the 10.37 train.

The Parishes Townships or Hamlets (for Gunhouse is properly a hamlet) which the line passes thro between the Trent and Ancholme are

[These	Township	Brumby	Parish of Frodingham
inserted	Township	Gunhouse	Parishes of West Halton and Frodingham
by J. H.			
in	Township	Frodingham	Parish of Frodingham
pencil	Township	Scunthorpe	Parish of Frodingham
	Hamlet	Low Santon	Parish of Appleby
	Hamlet	High Santon	Parish of Appleby
	Hamlet	Thornham	Parish of Appleby
	Parish]	Worlaby	[Parishes inserted by J. H. in pencil]

and it may be as well to insert Parish of Appleby as I think Thornham has not always been considered a Township—I am not certain about this.

The line commences at the Trent in the Field we are just purchasing of Chesman. I think notwithstanding the line is rather short we shall manage it without much difficulty.

In J. H.'s hand at the end of the letter:

Parish Elsham
,, Wrawby
Hamlet Kettleby—Parish of Bigby

Parish Bigby
Do Barnetby le Wold
Termini—
Trent in Township of Brumby Parish of Frodingham
M. and S. and L. Railway in Parish of Barnetby le Wold with a . . . branch to the Market Rasen branch of the same Railway in the hamlet of Kettleby in Parish of Bigby.

5. R. W. to J. H.; from Appleby Hall, 7 Nov. 1860:
Any limits of deviation will be included in the Townships I named —our line being mostly *made* and all fenced in the limits of deviation will be very small.
I find Lee cannot spare a plan to take to London. As soon as I return from London I can give all the information for references (occupiers, etc.) in ½ an hour.
I generally go in London to one of the Hotels in St James Street as being near the Carlton where I always live—but if I find it will facilitate matters I will stop at the Tavistock where Mr Dawes is. I will telegraph where I am if I have to send for you up. Roseby has got back and goes with me to London.

4. Telegram: R. W. (Tavistock Hotel, London) to J. H.; 7 Nov. 1860:
Come here by first train tomorrow (Thursday).

6. W. C. Atkinson to J. H., both in Brigg, 12 Nov. 1860:
I have just completed the plotting of the Survey of the Railway, and beg to inform you that the junction will be about five furlongs S.W. of the Barnetby Station.

7. Thos. Coates for Dyson and Co. to Nicholson, Hett and Freer; from 24 Parliament Street, Westminster, S.W., 12 Nov. 1860:
Since my other Letter was written I have had a conversation with Mr. Baxter upon this matter. He expresses his full concurrence in the construction of the Railway by your Clients—he believes that the traffic brought to that Railway from the South Yorkshire would of itself make the undertaking lucrative; but he apprehends that if the Company owning the Railway are identical with the owners of Minerals upon the Railway, and if the Company have the right to fix the tolls, and therefore to exact maximum tolls, for the carriage upon the Railway of their rivals, that power might be used oppressively and work even a prohibition of all Minerals but their own.
He assures me, too, that he has seen Mr. Watkin, who believes himself to have reserved for the Sheffield Company by the agreement the right to fix the tolls for traffic arising and carried beyond your Railway, that traffic being, as it is affirmed, comprised within the term "through traffic".

Finally he says that rather than leave in any hands the obnoxious power which he deprecates, the South Yorkshire and the Sheffield Companies will apply for powers to make a Railway parallel to yours; or again, they would be content to purchase Mr. Winn's Railway.

Meanwhile he looks forward to an amicable solution of the difficulty, and does not object to my acting, at all events for the present, on your behalf. He tells me, too, that your Clients and you are expected in Town on Wednesday.

8. D. and Co. to N., H., & F.; from London, 12 Nov. 1860:

The words you have inserted in red ink on page 2 are an improvement.

The words at page 4 seem to us quite sufficient.

We recommend you to insert the notice in a Lincolnshire Newspaper of established circulation, even though not published in the parts of Spilsby; and we adhere to the opinion that Doncaster is the best place for the Yorkshire advertisement.

The expression "already constructed or constructing" at page 6 is founded on the supposition that although the line from the Trent to the Ancholme is not yet constructed, yet part of the Railway is constructed; and of that part as well as of the incomplete part we shall deposit plans and sections.

[Added below the signature] We return the Notice; and shall assume it to be in a condition for insertion in the London Paper unless on Wednesday next we hear from you to the contrary.

9. Jno. W. Lancaster for Lithographic and General Printing Offices to Thomas Freer; from 9 New Bridge Street, York, 12 Nov. 1860:

In reply to your Note received this morning I write to say that I shall be glad to execute the plans named therein and shall also be glad to come over to Brigg respecting them should you think it necessary for me to do so.

The Plans and Sections (unless the Standing Orders are altered) will have to be the same size as the Bourton Plans which I have enclosed for your inspection by Book Post. Please let me have them back again although any time will do.

If you can send me a Copy for the Title I can be proceeding with it at once. At some time say how many Copies will be required . . .

[Added after sig.] 2 Miles with Sections are on each Sheet.

10. T. C. for D. and Co. to N., H., & F.; from London, 14 Nov. 1860:

The interest of the South Yorkshire Company is so nearly identical with that of your Clients, that I cannot conceive any ultimate disagreement between you.

The habit is to number properties according to parishes; recommencing the series of numbers with each parish. There's no rule about the matter; but for the parish deposit this method of numbering is most convenient; and in a long line the numbers would reach hundreds often, thousands sometimes, and would occupy too much space. Township and Hamlet boundaries need not be inserted in the plan.

The copy of the plan, section, Book of Reference and Notice with the Parish Clerk is sufficient for all the Townships in that parish and the Hamlets.

11. J. W. L. for Lith. and G.P.O. to N., H., & F.; 15 Nov. 1860:

In reply to your favor I write to say that 50 copies of the Plan referred to (say 8 Sheets) will be about from £27.10.0 to £30.0.0 and an additional 50 about £9 or £10 more.

To get them out in ordinary time we should now have the Tracings in hand but if pushed should require say 7 days clear.

If you can at once send Copy for any sheet of 2 Miles, it will be saving time. In reply please say what number of Copies you will have printed.

12. T. C. for D. and Co. to N., H., & F.; from London, 16 Nov. 1860:

Since I saw your engineer today, I have seen Mr. Baxter on other matters. Upon adverting to this undertaking he told me that Mr. Watkin had communicated to him a note of the arrangement which that gentleman had made on behalf of the Sheffield Company with Mr. Winn.

Of that note I send you a Copy; and I am satisfied that if I am authorised by you to accede to similar terms or to confirm these terms with respect to the South Yorkshire Company the opposition of that Company will be at an end.

[On the back of the letter, the alterations, deletions, and italicised words being in red ink] ~~8th November 1860 The running Companies vizt~~ the South Yorkshire *Company* and the Manchester Sheffield and Lincolnshire *Company* to have the power of fixing rates for traffic *carried by either of those Companies* to, from and over ~~Mr. Winn's~~ *the Trent Ancholme and Grimsby Railway* in connection with their respective districts, and ~~Mr. Winn~~ *the Trent Ancholme and Grimsby Railway* to take ~~his~~ *their* mileage of such rates less 40 per cent working expenses, provided ~~he~~ *they* receive~~s~~ a minimum toll of sixpence per ton on Ironstone and fourpence per ton on coal *carried on the Trent Ancholme and Grimsby Railway or on any portion thereof and without any deduction for terminal or other charges*, cases where it is desirable in the general interest to make a lower exceptional rate for the time being in which case ~~Mr. Winn's~~ *the proportion of the Trent Ancholme and Grimsby Company* to be settled in case of dispute by arbitration. *The Trent Ancholme and Grimsby Company to pay a mileage rate not exceeding one halfpenny per ton per mile for Traffic carried by them to from and over the South Yorkshire or Manchester Sheffield and Lincolnshire Railways.*

13. R. W. to E. Watkin, 17 Nov. 1860: [Headed "Copy in part"]

With regard with [*sic*] the suggested arrangements I assent to the 6d. minimum rate for Ironstone and 4d. for coal. With respect to the last clause about exceptional cases I am afraid it would lead to ultimate disputes as it stands and I think something more definite should be substituted if possible. I conceive if such a case arose it would be between us and the S.Y. or us and the M.S. & L. and not all the three, and tho I have not the least doubt that any such case would be settled with perfect ease between the M.S. & L. and ourselves I am by no means so sanguine as regards the S.Y.

There is another point which I omitted to name to you yesterday viz Terminal charges. According to the arrangement proposed the S.Y. would fix the rates for Coal to Grimsby of which we should receive a mileage subject to the minimum sum of 4d. and ½d. rate less 40% would leave about 5d. so that by putting on a terminal charge at Barnetby the S.Y. might easily so arrange that we should never receive more than 4d. for any distance. I became acquainted to some extent with the subject of terminal charges in a coal case we had with the Gt Northern some years ago, and I believe you will agree with me that a stipulation ought to be made to prevent the S.Y. exacting such a charge.

You can talk these points over with Roseby and settle with him what course it is best to adopt, it will meet with my approval, of course, in any arrangement being entered into with the S.Y. they must altogether withdraw their new scheme. If you want me in London and will telegraph me I will come up by next train.

14. J. W. L. for Lith. and G.P.O. to N., H. & F.; from York, 19 Nov. 1860:

Prompt and every attention shall be paid to your Commands on the arrival of your Messenger tonight, and with thanks.

15. T. C. for D. and Co. to N., H. & F.; from London, 20 Nov. 1860:

Permit us to press on you the propriety of answering without delay the proposition contained in my letter to you of the 16th on behalf of the South Yorkshire Company.

If your Clients do not confirm with respect to the South Yorkshire Company the terms contained in the Memorandum annexed to my letter, that Company will proceed with their project; and in the meanwhile they must take and are taking costly steps essential to that proceeding.

This state of things renders an ultimate settlement more difficult. I do not fear a contest with the South Yorkshire Company about the possession of this district, so far as the possession of the district goes.

In such a contest I have no doubt that your Clients will succeed. Nevertheless I think strife between parties essential to one another ought by all reasonable concessions to be avoided.

16. D. and Co. to N., H., and F.; from London, 20 Nov. 1860:

We send you herewith a mem. of the deposits to be made this month—also form of notice to Landowners—instructions as to service—and letter to outliers, and of acknowledgement.

17. T. G. Corbett to T. F.; from Elsham Hall, 20 Nov. 1860:

Dodds will be from home tomorrow. He will call upon you on Thursday and give every information you may require.

18. J. W. L. for Lith. and G.P.O. to N., H., & F.; from York, 21 Nov. 1860:

I beg to acknowledge receipt of Sheet No. 1 Tracing containing Scale and beg to say that Proofs of three Sheets of Plans as also Title will be sent from here by Great Northern Train leaving York at 3.45 in the morning. You will therefore please see after the same should it not be delivered in due course.

I shall be glad if you will examine and return as early as possible part if not the whole.

19. Acknowledgment of "Receipt of further Tracings" from J. W. L. for Lith. and G.P.O., York, to N., H., & F.; 22 Nov. 1860.

20. J. W. L. for Lith. and G.P.O. to N., H., & F.; 23 Nov. 1860:

I beg to acknowledge receipt of parcel to hand this morning with proofs returned and to say that having made the corrections marked I am *proceeding* with the printing of 20 copies of each plan—also of parcel to hand this afternoon containing four tracings. I shall send away by to-nights train a proof of one plan—and shall be glad to receive same back as well as those forwarded last night at your early Convenience.

21. B. Johnson for J. W. L. for Lith. and G.P.O. to N., H., & F.; from York, 24 Nov. 1860:

Duplicate-Copy of this sent by post.

In reply to your letter of the 23rd I write to say that the plans can be completed by the time stated—but it will be necessary to have some party here (say on Monday afternoon) to examine and pass the proofs.

Two or 3 Sheets of proofs will be sent away by Train leaving here at 3.45 A.M. (Sunday) and fully understand that nothing after such train will be sent as I shall expect all following proofs to be looked over here. If you can save any time by returning the proofs herewith per early Train please do so—if not let them be forwarded by the person you intend sending over.

[At the side]. The last Sheet is not yet to hand 7 P.M.

22. J. W. L. for Lith. and G.P.O. to N., H., and F.; from York, 24 Nov. 1860:

[The original of 21 with * before "Two or 3 Sheets" and another * after "by returning" in the last sentence. At the end is added: "The last Sheet is not yet to hand—5 P.M."].

23. T. F. to J. H.; from York, 26 Nov. 1860:

We have examined and corrected all the proof sheets except 2 —one of which is to be done tonight and the other early in the morning.

Mr. Roseby and Mr. Lee have had a long interview with Mr. Atkinson as to the intended Tunnel etc which has ended in a determination to have the plans as they have been prepared.

We find it necessary to insert a few additional numbers, which will have to be also inserted in the References—viz.:

Appleby	*Worlaby*	3a Field	C. Winn Esq.
		4b	*A. H. Johnson*
			George Gurnell
		19a	*Tho. Dee*
		23a	*Tho. Dee*
		42a	Plantation
		46a	Field

[Names in italic have been added in pencil. At the top of the page is added in pencil "Frod^{m} 61^{a} Field C. W. John Drury".]

If the references for Appleby have been copied these numbers will have to be interlined. If not copied they can be inserted in their proper order.

I fully expect to be home by the 8 o'clock train tomorrow night.

I arranged with Mr. Paxton in Hull today to send 50 more Sheets of the Reference paper to Mr. Cressey by the first Train tomorrow morning.

24. R. W. to J. H.; from Appleby Hall, 28 Nov. 1860:

I write a line to tell you that I have just got the agreement back from Mr. Watkin signed by the S.Y. Co. so that there is an end of their opposition and line. The Bridge over the Trent is to be entirely of Iron, Iron piles etc etc.

25. J. H. to R. W.; from Brigg, 28 Nov. 1860: [Copy]

I am much obliged by your early announcement of the withdrawal of the South Yorkshire competing Line, and beg to congratulate you upon having got rid of opposition in that quarter.

The evidence which the South Yorkshire Company will give in Committee, in support of their Bill for the Bridge, will materially strengthen your hands as regards the importance of your Railway.

26. T. F. to J. H.; from Tavistock Hotel, London, 30 Nov. 1860:

I have made the Deposits today. Mr. Roseby came up by the Mail Train and accompanied me to Messrs. Dyson and Co's—and also to the offices. Mr. Coates was so much occupied that he could not talk to me about the Bill today—and thinks it will be best to wait until he has the result of the meeting between Mr. Winn and Mr. Dawes next week.

He had received Mr. Baxter's directions *not* to proceed with the Rival Scheme to ours.

We saw the plans for the Bridge etc deposited—it will be *72 Feet* above high water mark—with an opening of 50 Feet in the centre.

. . . . .

I hope to reach home by the last Train tomorrow night.

27. D. and Co. to N., H., and F.; from London, 28 Nov. 1860:

As the Bill has to be prepared and printed, and deposited by the 23rd of Dec[r] we propose setting about the preparation of it, if you see no objection. An early reply will oblige.

28. J. W. L. for Lith. and G.P.O.; from York, 3 Dec. 1860:

[Acknowledgment of receipt of proofs] which I hope to send off completed tomorrow Tuesday.

29. J. W. L. for Lith. and G.P.O. to N., H., & F.; from York, 4 Dec. 1860:

By the Gt Northern Train leaving here at 9.45 P.M. this evening I have forwarded the Forms and circulars for Trent Railway which I hope will reach you in due course.

They are not so nicely finished as I could have wished oweing to the short time allowed but I trust they will be found correct.

Should you be likely to require more I shall be glad to know as early as convenient. The forms shall be kept standing until I receive your reply.

30. R. W. to J. H.; from Appleby Hall, 5 Dec. 1860:

I had Mr. Dawes here yesterday, and I think we have nearly settled our Railway arrangements subject to his Brothers approval. He has to go to London on his reference business on Sunday night—on Monday morning he has a consultation, the reference not beginning again till Tuesday, so that Monday afternoon he would be disengaged. My idea therefore is to go up to London on Monday, getting there per Retford by Manchester Express at 3.5, and I think we might get an interview with Mr. Coates that afternoon in which Mr. Dawes would be able to take part. I must be back here Wednesday as we have some friends coming to us that day.

I am sorry to hear from Roseby that you have been so ill, and I fear from what I have heard that you are still so. I beg you will not think under such circumstances of undertaking, in such weather, the journey with me to London, as I have no doubt Mr. Freer would join me and do everything that was necessary.

31. D. and Co. to N., H., and F.; from London, 5 Dec. 1860:

We shall be glad to receive your Instructions as to the Draft Bill as soon as possible, for you are aware, that it has to be printed and deposited before the 23rd Instant.

32. R. W. to J. H.; from Appleby Hall, 7 Dec. 1860:

I am much obliged by your note. Monday at 4.15 will suit perfectly for being at Mr. Coates's. I am sorry to say I have been unwell since Tuesday last and confined to the House and greatly fear I shall not be able to go to London on Monday. I have written for my Brother to come here tomorrow to be ready to supply my place on Monday if necessary. The agreements with the M. S. and L. and S. Y. Railway Companies shall be sent to London, or copies of them, and Mr. Coates shall also know the nature of our arrangements with Mr. Dawes. It is not yet quite completed but I expect hearing from him on the subject tomorrow, but it will be of such a nature as not to require insertion in the Bill I think. With regard to the agreement with Mr. Corbett I do not see that there can be any necessity for inserting it in the Bill, as I know that it is not a usual thing to do in such cases. The agreement will be between him and the Co. or me on behalf of the Co. as he prefers, but he says he is quite satisfied with the letter I wrote him which he considers, as I do, in the light of an agreement.

It is not very important whether we buy the land for his siding (if ever wanted) or not but I think when he comes to consider it, that he not only would not require it to be done, but will not even assent to it; most undoubtedly I would not were I in his case; I entirely agree with you in your view of this matter.

With respect to sidings for Lord Yarborough we are quite ready to enter into any fair and reasonable arrangement on the subject, but it must obviously be an agreement between Lord Yarborough or his Lessees and my Father. The Co. can of course entertain no objection to any sidings being put in, as it must obviously be for the benefit of the line.

The same remarks will apply to Lord Beauchamp but it appears to me that the agreement for accommodation for him should form a part of the arrangements to be made with him on the subject of Minerals generally. In this I think you will agree, perhaps, when you or Mr. Freer are in London you could call on Mr. Walford and see if any progress can be made in the matter.

What we most want now, as it appears to me, on the subject of the Railway is the estimates for the new, or valuation of old. I expected Roseby here today but he has not been yet.

33. J. H. to D. and Co. (copy); from Tavistock Hotel, London, 11 Dec. 1860:

If you strike off copies of the Bill before sending draft for perusal, be good enough to forward a copy to George Dawes Esqre, Milton and Elsecar Ironworks, Barnsley, as well as to Mr. R. Winn, Appleby Hall, Brigg, and ourselves. If you send us drafts in the first instance, Mr. Winn will forward it to Mr. Dawes.

34. D. and Co. to N., H., and F.; from London, 12 Dec. 1860:

We send you the form of an Estimate for the Engineer to sign. He will understand that by the word "Undertaking" which the Estimate adopts from the Standing Orders is meant the undertaking which remains to be accomplished under the Act. Thus it will exclude the value of the land and the cost of the works already made between the Trent and the Ancholme.

On the other hand we shall want for the Bill the estimate of the whole Undertaking, so as to measure the capital of the Company.

We send too the form of a Declaration under the 40th Standing order which we recommend that Mr. Winn should sign as well as you.

34a. W. Sowerby, Jnr., to T. F.; from Messingham Hall, 12 Dec. 1860:

Mr. Parkinson's Christian name is William, and his address Dinnington, Rotherham. He is however at present in London with Father. They went up yesterday to the Cattle Show.

P.S. They return Monday next.

35. J. H. Dunn for W. H. & G. Dawes to N. H. & F.; from Milton and Elsecar Ironworks, 12 Dec. 1860:

We have your favour with the Parliamentary Notices.

Our Mr. Geo. Dawes is at present in London but will be here on Friday next when they shall be properly attended to.

36. T. C. for D. and Co. to N., H., & F.; from London, 12 Dec. 1860:

This Bill could not have been printed today in time for post; I therefore send down a Manuscript Copy of it. Meanwhile I have sent it to the printer, because I am satisfied that for the most part it will meet the wishes of our clients; and by tomorrow evenings (Thursd^{s}) post you shall have six copies.

I send you too the Drainage Clauses. They are drawn up in a style which has now become obsolete; and I have abridged them somewhat.

The mere alteration of phraseology would not however have induced me to trouble you with them, if I had not also raised one or two questions in the margin which you ought to consider. When you have done so will you be good enough to return them to me. This, you will I have no doubt do without delay, that they may be printed.

37. D. and Co. to N., H., & F.; from London, 14 Dec. 1860:

We send you herewith the draft Petition for the Bill, which you will be good enough to get engrossed on Parchment and signed.

Pray return it to us at your early convenience.

38. J. W. L. for Lith. & G.P.O. to N., H., & F.; from York, 14 Dec. 1860:

I have forwarded by tonights train 6 copies of T.A.G. Railway plans, which I hope will be sufficient and although the full quantity of 2 or 3 sheets are printed yet I have been obliged to delay them on account of the great run on the market for this size and class of paper but expect it every day.

Please make the corrections required in those remaining to be struck off . . .

39. N., H., & F. to D. and Co (copy); from Brigg, 15 Dec. 1860:

We send by Book Post, one of the printed copies of this Bill, with some marginal observations upon which we purpose seeing you on Monday about 4 p.m. We will bring the Ancholme and Sewers Clauses. Mr. Winn wishes to have a clause for providing drains under the Railway from his Warping Drain to the lands lying on the South side of the Railway. Messrs. Dawes by the terms of their Lease are bound to provide such communications.

40. T. F. to J. H. (?) (copy); from Brigg, 17 Dec. 1860:

I have been to Frodingham this morning and seen the Award, and find that [*sic*] the boundaries between Frodingham and Brumby and Frodingham and Scunthorpe but that nothing is said about the boundary of *Gunhouse*—or to throw any light on the meaning of the red ink Line, along the Award Plan, which I thought was intended to denote the boundary between Frodingham and Gunhouse. Mr. Weigall examined the Award and Plan with me and we went in to the village to see the Parish Clerk and from what he said I am disposed to think that there is a *Hamlet* of Gunhouse in the Township of Scunthorpe in the Parish of Frodingham (of which the Gunhouse Ings and Gunhouse Carrs form part) and that all the houses in this Hamlet are rated to the rates of *Scunthorpe*.

The *Township* of Gunhouse for which there is a Guardian-Overseer, and Surveyor of Highways appears to be all in West Halton Parish.

Mr. Weigall has promised to get me some further information today and send it to Brigg tomorrow. If I get it you shall have it forwarded to Town.

41. Rev. E. Mitford Weigall to T. F.; from Frodingham Vicarage, 18 Dec. 1860:

I was in Gunhouse yesterday, but came back too late to write you by post. I find that the occupiers of Gunhouse Ings and Gunhouse Carrs pay Poor Rate to the Township in which the Ings or Carrs are situated. As for instance: Robert Taylor of Drain Head, occupies part of the Ings and Carrs situated in Frodingham; and he pays Poor Rate to *Frodingham*.

The same rule holds good I believe with regard to the Gunhouse Ings and Carrs in Scunthorpe—and as far as I can make out the Guardian and Overseer of Gunhouse have only to do with that part of the Township which lies in the Parish of West Halton.

The parts of Gunhouse situated in Frodingham and Scunthorpe do not maintain their own Poor: they come upon Frodingham and Scunthorpe—and the Highway Surveyors of these townships have to look after the portions of road in Gunhouse which lie in their respective Townships.

42. R. W. to J. H.; from Appleby Hall, 17 Dec. 1860:

My Father has returned me the enclosed unsigned as he says that as his name does not appear in the bill he does not think that he can be looked upon as a promoter properly speaking and he therefore fancies I should be the one to sign the declaration.

What do you say on this. If I am to sign the document a fresh form will require to be drawn up, if you still think it better for my Father to sign, let me have the enclosed back and I will send it him by this post. Mr. Corbett writes me word he is going from home today, and cannot see me before Thursday or Saturday. I think there is no hurry about the matter as it appears Mr. Coates will not introduce the agreement with Mr. Corbett into the Bill. I am going from home for a night at 2 o'clock today, please send my man back as soon as possible or I shall not have time to send the declaration back to my Father before I leave if you still want his signature.

[In pencil at top] The declaration was returned to Mr. Winn mentioning Mr. H. absence and that Mr. F at Winterton.

43. J. H. to Charles Winn (copy); from Tavistock Hotel, 17 Dec. 1860:

I send by this post, for your signature, a Petition for this Bill to the House of Commons. I shall be much obliged if you will sign the

Petition and forward it tomorrow to Messrs. Dawes, Milton and Elsecar Ironworks . . , to whom I will write.

[After signature] A Lord of a Manor is not entitled (as such) to notice of a Bill, unless the Railway is intended to cross some common or waste land in which he is interested.

44. J. H. to Messrs. Dawes (copy); from Tavistock Hotel, 18 Dec. 1860:

We have forwarded to C. Winn, Esqre, for his signature, the Petition for this Bill, with a request that he will transmit it to you. It is requisite that *both* of you sign it, and we shall be obliged to you to forward it to Messrs. Dyson . . . Westminster . . . , without any delay. The Petition *must* be filed at the Private Bill Office on or before Saturday next.

We have corrected the omission in the first proof of the Bill, by adding the names of yourselves to those of Mr. Rowland Winn and Mr. Edmund John Winn in Clause 2 incorporating the Company, amd also in Clause 14 as first Directors. In Clause 7 we have struck out the mention of your nominees, in compliance with the terms of your agreement made with Mr. R. Winn with reference to your shares. In clause 5 an alteration is made authorizing the delivery of Mr. Winn's share certificates to his nominees, which he may substitute his sons [*sic*], fixing the amount of his shares to be allotted under that clause, at the price to be paid for his land . . .

May we trouble you to write us *here*, as well as at *Brigg*, stating that the Petition has been forwarded to Dyson & Co.

45. T. F. to J. H. (copy); from Brigg, 18 Dec. 1860:

After you had left home yesterday and during my absence Mr. Winn sent the enclosed letter as to the declaration required to be made by Mr. Winn. Mr. Roland [Hett] returned the Declaration and stated that we were both from home.

There seems to be nothing in the objection which has occurred to Mr. Winn—but probably it would be best for you to write to him or to Mr. R. Winn, and say so—of his having mentioned that point to Mr. Coates in case you think it necessary to do so.

I forgot to say in my note of yesterday that in the Frodingham Award the allotments in the Gunhouse Carrs and Ings are set out thus "All that allotment in *Gunhouse Ings or Carrs in Frodingham, etc.*

I have not yet heard from Mr. Weigall.

46. J. H. to T. F. (copy); from Tavistock Hotel, 18 Dec. 1860.

I have had the Petition for this Bill engrossed, and have forwarded the same to Mr. Winn, Nostel, for signature, with a request that he will transmit it without delay to Messrs. Dawes (to whom I have written) for their signature. They are to forward it to Messrs. Dyson and Co.

With reference to the estimate of expence, it *must* be here not later than *Thursday* morning. We want the estimated expence of the *whole* undertaking (including the purchase of land and contingencies), and also an estimate of the amount which will remain to be expended upon it after Saturday next. To find this, must be deducted from the estimated expence of the *whole* undertaking, the value of the land from Trent to Ancholme provided by Mr Winn, including the Ironstone thereunder, and the value of the works executed by Messrs. Dawes, and of such materials as they have appropriated to the formation of the line. These particulars must be sent to Dyson and Co., as I purpose returning tomorrow unless any thing should occur to render my further stay desirable.

[Addition] You had better see Mr. Roseby or Mr. Atkinson immediately as to the estimates.

47. G. Dawes to N., H., & F.; from M & E Ironworks, 19 Dec. 1860:

Your favour of yesterday is duly to hand with the Petition—which I have signed and sent on by this post to my brother to sign with a request he would forward in turn to Messrs. Dyson and Co.

48. J. H. to C. Winn, Nostell Priory (copy); from Tavistock Hotel, 19 Dec. 1860:

I have received here a letter from Mr. Winn in which he mentions that you think he, not you, ought to sign the Declaration forwarded for your signature, owing to your name not appearing in the Bill. This is a mistake. You are stated in the Bill to have provided land for the Railway between the Trent and the Anch., for which you are to be paid by Shares in the Company. You are in fact the principal promoter of the undertaking, and shd. therefore sign the Declaration. It is of no importance that you are not in the Bill as a Director. I will request Mr. R. Winn to return the Declaration to you for signature and I shall be must [*sic*] obliged if you will forward it to me, *at Brigg*, at your earliest convenience. I am going down today.

I hope you have signed the Petition and forwarded it to Messrs. Dawes, as it *must* be filed in the Private Bill office on *Saturday* next, or we shall be too late. If you have not already signed and forwarded it, I am afraid I must ask you to sign it and send off a messenger with it immediately to Messrs. Dawes, that we may insure its being signed by them, and sent to Messrs. Dyson and Co., 24 Parliament Street, Westminster, so as to reach them on Saturday, morning. It should have three signatures; therefore Mr. Edmund J. Winn may sign it, as well as yourself, if both the Mr. Daweses cannot be met with.

I have seen Mr. Coates our Parliamentary agent, this morning, and he quite concurs in what I have written.

May I trouble you to inform me at Brigg, by Telegram, what has been done to the Petition.

49. J. H. to R. W. (copy); from Brigg, 19 Dec. 1860:

I send over my servant with a copy of a letter which I wrote from London this morning to Mr. Winn at Nostel. As the Declaration was returned to you unsigned by Mr. Winn, I am apprehensive lest he should have hesitated to sign the Petition for the Bill which I sent to him last Monday. Unless the Petition is filed on *Saturday next*, we shall be, I am afraid, altogether stopped in our proceedings. I hear that Mr. Edmund Winn came to Appleby this morning. He may know whether the Petition has been forwarded to Messrs. Dawes, and you will be able to judge whether any further action must be taken by him or yourself about it.

If there appear to be any question as to the Petition reaching London on Saturday, perhaps it would be best for yourself and Mr. E. Winn to come over and sign a petition, to be used in case of need.

50. G. D. to N., H., & F.; from M. & E. Ironworks, 19 Dec. 1860:

I have signed the Petition and sent it on to my brother requesting him to forward direct to Messrs. Dyson and Co. tomorrow and I trust he will do so.

51. Charles Winn to J. H.; from "Nostel", 1 o'clock P.M., 19 Dec. 1860:

I have just returned from the Featherstone Station near here, from where I have sent you a message by telegram which you will receive in less than half an hour from this time. The purport of it is to say that I signed the *Petition* on the day I received it, and forwarded it by the same days post to the Messrs. Dawes' addressed agreeably to your instructions so that I trust it will ere this have been returned to Messrs. Dyson and Co.

As to the Declaration to which you allude, my son Rowland Winn has it; and will no doubt see you respecting it as soon as he becomes aware of your having returned to Brigg.

52. Telegram: C. W., Nostle [*sic*] to N., H., & F.; 20 Dec. 1860:

Petition signed. By C. W. as soon as received and forwarded to Miss Dawes immediately. Mr. R. W. has the Declaration at Appleby.

53. R. W. to J. H.; from Appleby Hall, 20 Dec. 1860:

I return the declaration to which I have got my Father's signature having told him he had better sign it, and that it need not be used unless it were necessary. He seemed to wish to have nothing to do with the Bill at all and writes that he wishes the shares to be taken for the land to be in my Brothers name and my own.

With regard to the petition I know nothing about it as my father does not mention it, and think the only safe plan will be for me to ride over to Brigg this morning (which I will do) sign a pe[ti]tion and send some one off by the 10.37 train to get Mr. Dawes signature and my Fathers. He had better go to Mr. Dawes first as my father is certain to be at home at any time not being able to get about.

54. T. C. for D. & Co. to N., H., & F.; from London, 21 Dec. 1860:

The petition has reached us; it is in due form.

Mr. Roseby had brought his estimate:

Sum expended including value of land from Trent to Ancholme	37,247.10
Sum remaining to be expended	80,088. 5
Total Capital	£117,335.15

These figures I have dealt with in the Bill in the manner indicated in red ink [at the side: 40,000 l.
80,000 l.
120,000 l.]

I do not think £2665 at all too much to add to the estimate.

The sum to be deposited will therefore be £6400.

This far exceeds what was contemplated, so far as I recollect; but we must deal with the facts as they are.

The Bill Petitions etc. will be deposited tomorrow (Saturday) morning.

55. G. D. to N., H., & F.; from M. & E. Ironworks, 21 Dec. 1860:

Your letter to our W. H. Dawes' is duly received and we have written him to Moseley Hall, nr Birmingham, upon the subject as we forward the papers to him there. As he is not down here more than two or three times a year and then only for a few days, will you in future please address him direct.

56. R. W. to J. H.; from Appleby Hall, 25 Dec. 1860:

I have your letter this morning informing me that the sum already expended upon the Railway is estimated at £40,000 and the sum remaining to be expended £80,000 the deposit on which latter sum will amount to £6,400.

Mr. Atkinson informed me that the quantity of land was estimated at an average of 6 acres per mile and the value of £100 an acre—and as the distance East of the Ancholme is 5 Miles about 30 acres will be required, in value estimated at £3000 the deposit on which will be £240—which will be the proportion of the deposit to be paid by my Father—leaving £6160 as Messrs. Dawes share. I conclude either you or Mr. Roseby will communicate this at once to Mr. Dawes. I think Roseby will have to see him immediately about the estimate, and I fear this hard frost will retard the works for the present which is unfortunate. I hear Roseby is laid up extremely ill at

Brigg, in consequence of which I have not seen him since his return from London. You are probably aware of this. Will you send me a few copies of the Bill as deposited as soon as you get them.

[On the back in R. W.'s writing] The following is a copy of the clause in the agreement with Messrs. Dawes on the subject of the deposit

That Mr. Winn pay the Parliamentary deposit upon the estimated cost of the land to be purchased East of the Ancholme and Messrs. Dawes on the estimated cost of the works still required to complete the Railway.

57. R. W. to J. H.; from Appleby Hall, 26 Dec. 1860:

I will go to the Board tomorrow, and afterwards see you about the Railway. Don't write to Mr. Dawes today. Perhaps tomorrow Roseby will be well enough to talk the subject over with us and we will then decide what to do. My Father has *not* assented to the South Yorks. scheme—he has sent me the papers to fill up as I like. I will bring them with me tomorrow and we can arrange what to do with them. I will also bring in the South Yorks. Bill—which you have sent me.

Roseby I hope is much better as he has himself written me a note this morning.

58. D. and Co. to N., H., & F.; from London, 27 Dec. 1860:

The estimate in Duplicate, and the Declaration under the 40th Standing order have reached us.

We have sent to you the Bills you ask for.

The return of Assent does not prevent a Landowner from petitioning against the Bill and being heard. His change of opinion is of course a matter for comment by counsel, and is a thing to be accounted for by the person who so vacillates. But that is all. So with a return of "neuter". The absence of all answer leaves the Landowner's hands quite free. No answer or an answer of neuter is deemed equivalent to assent.

We ought to have the £6,400 if [*sic*] cash on Monday morning the 14th Jany. If the deposit is to be made by the transfer of stock (which does not seem worth while in this case) things ought to be in course of preparation on Friday the 11th.

59. R. W. to J. H.; from Appleby Hall, 29 Dec. 1860:

Sherwood went yesterday to the various tenants who have had the notices respecting the railway sent to them. He ascertained that at any rate most of them had been sent in to you. I think he will call upon you this morning and give you any he may have collected. I have not seen him this morning.

I think you should endeavour to get Mr. Corbetts assent today by some means if possible so as to be able to return him as an assenting party. I am surprised at Mr. West, as he most undoubtedly told me he should be strongly in favour of the line unless he found the College opposed to it. He remarked that the living was small and he could not afford to sacrifice income by loss of land, but if that was compensated for he could entertain no objection. I think I must write to the College and explain this as I represented him to them as being personally in favour of the line.

It seems to me that we almost must return the South Yorks papers as dissenting as we object to their having any line East of Trent. This however you must decide as you think best. Under any circumstances my Father cannot assent.

60. D. and Co. to N., H., & F.; from London, 29 Dec. 1860:

We beg leave to acknowledge the receipt of the Lists of Owners etc. in Duplicate, which are in due form.

61. D. and Co. to N., H., & F.; from London, 29 Dec. 1860:

We send you herewith Draft Requisition for Warrant of Private Bill office clerk for payment of money into Bank of England.

We must have the requisition at the latest by the 11th January, and we shall be glad to have it a day or two sooner if possible. If the deposit is not to be made in cash, or only partly so, you must, when you give us the requisition, hand us full particulars of how the deposit will be made—Numbers and dates of Exchequer Bills, and particulars of Stock, which should stand in the names of the requisitionists. If Stock is to be transferred, we ought to have the requisitions by the 8th Jan^{y}, as Saturdays and Mondays are no^{t} transfer days.

62. J. W. L. to T. F.; from York, 29 Dec. 1860:

The Plans referred to in your Note of this Morning shall be got out of hand without delay. Please say by return whether you are likely to require any more of the printed forms in connection with the Same before taking down the Type, and should you be able to send me an Order at same time for Stationery I shall be glad and can send altogether . . .

63. D. and Co. to N., H., & F.; from London, 31 Dec. 1860:

You are quite right to insert the name of *William* Parkinson in the list of owners. There's no excuse for perpetuating error.

The lists etc. have been duly deposited.

64. J. Roseby to J. H.; from Brigg, 4 Jan. 1861:

Could you favour me with your copy of the South Yorkshire plan of the Trent Bridge and their copy of the Bill this Evening. I will return them in the morning.

Mr. Tootal is here and I want him to explain to Mr. Dawes, what the S.Y. Company want to do.

65. J. R. to N., H., & F.; from Brigg, 5 Jan. 1861:
I beg to return you the copy of the South Yorkshire Bill for which I am obliged.
Have you any more copies of the Plans and Sections. Mr. Tootal is going to meet Mr. Dawes and wants to take a copy with him.

65[a]. N., H., & F. to J. R.; from Brigg, 5 Jan. 1861:
We have not received any more copies of the Plans and Sections from York. We sent a copy to Mr. George Dawes some time ago.

66. R. W. to J. H.; from Appleby Hall, 5 Jan. 1861:
I only got back from London late last night where I have been nearly a week for the purpose of meeting Messrs. Dawes, and the Railway Company and trying what arrangements can be made on the subject of our line. There is to be a meeting (at Doncaster probably) in a few days to settle the matter, but I think it will end in the M. S. & L. taking $\frac{1}{3}$, the S.Y. another, and ourselves and Lessees a $\frac{1}{3}$. I think all parties seem willing for that. We shall take the land at agricultural value with a fixed sum for minerals in shares and shall deal liberally in this respect, in consideration of good rates which after all is the main question with us. I think from what Mr. Watkin said that Mr. Baxter will write you on the subject. The Railway Company desire to reserve a right of buying up our $\frac{1}{3}$ shares. This I don't object to, as with their $\frac{2}{3}$ interest they could any time swamp us, and it might lead us into difficulties with them. In haste . . .

67. J. W. L. to N., H., & F.; from York, 9 Jan. 1861:
The Plans are sent off tonight by luggage train and which I hope will reach you in due course and give satisfaction.

68. D. and Co. to N., H., & F.; from London, 9 Jan. 1961:
The Requisition has reached us: it is in due form.

69. D. and Co. to N., H., & F.; from London, 10 Jan. 1861:
We send you herewith draft Statement of proofs as to the compliance with the Standing Order—also affidavits as to the service of notices—and the deposit of plans—and a Mem. as to the mode of giving the proofs. The affidavits do not require to be stamped.

70. D. and Co. to N., H., & F.; from London, 11 Jan. 1861:
We have the Directions of the Accountant General, and pray do not forget that the money (£6,400) must be deposited before 3 o'clock on Monday.

71. J. R. to George Dawes (copy); [from Brigg], 12 Jan. 1861:
Mr. Hett has just called to say that he has a letter from Messrs. Dyson the London Agents to say that the deposit must be deposited

before 3 o.c. on Monday. Do not neglect. Messrs. Dyson and Co. addr 24 Parliament Street, Westminster.

72. G. D. to "J. Rosby Junr" (copy); from M. & E. Ironworks, 12 Jan. 1861:

Since I saw you on Monday I have had to pay about 4000 unexpectedly. this with the heavy pull to the Earl last March and one or two other matters has exhausted my funds. I intended for the Railway upwards of 13000£ and every shilling paid within a month only—next week Mr. Winns bill is due which adds another to the lump and indeed has so exhausted my resources that it is utterly impossible I can find the deposits on Monday therefore will you consider over what is best to be done. I suppose if the deposit is not paid on Monday the bill will be lost this year. Will you see Messrs. Nicholson, Hett, Freer, and conclude with them what is to be done. Would they advance the Money think you on Security of the line. There would be no harm asking them. I see by the agreement I was wrong in my notion that Mr. Winn was to find half.

73. J. R. to N., H., & F.; from Brigg, 13 Jan. 1861:

I enclose copy of letter received this morning from Mr. Dawes, (the original I have sent on to Mr. Winn).

I am going to see Mr. Winn on the subject, this afternoon but would like to see you before I went.

I feel reluctant to call on business matters on a Sunday but with your permission I will do so about 2 o.c.

74. R. W. to J. H. (in pencil); 13 Jan. 1861:

I have seen Roseby, and heard what Mr. Dawes has written him and what has passed between him and yourself since he got Mr. D's letter. I do not think it would be desirable for my Father to advance the money for the deposit unless it were as a kind of mortgage on the line itself, and even then I believe it would be more to our advantage to take advantage of the provisions of Messrs. Dawes lease and compel them to complete the line between the Trent and Ancholme by the 1st of Jany 1862 and apply next year for a Bill to Barnetby. Under all the circumstances I have thought it best that Roseby should go to Manchester this afternoon and see Mr. Watkin and consult him. I think it is possible he may find the means rather than let a difficulty arise; and if so I think it is better than our in any way breaking thro the agreement already entered into with Mr. Dawes. So far as we are concerned I have not the least doubt that the terms of the lease is a better bargain than the subsequent agreement.

75. (Draft) letter N., H., & F.; to D. and Co; from Brigg, 13 Jan. 1861:

From a communication received from Mr. Dawes we find there

is a hitch about his share of this deposit, and we very much fear that you will not be put in funds to enable you to make the deposit before 3 o'clock tomorrow, and probably not during the day. Possibly it may be arranged that you shall have the amount in your hands some time tomorrow night, which would be useful, we apprehend, on an application to dispense with a strict compliance with the Standing Orders on this point. With this object, if you receive no communication before leaving the office tomorrow night, will you send a note (to be opened by Mr. R. Winn or Mr. Roseby) addressed to them at the Tavistock Hotel, Covent Garden, stating where one of your firm could be met with after the arrival of the 10 o'clock Train tomorrow night, to take charge of the money.

We presume that the deposit would be received after tomorrow, subject to the result of your application to dispense with the Standing Order. Write us fully by return.

[On the back—crossed out]: 12 Jan 1861. We have no doubt you will receive the £6,400, for this deposit, not later than Monday morning. We understood the deposit was to be made on Tuesday.

76. R. W. to J. H.; from Appleby Hall, 14 Jan. 1861:

I am beyond measure disgusted at this mishap respecting the Railway. Mr. Dawes is very much to blame for not acting up to his engagement, or at least not giving more timely notice when it might have been possible to make some arrangement. The more I consider this subject the more I am persuaded of the inadvisability of my Father advancing this money for Mr. Dawes. The fact is under their Lease they were bound to form a line from the *Ancholme to the Roman road* last summer (which they did sufficiently for present purposes) they are also bound to complete a railway in all respect adapted for locomotive traffic, and with a gradient not exceeding 1 in 72 (which is quite workable and not so bad as some of the South Yorks gradients at present near Barnsley) from the occupation road leading from Santon to Scunthorpe (which we call the point A) to the Trent on or before the 1st of July next, and before the 1st of Jany 1862, they are bound to complete the entire line from the Trent to the Ancholme. On giving 6 months notice at any time we may purchase from Messrs. Dawes the entire line at cost price less wear and tear allowing Messrs. Dawes however to have a seperate [*sic*] single line of Railway from the point A to Trent for their own exclusive use if they desire it but they are debarred from carrying any goods except for their own use. In my opinion this is a much better bargain for us than the one subsequently made in London for a public line—but as it was a great object with us to get thro to Grimsby I certainly think the arrangement made in London was a prudent one, and I do not think it would have been wise to have pressed Mr. Dawes for harder terms, for as he was laying out so much money it was an object with us to keep him satisfied with his undertaking and I think he was entitled to liberal treatment—he has on more than one occasion expressed his entire satisfaction with the London arrangement. Now however the matter has assumed a different shape. By the agreement under the lease, we have the security of the Lease itself for their doing what they undertook and also the security of the works they have already done as they would forfeit their Lease, and consequently the money expended if they did not comply with the terms. I saw however at once that in abandoning this we were giving up all the security we had, unless Messrs. Dawes found the whole of the deposit for the necessary works, and as you know I was very particular in the agreement made with him on this head. If we now find the deposit for Messrs. Dawes we in fact have no hold upon him whatever, for even if we took an I.O.U. from him it is worth nothing, if, in the course of Trade, things should go wrong with him—and even if we secured the money on the works already done it amounts to nothing because by his lease if he fails in carrying out the conditions of it he forfeits the Lease itself and with it of course the works he has already done and even if it came to a question of his being able to remove the Iron Rails and Engines, I conclude an action would lie against him for non fulfilment of the contract he had entered into by his lease so that we should not allow these to be removed nor under any circumstances could he, in terms of his lease, do so without first offering them to us at their then value. The Railway clauses in the lease are all to remain the same as they were before any intention existed of going to Parliament as it was considered that it was necessary to provide against the contingency of the Bill being thrown out. The agreement made in London is now undoubtedly at an end, if we choose to consider it so, as Messrs. Dawes have failed to perform their part of it, and we must fall back upon the lease unless any other arrangement can be *prudently* adopted which will take a good deal of consideration—but at present I do not see my way to it at all I must say. We shall hear tomorrow what Roseby does at Manchester. I will ride over to Brigg tomorrow morning after the post gets here. I shall be at Brigg at 12 or soon after.

77. T. C. for D. and Co. to N., H., & F.; from London, 14 Jan. 1861 "6 p.m.":

The money has not yet arrived. We shall write to the Tavistock as you direct. In this case I do not doubt that the Standing Orders will be dispensed with. The whole scheme is too creditable and bonâ fide to be lost by the loss of a day in the deposit.

78. Telegram: J. R., Tavistock Hotel, London, to J. H.; 15 Jan. 1861:

Come to London this evening with Mr. Winn, and bring leases and agreements. I have seen Mr. Coates, and Mr. Watkin who advise the deposit to be paid. If Mr. Winn is not at Brigg, send my man Appleby with this message. The deposit must be provided for.

79. D. and Co. to N., H., & F.; from London, 18 Jan. 1861:

We send you herewith copy letter we have received from the Board of Trade as to Level Crossings etc., and it would be for the Engineer to attend to the directions contained therein as soon as possible.

80. D. and Co. to N., H., & F.; from London, 18 Jan. 1861:

This Bill will be before the Examiner on Friday the 1st February.

81. D. and Co. to N., H., & F.; from London, 24 Jan. 1861:

The Compliance with the Standing orders must undoubtedly be proved on the 1st Feby: so that the witnesses are in town at ten o'clock in the morning of that day they will be in time. Mr. Freer's attendance will be advisable; and Mr. Roseby's almost essential: the attendance of the Surveyor is quite superfluous.

You need not embarrass yourself about Mr. Parkinson's case. The right man had, and acknowledges having had notice. So with Mr. Wells's case: the right parties had notice and none object. If on reflexion we think it worthwhile to give any explanation of these mistakes in the Book of Reference, Mr. Freer can give them orally.

82. R. W. to J. H.; from Appleby Hall, 29 Jan. 1861:

I hear the Railway Bill is to come before standing orders on Friday. I hope you will not want Roseby to go up. I cannot let him go unless it is a matter of *absolute necessity*, which I do not think it is. I think Mr. Atkinson and Mr. Lee who surveyed the line must be all you require. There is so much for Roseby to do now here, and there have been so many delays occasioned by his late absence for 10 days, that I cannot let him go to London again this week it if can be avoided.

83. R. W to J. H.; from Appleby Hall, 1 Feb. 1861:

When I was in London the other day I saw Mr. Dickson of Preston, who came up on some business with Mr. Beale. I requested him before leaving London to call on Mr. Coates, and explain to him the nature of our arrangements with Mr. Dawes, and consequently what clauses we should require inserting in the Bill, for our protection when the line passed to a public Company. He now writes me word that he saw Mr. Coates who will prepare such clauses as he thinks will meet the case and then communicate with both yourself and Mr. Dickson. If anything strikes you perhaps you better write yourself to Mr. Dickson (Buck and Dickson, Preston). I have heard nothing from

Mr. Baxter or Mr. Watkin since I returned from London, and do not know when the next meeting is to be perhaps we shall know something when Roseby gets back from London, which I hope will be tomorrow. I see the Trent Bridge has *not* complied with Standing Orders.

84. R. W. to J. H.; from Appleby Hall, 11 Feb. 1861:

I will attend at Winterton on Friday should nothing unforseen [*sic*] occur.

Railway

I have got a sketch of a proposed agreement about the line from Mr. Baxter—it is the same as I told you. I will bring it to show you the first time I am over at Brigg, as I should like to talk it over with you. You have probably heard that the South Yorks is to be leased to the M. S. & L.—if the proprietors assent as no doubt they will . . .

85. Baxter, Rose & Co. to N., H., & F.; from 6 Victoria Street, Westminster Abbey, 13 Feb. 1861:

South Yorkshire Railway (Keadby Extension)

We have sent you (by Book Post) a copy of the deposited Plans and Sections in this matter.

Trent Ancholme & Grimsby Railway

We shall be glad to receive a copy of these Plans and Sections as suggested in your letter.

86. B. R. and Co. to N., H. & F.; from London, 15 Feb. 1861:

We have duly received a copy of the deposited Plans and Sections herein, for which we are much obliged.

87. T. C. for D. and Co. to N., H., & F.; from London, 15 Feb. 1861:

It is probable that this Case will be before the Standing Orders Committee next Tuesday, and it is of great importance for us to have the correspondence to which your Letter alludes.

Especially we would wish to have the Letter written, we think, to Mr. Roseby on the Saturday Evening—which was the first intimation that Messrs. Dawes's share of the money would not be ready.

This Bill was so low down in the List that it comes before the Standing Orders Committee earlier than we had expected and I am afraid that we must hurry you to send up these Documents so that they should reach us on Monday morning.

88. R. W. to J. H.; from Appleby Hall, 16 Feb. 1861:

On Thursday I wrote to Mr. Baxter a letter and enclose a copy of it and of his reply received this morning—also an answer I have written him by this post.

I don't myself think there is much in any of the points except the last, viz. validity of any agreement entered into if not noticed in the act. This you must endeavour to ascertain. Mr. Dickson says he thinks an agreement under the seal of the Company will hold good and Mr. Coates said the same the last time I saw him in London, which was when you were there I think. From what Mr. Beale remarked I rather concluded such was *not* the case, however we must be clear on this point as after all it is much the most important consideration.

89. R. W. to J. H.; from Appleby Hall, 18 Feb. 1861:

Roseby says you want the enclosed. I have your note this morning. Mr. Baxter has not sent the agreement. What I sent you was an exact copy of what he said in the letter I had from him the day I wrote you, except the first sentence which I omitted being in a hurry. It was to say that Mr. Watkin could not remain to settle anything last Wednesday, but that he should see him again *this* week when he hoped to get an arrangement made. I think with you that we shall have to take counsels opinion.

As soon as I receive any further information I will let you know.

90. J. H. to R. W. (copy); from Brigg, 18 Feb. 1861:

I think the most prudent course would be to lay before counsel the Draft of the Deed proposed to be now executed by the two existing companies and the Messrs. Dawes and yourself, with such remarks upon it as may be thought desirable. You mentioned that Mr. Baxter was to send you an amended draft. Have you received it?

91. W. F. Clark to T. F.; from York, 19 Feb. 1861:

Employ either Mr. J. Bullar, 11 Kings Bench Walk, Temple, or Mr. J. H. Lloyd, 1 Kings Bench Walk.

We have frequently employed Mr. Bullar and he is very much occupied in drawing Bills for Companies and will I think be the very man for your purpose after you have got your arrangements into shape. I should if I were you run up and confer with Bullar and let him peruse your provisional agreement (if you have one) as so much depends upon being all right in your preliminary tackling—if you mention Leemans name to Bullar I feel confident he will give you every attention.

My wife desires to be kindly remembered—my boy is at Rugby and my daughter at a school in Kensington, so we are all alone.

Remember me to your wife.

92. R. W. to J. H.; from Appleby Hall, 20 Feb. 1861:

I shall be at the board at Brigg tomorrow, and after it is over will confer with you on the subject [of Railways].

93. D. and Co. to N., H., & F.; from London, 20 Feb. 1861:

The Standing Order Committee allow the Bill to proceed—and the Bill has today been read a 1st time in the House of Commons. We have still the House of Lords Standing Order Committee, to go before, but we do not anticipate any difficulty there.

94. D. and Co. to N., H., & F.; from London, 22 Feb. 1861:

Trent Ancholme and Grimsby Railway

This Bill was grouped yesterday and the Committee appointed to meet on Friday the 5th March.

Meanwhile the 5th March is the day upon which the time for petitioning expires.

South Yorkshire (Keadby Extension)

This Bill is in the same group—and the time for petitioning against it will also expire on the 5th March.

There are other Bills in the group which will occupy a considerable time; and these two must needs be taken last.

95. R. W. to J. H.; from Appleby Hall, 22 Feb. 1861:

I have no letter from Mr. Baxter today. I have therefore written him by this post, as we decided on yesterday, and you shall hear the moment I get his reply. Meantime I think you might be ascertaining whether an agreement under the hands and seal of the Company is binding in law; or whether it is absolutely necessary to have something inserted in the bill. I should not under the circumstances press for the latter if the former could be made to answer our purpose.

97. R. W. to J. H.; from Appleby Hall, 26 Feb. 1861:

I have just got the two enclosed telegraphs. I hardly know what to do—but I think the best plan will be to go to Doncaster as we arranged where you will see Mr. Dixon [*sic*] and settle the course necessary to be adopted, and we can go on from Doncaster to London by an afternoon train. I see nothing else for it but this, as time is so pressing. I shall write Mr. Baxter that I will see him in London on Thursday.

97a. Telegram (copy): R. W. to Buck & Dickson, Solicitors, Preston; from Appleby Hall (undated):

Meet me at Angel Inn Doncaster on Wednesday to see Mr. Baxter at eleven thirty and settle the Railway question.

97b. Telegram: Buck & Dickson to R. W.; from Preston, 26 Feb. 1861:

The writer hopes to meet you at Doncaster about twelve o'clock tomorrow.

97c. Telegram: R. Baxter to R. W.; from London, 26 Feb. 1861:

Watkin not ready. Useless to trouble you to come to Doncaster. Can you be here on Thursday, please write.

98. Coverdale Lee and Collyer Bristow (4 Bedford Row, London, W.C.) to N., H., & F.; the Angel Inn, Doncaster; to N., H., & F.; from London, 26 Feb. 1861:

Trent Ancholme and Grimsby Railway/Exparte Winn

We enclose the bill, copy draft agreement, and instructions with Mr. John Bullar's remarks thereon.

99. D. and Co. to N., H., & F.; from London, 27 Feb. 1861:

Herewith, we send you a Copy of the Petition of the Manchester Sheffield and Lincolnshire Railway Company against this Bill.

100. D. and Co. to N., H., & F.; from London, 1 March 1861:

Trent Ancholme etc. Bill

Since Mr. Winn and you left me I have had an interview with Mr. Baxter and talked to him about the Clause which we prepared as to the Conveyance of Minerals.

He tells me that Mr. Watkin absolutely objects to such a Clause, because he alleges that to convey minerals on such terms for all comers would be unprofitable. Mr. Baxter repeated to me the proposition which he made to you that the Bill should contain a power to the Company to contract with Mr. Winn—a superfluous power as it seems to me; and then that an agreement should be entered into with such recitals as would prevent the agreement from being used as a predecent for all other persons.

If the agreement is settled before the Bill goes into Committee in the Lords, I think that this process will give a sufficient security to Mr. Winn and for the tenants to whom the agreement extends—and I confess that the controversy does not seem to me of a kind to put the Bill in jeopardy.

101. D. and Co. to N., H., & F.; from London, 1 March 1861:

So. Yorkshire. Keadby Extn

The form of petition which you will receive herewith will give the Drainage Commissioners all the opportunity they want of being heard on Clauses and proposing Clauses.

103. R. W. to J. H.; from Appleby Hall, 5 March 1861:

I was unable to reply to your two letters by yesterdays post. As soon as you have arranged with Mr. Coates the best course to be adopted I shall be disposed to submit the whole proposal to counsel as I think the matter is of too large a nature to make it prudent to run any risk, in fact no one can foresee what may be the state of affairs 10 or 20 yrs hence and our obligations are for 100. I have no desire to press the insertion of the clause proposed by Mr. Coates the other day, in the bill, if any other strictly legal means of making us secure can be adopted—but secured we *must be.* I have no idea of leaving anything at the option of the Railway Companies—for tho I have no doubt both Mr. Baxter and Mr. Watkin would endeavour in all good faith to carry out strictly any arrangement they had been parties to, yet this agreement is for a term far exceeding the limits of their life time or my own which makes a legal binding arrangement absolutely necessary, and certainly nothing short will satisfy me. From what we ascertained in London it seems we have the Railway at present entirely without our own control. I shall be ready to take further steps whenever you find it necessary, but I suppose there is no immediate hurry.

104. D. and Co. to N., H., & F.; from London, 18 March 1861: Trent Ancholme and Grimsby Ry

This Bill is not at all likely to be on before Easter. Meanwhile I ought to apologise to you for not having written you earlier.

I am in conference with Mr. Winn and with Mr. Watkin and Mr. Baxter for protective Clauses and I am not without hope that we may come to a satisfactory result.

105. R. W. to J. H.; from Appleby Hall, 20 March 1861:

I have just heard from my brother in London, who after repeated attempts has at last succeeded in seeing Mr Coates. I copy the portion of his letter which relates to the Railway matters.

"I met Mr. Coates yesterday afternoon in the committee room and I had some talk with him, he tells me Watkins [*sic*] sticks to not having the 6d rate inserted in the Bill or secured by it; he says it will create a precedent which would hamper him in other cases, but he says he will consent to give us a fixed rate of 4½d for running over the line and that we may do the haulage, in other words he leaves us 1½d for engine power this would never do; I am told we ought to have from 2½d to 3d. While I was talking to Coates Watkin came up, Coates told him the matter we were on and asked if he had reconsidered the subject. Watkin at once said 'in ten minutes from now I will meet you at Baxters and will try to settle it'—and then he went off, as soon as he had gone Coates said 'it will never do for you and I to go there you see Watkin cant say anything without Baxter and he wants to get us to his office and have us committed to something, clearly we are better out of their way', so he sent word he was called to a committee, and could not go. Coates says he does not see any reason why the rate should not be entered in the Bill, or at any rate have an agreement drawn up and referred to in the act, at the same time he says *his opinion is* that an agreement *could* be made between ourselves and the Companies which would be binding on them without inserting it in the act. As to Mr. Elwes petition he thinks nothing of it; it is merely the ordinary wording and means nothing, the M. S. and L. petition is also nothing he says—but he thinks we certainly ought to have the line looked over by some engineer who is know[n] and could give evidence, shall I ask Watkin to let their Engineer look it over *or speak to Fowler about it*?"

I suppose we better [*sic*] have an engineer to look the line over. I have told my brother to enquire of Coates who he would like to have, but I think under the circumstances it better [*sic*] not be either the engineer of the M. S. & L. or of the S. Y. Roseby proposed Harrison of the North Eastern, as being a less experience[d] man than Fowler, but as he lives in the North (I forget where) we should have to take him to London and keep him there probably some days, so I conceive it might be quite as costly as having Mr. Fowler. The idea of our accepting Mr. Watkins proposal of doing the haulage at a reduction from the 6d of 1½d is simply absurd. What was agreed on in the event of the line remaining ours was that we should receive from the Companies a tonnage rate less 40% for working expenses—this I believe was nothing more than what was fair and reasonable. Why then should we now be satisfied with 25% in our own case? especially when the distance is so short that it is much more costly to work at *per mile* than a longer run. I have written Mr. Dawes to say that I must see him on an early day to talk the subject over and see what view he now takes of the matter. I will send this over by a messenger so that if anything strikes you, that you would like my Brother to talk over and arrange with Mr. Coates, you may write him by this post yourself. Otherwise I fear he may have left London, his address is Army and Navy Club, Pall Mall. I think it may end in our having to go on with the Bill ourselves putting in a clause as to the 6d. rate In this case I wish you would as far as you think you can modify the sewers and Ancholme clauses so that they may not be taken hold of in the way Mr. Baxter seemed disposed to do—as I think it would give them a handle against the bill. I think as regards the Ancholme if you could copy as nearly as possible the clauses in the M. S. & L. Act it would be the best.

106. Edmund J. Winn to J. H.; from Army and Navy Club, 21 March 1861:

Mr. Coates is ill and has not been to his office for the last two days, however they expect him to be there tomorrow and I have endeavoured to secure an interview with him, and will learn his opinion on the various points you mention. I do not expect we shall come to any terms with the M. S. & L.

107. R. W. to J. H.; from Appleby Hall, 22 March 1861:

I am going to meet Mr. Dawes on Monday on some matters and shall endeavour then to find out what view he takes about the Railway—and if possible come to something definite with him on the subject. Will you be so good as [to] send me by the postman tomorrow morning, the case you laid before Counsel (Mr. Lloyd) with his remarks, that I may show them to Mr. Dawes. You shall [have] them back early next week.

P.S. I have heard nothing further from my brother since I last wrote you.

108. D. and Co. to N., H., & F.; from London, 22 March 1861:

Herewith we send you a Copy of Lord Redesdale's remarks on this [T. A. & G.] Bill.

109. R. W. to J. H.; from Appleby Hall, 23 March 1861:

I have your parcel this morning with Mr. Bullers [*sic*] opinion which you shall have back early next week. I have this morning a letter from my brother, the following is a copy of the Railway portion of it—

"I have been to Coates this morning, find he was at the office for a few minutes but obliged to leave, not well enough to attend to business—however I saw his partner who does the business in his absence and seemed to be quite up to all that had been done about our line. I told him what I had come to see Coates about to which he replied 'if you take my advice you will let the matter rest just now your bill cannot come on before the 15 of April so there is plenty of time, if you try to come to anything with Watkin and the S. Yorks. ten to one you would fail, they would not meet each other, they dont themselves know at present how they stand with one another, and until these Liverpool Bills are done with Watkin has his hands too full to attend to anything else, under any circumstances I think you are all right, and you will see when it is time and they find you are independant [*sic*] they will come to you; dont think it necessary to believe anything Watkin tells you, he is a sharp man and a very slippery one, with regard to Fowler (the engineer) of course you could not employ a better man but I would not go to the expense of sending him down till nearer the time if you find that it is necessary'—all this seemed to me such good advice that I have acted on it and done nothing further."

I copy exactly what my Brother says. It is not very easy to see how this is to end, but we shall have a solution of it in a few weeks at any rate—I shall see Mr. Dawes in Yorkshire on Monday, and see if some arrangement cannot be come to with him to make us independent of the Companies.

110. T. C. for D. and Co. to N., H., & F.; from London, 1 April 1861:

Trent Ancholme etc. Railway

I have been confined to my house for a week by illness and so deferred writing to you the result of an interview I had with Mr. Baxter and Mr. Watkin on the 19 March.

Both adhered to the opinion, and (let me add) will I am sure continue to adhere to the opinion, that a clause in the Bill defining tolls for the conveyance of minerals between the Trent and the Ancholme will be attended with such inconvenience on the system of the Sheffield and South Yorkshire Railways as to render such a Clause inadmissible.

This opinion is confirmed by others conversant with Railways, whom I have consulted.

But they will consent to the insertion of a Clause enabling agreements to be made between the Company to be incorporated by the Bill and Mr. Winn; and they will be prepared to settle such an agreement before the Bill passes through Committee.

It seems to me that if you can settle the terms of the agreement, such an agreement may be enforced in Equity; and I have taken the liberty of suggesting to you the outline of such an agreement to guide you or your Counsel in the preparation of it, or in the settling of any Draft which may be laid before you by Messrs. Baxter.

I also send you the Draft of a Clause for authorizing the making of such an agreement.

Mr. Baxter will be at Doncaster during the remainder of the week, and perhaps you may find it convenient to see him there.

Meanwhile I will send to him, without binding us in any way, a copy of the Clause and of the outline of agreement.

111. T. C. for D. and Co. to N., H., & F.; from London, 2 April 1861:

Trent Ancholme Railway Bill

When I was making my communication to you yesterday I had not before me the letter of Mr. Rowland Winn dated the 2nd March, suggesting the form of the Clause, nor did I sufficiently bear in mind that Mr. Edmund Winn had told me that it was not only conveyance to the Trent of their Minerals which they desire to secure, but also conveyance to the Ancholme, and to any spots intermediate between the Trent and the Ancholme.

But I had not lost sight of these things in my conversation with Mr. Baxter and Mr. Watkin, although neither held out to me any promise or indeed any hope that these objects would be attained. Indeed the difficulty of conducting a local traffic of this sort by the Company upon part of what will ultimately be a through line, and the impossibility of defining the duty of the Company so as to keep it within reasonable bounds rendered me reluctant to press the matter.

Nevertheless it is entirely open, and in transmitting to Mr. Baxter the outline of the agreement I have warned him that the covenant does not comprise conditions which your clients deem indispensable.

Permit me to remind you that the arrangements between Mr. Winn and the two Companies do not admit of being postponed, and that this week affords perhaps the best opportunity for making those arrangements.

Note. In the last paragraph of the Outline of agreement after the words "reconvey the said Waggons", insert the words "free of charge".

112. T. C. for D. and Co. to N., H., & F.; from London, 4 April 1861:

Trent Ancholme etc Railway

I regret that arrangements which I cannot now alter will prevent me from being here on Saturday. Any time that you will fix after 12 o'clock on Monday will suit me.

Perhaps in your conference with Mr. Winn you will not lose sight of the following considerations:

First, we will suppose that you break off the negociation with the two Companies, and that you continue your application for an Act according to the original scheme.

This hypothesis involves the repayment of £6,200—the finding of the necessary Capital for the completion of the Railway as a passenger Line, and perhaps Capital for the working of the Railway. It involves either conceding or resisting running powers to the two Companies; if conceding, there must be a kind of priority reserved for local traffic; if resisting, we must contemplate considerable expense in the conflict, and we must lay the ground inevitably for the construction of a parallel line hereafter, supposing running powers to be refused.

Nor am I sure that if the Bill were obtained in the Commons it would pass the Lords, so far as the line between the Ancholme and Barnetby-le-Wold is concerned.

Second. We will assume the Bill to be withdrawn, the great expense hitherto incurred upon its prosecution wasted, and the project to be confined to the line between the Trent and the Ancholme. It is manifest that if we adopt this course the two Companies will next Session obtain powers to unite their Undertakings; perhaps over Mr. Winn's estate—probably avoiding that estate; and it may be that Mr. Winn and his tenants may so lose direct access to the Sheffield System and the Port of Grimsby and access to the South Yorkshire Coal Field.

I have made these suggestions to you not for the sake of reconciling your Clients to an oppressive bargain with the two Companies, but for the purpose of inducing you to advise such concessions as (consistently with Mr. Winn's security) shall avert very serious inconveniences. And it behoves us to remember that whatever embarrassments we have are of our own producing; in that Mr. Winn has thought it expedient to pledge himself and his heirs for the next century to become Carriers for his tenants; and also, in that we have been driven to seek pecuniary aid from the very bodies of whom it would have been desirable that we should have been independent.

I retain the opinion that a conference between Mr. Winn, you, and Mr. Baxter would tend to a solution of the difficulties.

113. R. W. to J. H.; from Appleby Hall, 5 April 1861, "Friday Night":

Mr. Baxter, Mr. Bartholomew came over to the Trent this afternoon. Their visit was for the purpose of bringing Mr. Fairburn of Manchester to see the site of the Bridge as he is going to contract for it. They had only 1¼ hours to spare altogether. Mr. Baxter went on on an engine as far as Scunthorpe to look at the Ironstone pit but had only time to remain there 4 or 5 minutes. He did not mention our arrangements with the Companies in any way and appeared to avoid it in fact there was very little opportunity of saying anything. We looked at the warping drain, and he appears to think that one opening would do for us. We also alluded to the land we wish to reserve. If you again wish to see me I will go over to Brigg tomorrow afternoon. I think however there is nothing more I can say at present. I think the most important object is to ascertain what sort of an agreement Mr. Buller thinks we should be safe in making in order to secure the 6d rule, especially—and my own idea was that from what Mr. Coates said a short time ago to my brother that it was policy not to press the Companies for an immediate arrangement unless they make a move in that direction themselves. You will hear however more particularly what Mr. Coates thinks and why he has changed his views—with regard to his remarks in his last letter to you—I should have no idea whatever of breaking off negociation with them, so long as we get some legal security for our arrangements with them and are advised by Mr. Buller that we are safe. If we could not make safe terms with the Companies we must certainly repay the £6,200 and there would be 4 years in which to find capital for completing the line to Barnetby. We have long ago undertaken to give the Companies running powers, and could certainly not refuse that now—it is a point long since settled. I am very ready for a reasonable agreement with the Companies so long as we can get due security there does not seem to me any doubt about getting an arrangement, the point is the *security for it*, and this Mr. Buller will best advise us in as it appears to me. I cannot at all agree in the last sentence of Mr. Coates's letter, viz. that any embarrassments we may have, have been produced by "Mr. Winn having thought it expedient to pledge himself and his heirs for the next century to become Carriers for his tenants" in truth it did not amount to that, as we should only have become carriers under certain circumstances, and at a rate which from what I have already seen would be very remunerative when the works get more developed. Had however no such bargain existed I should still have insisted on a fixed rate of 6d. to the Trent as the *main point* to be obtained in any arrangement with the Companies, as I consider it an important safeguard.

[On the back in pencil by J. H.]: The arrangement as to the carrying of Minerals is this. Messrs. Dawes in their Lease contract to convey the minerals at the fixed rate and Mr. Winn covenants with his other lessees to give them the benefit of Dawes' covenant.

114. J. H. to R. W. (copy): from Brigg, 6 April 1861:

I do not think it is requisite that I should see you again before going to London. After seeing Mr. Coates and Mr. Bullar, I will communicate with you.

115. J. H. to T. C. (copy): 8 Apri 1861l:

The Coal rate suggested by Mr. R. Winn at the foot of the agreement prepared by you has reference to a stipulation in the Lease to Messrs. Dawes that *all coal* brought by Water Carriage to the Trent or Ancholme and there put into the Railway must be conveyed by **them** along any portion of the new line between those Rivers at a fixed rate per mile. This is a matter that concerns the new Company.

116. J. H. to R. W. (copy); from Old Hummums, Covent Garden, London, 9 April 1861:

I had a long interview yesterday with Mr. Coates and Mr. Shrubsole his partner, and the result was that we settled the terms of an amended agreement (of which I send you a copy) with respect to the fixed Toll for conveying Ironstone, and Iron to the Trent and Ancholme, and intermediate places, and for the conveyance of coal from the Trent and Ancholme. Mr. Dickson in his letter to me states that the Coal rate introduced by you into Dawes's lease is 1½d. per ton per mile. I see we have not literally carried this out in the agreement, which stipulates for 6d. per ton for any distance. If material this can be altered. It is, however, Mr Coates' full conviction that the whole of the stipulation will be resisted by Mr. Watkin and not acceded to, with the exception of that relating to the conveyance of Ironstone and Iron to the *Trent*, and that possibly the mention of Iron will not be sanctioned.

The proposed Clause and agreement are before Mr. Lloyd, Mr. Bullar not being in Town. Mr. Coates has no doubt the agreement might be enforced in equity.

I understand that neither Messrs. Dawes' Lease nor Mr. Beale's is yet signed. It seems important that either the terms of the proposed agreement should be made in conformity with the terms in the Leases, or that the Leases—especially Dawes's should be altered so that Beale may not be able to insist under his agreement upon other terms than those secured by the proposed agreement.

There is however this difficulty that if the Bill should not pass you want the Coal rate in Dawes's Lease—I do not find that 'Iron' is stipulated to be carried for Dawes either at the 6d. or the 1½d. rate.

I have not at present seen either Mr. Baxter, or Mr. Rackham, Mr. Elwes' family Solicitor.

Since writing the above I have had a conference with Mr. Lloyd, whose impression is that the proposed agreement will be a binding one. He, however, wishes to have an opportunity of considering the matter more carefully and promises the papers on Friday.

Will you consider the Suggestions for agreement and my letter, and let me know which of the matters you think may be given up in necessity. It is unfortunate that Mr. Lloyd is so much occupied as to be quite unable to take up the papers at once. The other agreement will require immediate attention as soon as this more essential one is arranged, and I may have occasion to summon you at any time.

Mr. Coates thinks we shall be in Committee about the 22nd instant.

117. J. H. to T. F.; from Old Hummums . . . 10 April 1861:

The main difficulty with the Sheffield Company (with respect to a fixed rate for the conveyance of Minerals to the Trent and Ancholme) will I think be got over satisfactorily to all parties. Mr. Lloyd's impression is that a binding agreement on the subject may be made without embodying it in the Bill, but I shall not have his definitive opinion before Friday. Mr. Coates thought we should not be in committee before next Monday week. Today, however, he thinks it possible the case may be on in a week. I shall arrange with him as to the evidence tomorrow or on Friday. I have no hope of returning home until the whole matter is in shape. You had better see Roseby and Mr. Atkinson, as I anticipate both will have to come up. I did mention the matter to Mr. John West, and he would I think give evidence if required. One or two witnesses of that class will I expect be wanted. I am writing to Mr. Winn.

Since writing the above I have seen Mr. Rackham and feel satisfied they do not really mean to oppose in committee, though I have no statement to that effect. He will write Mr. Barnard tonight and I shall see him on Friday.

118. R. W. to J. H. (in London); from Appleby Hall, 10 April 1861:

I will endeavour to return you the draft agreement you have prepared with Mr. Coates by this post, but I want to have it copied and I am not sure if I can get it done in time. I think 1st *It is essential* to have a rate for Ironstone to the Trent of 6d.

Also a Coal rate from the Trent in the event of the Bridge bill not being obtained, or the Bridge not being made, and that either a 6d. rate or 1½d. per ton per mile will do.

2d That *it is desirable* to include the Ancholme as well as the Trent, and to make the 6d. rate apply to *Iron* as well as to *Ironstone.*

3d That it is *not necessary* to insist on the words "from any point to any point".

I think we can alter Messrs. Dawes lease to meet this in a way that will satisfy both him and Mr. Beale. I cannot see that Mr. Watkin can object to give us a coal rate if the Bridge is not made, if it is we should not require it. I think I cannot say any more today.

119. J. H. to R. W. (copy); from Old Hummums . . . 10 April 1861:

Assuming that it may be requisite to specify the dimensions of the opening to be constructed under the Railway for warping purposes, will you have the goodness to inform me whether the *present bottom* of the Warping Drain is low enough, and if not to what depth below that it would be necessary to excavate. I wish to be in a position to define the depth of the opening to be made under the Railway as well as the width. I ascertained from Mr. Atkinson that the bottom must be 55 ft in width, with a batter or slope of 1½ foot horizontal and 1 foot perpendicular.

You mentioned that Mr. Tolson White, and another gentleman had been over the Line. What portion did they inspect? What was the name of the second gentleman? I think it possible their inspection had reference to the Keadby Extension.

Will you forward to me any letters or copies of letters in your possession having reference to your understanding with Mr. Corbett. My understanding is that the Company are to put down Rails from the line to the brickyard in Elsham Car and to the Worlaby Causeway, upon Mr. Corbett's land, and to be at the expence [*sic*] of the requisite points upon his land to connect with the line—a siding to be constructed by him from his Ironstone quarry or mine.

I wrote the earlier part of my letter in the morning. I have since seen Mr. Rackham. He will write to Mr. Barnard tonight and I am to see him on Friday. I have no fear of any contest before the committee upon Mr. Elwes' petition. The question seems to be whether our valuer and Mr. Bradley, Mr. Elwes' agent can meet and make an arrangement as to price and accommodation works, before going into committee. I am afraid not. Mr. Coates now thinks the case may come on about Wednesday next. There is much to arrange with Mr. Baxter previously, and I must ask you to hold yourself in readiness to come up. I am anxious to have Mr. Lloyd's opinion before conferring with Mr. Baxter.

120. R. W. to J. H.; from Appleby Hall, 11 April 1861:

I have your letter this morning. I have understood that there is about 4 to 5 ft. of silt in the bottom of the warping drain which would be washed out by the tide as soon as the warping operations were commenced, but I rather think the thickness varies somewhat. My brother is in London at the Army and Navy having been sent for by Mr. Baxter to give evidence on the Barnsley Coal railway as they call it. If you want anything consult with him, and I shall be ready to join you any day. When will the Bridge Bill come on. A person of the name of Brown of Barnsley, a surveyor, as I understand, came with Mr. Tolson White but they only went to the Ironstone pits with Mr. Tootal, we cannot make out by whom they were sent, it was certainly nothing to do with our line and I fancy they must be engaged on the Barnsley coal line, and had come to look at the Ironstone, in connection with its probability of increasing the demand for Barnsley Hard coal for smelting purposes. I expect you will find they are engaged on the Coal line. With respect to Mr. Corbett—I have never written him but one letter as to the terms of crossing his land—the original I left with you and have not another copy. I know the terms or I understood them to be

A branch to be put to the Worlaby Brickyard (the position of which he could perhaps be induced to alter—to nearer the line—as there are *no buildings* whatever at present).

A siding at the Worlaby Causeway.

A station at the Brigg and Elsham turnpike with proper accommodation.

A siding to his Ironstone if he ever hereafter finds any and desires to work it.

I believe this to be exactly what I said in my letter to him—and his reply is

"The arrangements you enumerate are quite satisfactory and a full reply to my letter to Messrs. Nicholson Hett and Freer of the 10th Inst." i.e., November.

I understood that the sidings and points were to be put in by the Company.

I am glad to hear what you say about Mr. Elwes opposition. I shall be ready to come up any day—I should like to be there when the Bridge Bill comes on.

121. J. H. to R. W. (copy); from D. & Co's offices, London, 11 April 1861:

I have seen Mr. Tolson White and Mr. Brown, another engineer, and I find they are to give evidence in support of the Barnsley Coal Railway promoted by the South Yorkshire Company. One point of this evidence is to be that the coal is wanted in our Ironstone District, and it was with a view to enable them to speak upon this point that they recently went over the line. Mr. White tells me that Mr. Edmund Winn is come up for the purpose of giving evidence on that Bill. The Bill is expected to be in committee tomorrow or on Monday.

It appears to Mr. Coates as well as to myself that you should be in Town on Monday *morning*. Between ourselves Mr. Coates complains that he cannot get Mr. Baxter to attend to this and several other matters of importance. I hope we shall have made some progress with him before your arrival.

122. J. H. to R. W. (copy); from "London", 12 April 1861:

Mr. Lloyd has not yet settled the clause and agreement, but now promises to let me have them tomorrow.

Nothing is arranged with Mr. Baxter as to the agreement, but Mr. Coates has an appointment with him for tomorrow morning. I am to see Mr. Coates afterwards. Mr. Edmund Winn doubts whether Mr. Baxter is in a position to make the proposed arrangements. We may have to go on independently. Will you arrange that this shall be done if requisite. I have seen Mr. Rackham, who states that Mr. Elwes will *not* appear on his petition, so that we shall be virtually unopposed. You must nevertheless be here on Monday morning.

Mr. Burke opened the case of the Barnsley Coal Line this morning, and the examination of witnesses will commence at 11.30 on Monday.

Lord Redesdale is raising a difficulty about the Line, on the ground that it is for Mr. Winn's private advantage.

123. J. H. to Edmund Winn at Army and Navy Club (copy); from Old Hummums . . . 12 April 1861:

I have arranged with Mr. Coates to call upon him tomorrow at 12, and I shall be glad if you can conveniently meet me. Mr. Coates is to see Mr. Baxter at 10.

124. R. W. to J. H.; from Appleby Hall, 12 April 1861:

What you tell me about Mr. White etc. is just what I anticipated. I will be in London at 3 o'clock on Monday, unless I hear from you to the contrary. If there is no occasion for my going so soon you must let me know.

125. J. H. to T. F.; from "London"

(*a*) 12 April 1861: [in pencil]

You will be glad to hear that Mr Elwes will not appear upon his Petition, and that we shall be practically unopposed. We have, however, not been able to conclude any arrangements with Mr. Baxter, and I do not know whether we shall not have to go on independently. It is very annoying to be in this uncertain state. Mr. Coates is very much bothered about it. I have written for Mr. R. Winn to be here on Monday morning. We expect to be in committee in the middle of next week, but may be thrown over to the week following. As far as I can see, I must remain to watch the case, and act according to circumstances. I have written to ask Roslin [J. H.'s eldest son and a member of the firm] to join me. Will you send by him the lists of assents, dissents and neuters.

I am to see Mr. Coates tomorrow as to evidence, which will be pretty nearly formal.

[At the side: "Written at the House of Commons"]

(*b*) 13 April 1861:

We progress very slowly with our arrangements with Mr. Baxter, but I have good hopes that we shall come to terms. The Bill cannot now be taken before Thursday, and perhaps may not be disposed of before Monday. Mr. R. Winn comes up on that day. I believe Mr. Roseby only will be wanted as to the estimate, and the work executed. He need not come up until he hears from me or Mr. Winn but he must be in readiness.

126. J. H. to R. W. (copy); from London, 13 April 1861:
Mr. Edmund Winn met me at Mr. Coates' this morning, and will give you particulars of our interview. But little progress has been made, but I think the essential provisions of the main agreement will be arranged. I have not yet got the papers from Mr. Lloyd. Some progress as to the settlement of the Warping Clause and the Sewers Clauses to be inserted in the Keadby Extension Bill has also been made, Mr. Baxter having requested Mr. Coates to arrange them. Nothing has been done as to the other agreement. We are to meet at Mr. Coates' at 4 on Tuesday, when I hope Mr. Watkin will attend and that we may get the terms settled. I think it is desirable that you should come up on Monday, that we may have an opportunity of consulting upon any matters which may be unsettled.

127. R. W. to J. H.; from Appleby Hall, 13 April 1861:
I have got your letter of yesterday. I have had a somewhat extraordinary letter from Mr. Dawes from which I understand him to decline finding any portion of the £6000 deposit, that is to say to join with us in a security for it. He does not say so in direct terms but I could conclude his meaning to be such. I shall not advise my Father to do more than join Dawes in raising the money as I proposed to him (Dawes) the other day at Barnsley, in case we could not make any terms that were safe with the Railway Companies—and to which he then fully assented. I cannot think in common prudence my Father ought to raise the whole of the money himself, and become in fact security for Dawes afterwards completing the line, which he tells us oweing [*sic*] to the state of the Iron trade he could not now do—and of course cannot say when he would be able. I will write Mr. Dawes by this post and say I am told it is possible, oweing to the two Railway Companies being in such an unsettled state as to their own affairs, we may find they are unable to complete an arrangement with us, and in that case it is necessary for him to make up his mind what he will do, whether find the deposit or a portion of it, or abandon the Bill. I shall tell him he must arrange to be in London on Monday. I dont think our Bill could be in committee next week.

128. J. H. to J. R. (copy); from Old Hummums . . . 16 April 1861:
The Keadby Extension Bill is to be in committee on Thursday, and our Line [T., A. & G. Railway] will be taken immediately after-

wards. You should therefore come up tomorrow. No other evidence than yours will be wanted, as there will be no opposition.

You will have to state the length of the Line from Trent to Ancholme, and from Ancholme to Barnetby Junction, and to say how much has been constructed, and to give particulars of the Estimates.

129. D. & Co. to N., H., & F.; from London, 16 April 1861:

We beg leave to call your attention to the Copy of a letter we have this day received from Colonel Yolland. You will find the copy on the other side.

[Other side]: (Copy). Colonel Yolland presents his compliments to Messrs. Dyson & Co. and begs to say that he would wish to see the engineer of the Trent Ancholme & Grimsby Railway as soon as may be convenient.

130. J. H. to T. F.; from London, 16 April 1861:

The Keadby Extension Bill is fixed to be in committee on Thursday, and I have written to request Roseby to come up tomorrow. No other witness will be required. Will you have the goodness to tell Roland that Roseby is coming up, so that if Mrs. Hett has anything to send to me, he may be asked to bring it.

We have not yet completed our arrangements with Baxter. I certainly cannot leave Town before Friday, if then.

131. J. R. to J. H. (at Old Hummums); from Brigg, 17 April 1861:

I am in receipt of yours of yesterday and will attend to your instructions. I will be in London on Thursday evening.

132. J. H. to E. J. Winn at Army & Navy Club, Pall Mall (copy); from Old Hummums . . . 17 April 1861:

Mr. Coates has appointed to see Mr. Baxter tomorrow morning at 9.15 as to our protection clauses in the Keadby Extension Bill, and I have arranged to call upon Mr. Coates, with Mr. R. Winn, at 11.

(Copy): J. H. to R. W. (at Carlton Club); 17 April 1861:

Mr. Coates has appointed . . .11.

134. J. H. to W. C. Atkinson (copy); from Old Hummums . . . 18 April 1861:

I shall be glad if you can call upon me here at 10 o'clock tomorrow morning.

135. J. H. to R. W. (at Carlton Club) (copy); from Old Hummums . . 19 April 1861:

I have arranged with Mr. Coates to call upon him with you at 2 o'clock tomorrow. He is to see Mr. Baxter previously.

136. D. and Co. to J. H. (at O.H.); from London, 20 April 1861:
We send you herewith a Copy of Colonel Yollands Report upon the Level Crossings etc. in this [T.A.G.] Bill.
We also beg leave to inform you that this Bill will be taken in Committee by the Chairman of Ways and Means on Tuesday next (23rd).

137. J. H. to R. W. (at C.C.) (copy); from O.H., 22 April 1861:
I have called upon you with a draft agreement received this evening from Mr. Baxter, with his note. I have also brought a copy of the draft agreement prepared by Mr. Lloyd, and of the Clause in the Bill by which it is authorized to be made. I think the *two* agreements are essential, the one being for Mr. Winn's benefit in his individual capacity, the other comprizing arrangements between the Companies.
The appointment you will see is for half past 9. I will call at the Carlton soon after 9. You will see I have made some remarks upon Mr. Baxter's draft and some additions and alterations.
I have the papers for you to consider.

138. Robert Baxter to J. H. (at O.H.); from 6 Victoria Street, Westminster Abbey, S.W., 22 April 1861:
I have at last settled this [T., A. & G. Rly Bill] draft with Mr. Watkin this morning. I enclose it to you.
I have just received your draft. It cannot be necessary to have two and I therefore must ask you to look at the one I send and with which we will deal tomorrow morning at half past 9 when Mr. Winn will be with me.

139. J. H. to B. R. & Co. (copy); from O.H., 22 April 1861:
I have had a long conference with Mr. Coates as to the final settlement of this Bill for the Commons Committee. Mr. Coates states that it is not advisable to leave anything for settlement with regard to rates before the Lords' Committee. It is therefore essential that the arrangements with the Sheffield and So. Yorkshire Companies be at once agreed upon, and reduced into writing before attending before Mr. Massey. I send for your perusal draft agreement respecting the conveyance of Ironstone etc. be ore the Trent and Anch. and a copy of the draft agreement sent by you to Mr. R. Winn with alterations and remarks. Mr. Winn understood you to say you should send him an amended draft, but he has not rec'd it. Will you let this matter have immediate attention.

140. J. H. to T. C. (copy); from O.H., 22 April 1861:
I enclose draft copies of two agreements which I have sent to Mr. Baxter for perusal, the one having reference to the conveyance of Ironstone etc. to the Trent and Ancholme, and the other being a

copy of a draft prepared by Mr. Baxter, with my alterations and remarks. I have stated that it is essential that the arrangements be at once agreed upon and reduced into writing before attending Mr. Massey. I have not been able to enclose the agreement secondly mentioned.

141. J. H. to T. F.; from London, 23 April 1861:

After a very irksome delay I hope we have now got this matter into shape. We go into Committee on Thursday and I hope to be at home on Friday. Will you send, by return, the statement prepared by Mr. Torry, showing the number of carriages etc. passing along the Turnpike Road to Barton, a copy of which I sent to the Board of Trade. It will be found, I expect, in the Railway box.

142. J. H. to T. C. (copy); from O. H., 24 April 1861:

I send you a copy of the clause as to agreements with Mr. Winn. I have satisfied Mr. Baxter as to the Ancholme Bridge.

[On the back]: Other evidence as to level crossings applies to 84 Frodingham/ 23 Appleby/ 32 Appleby/ 7 Wrawby.

143. D. & Co. to N., H., & F.; from London, 6 May 1861:

We send you by this post prints of this [T.A.G.] Bill, as passed by the Commons Committee. You will be so good as to get a Bill or Bills signed by all the parties named in the Bill as subscribers or Directors. They need not all sign the same Bill, but each must sign some Bill or other—it is to signify their consent to their names appearing as Subscribers or Directors.

143a. D. & Co. to N., H. & F.; from London, 6 May 1861:

We will thank you to let us have £400, on account of the Bill at your early convenience.

144. D. & Co., to N., H., & F.; from London, 7 May 1861:

We send you herewith further proofs herein for the House of Lords.

145. R. Dudley Baxter to R. W. (copy); from 6 Victoria St., S.W., 8 May 1861:

I have sent you, for my Father, a copy of the Trent and Ancholme Bill as amended, by which you will observe at page 10 that the level crossings sanctioned are in Nos 2, 32 and 7 on the plan.

I have also sent you the engrossment of the General Agreement to which you can obtain the signatures of your lessees.

With respect to the agreement as to the sixpenny rate Mr. Hett brought one to my father but subsequently took it away saying that you would be satisfied with the clause in the general Agreement.

146. R. W. to J. H.; from Appleby Hall, 9 May 1861:

I have just got the enclosed from Mr. Baxter with copy of Railway Bill which I also send for you to look thro as well as the general agreement. You will observe what Mr. Baxter says—I think there must be some mistake—you must get it set right at once—I also will write. In post haste.

P.S. Let me know if the general agreement is right.

147. R. W. to J. H.; from Appleby Hall, 11 May 1861:

You said you were going to write to me about Mr. Baxters agreement etc. but as I have not heard, I fear lest the postman may have forgotten to deliver it if you sent me a parcel as is not very unfrequently the case. I find Mr. Geo Dawes will be in London next week and if we can only get the agreement arranged I would get him to call at Mr. Baxters office and sign it whilst he is in Town—and request Mr. B. to get it signed by the Railway Companies at once.

148. J. H. to R. W. (copy); from Brigg, 11 May 1861:

I wish to see you about this matter [T.A.G.], and therefore propose to call upon you on Monday next at 1 o'clock.

149. J. H. to R. W. (copy); from Brigg, 11 May 1861:

Referring to Mr. R. Dudley Baxter's letter to you of the 8th instant, I beg to observe that Mr. Baxter is in error with respect to my having taken away the draft of the special agreement as to the sixpenny rate, saying that you would be satisfied with the clause in the general agreement. On the contrary I left the draft with Mr. Baxter at his house in Queen Square, after having seen you at the Carlton upon the alteration proposed by him. Those alterations I informed him you would assent to in the main, but that they would require to be modified in the spirit of Mr. Lloyd's clauses, so as to stipulate for the conveyance of all Ironstone on the Railway to *and along* any branches and *sidings* to the Trent and Ancholme, and for the conveyance without charge of empty waggons to the places from whence they had been conveyed loaded. I mentioned that you had not completed the leases to the persons whom you spoke of as lessees, but that the *terms proposed to them* included the conveyance of minerals for them at the 6d. rate. I also observed that you would look to Mr. Baxter to see that the provisions on the above points were sufficient for you. I also mentioned that the terms of the special agreement, which was to be completed after the act was passed, should in the meantime be embodied in the general agreement, but I never for a moment thought of the special agreement being dispensed with. I gave Mr. Baxter the names of the parties to whom, in addition to Mr. Winn, the special rate was to apply, namely Messrs. William Henry Dawes and Geo. Dawes, Mr. Samuel Beale, Messrs. Bell, Brothers, and Messrs. Losh [?] Wilson and Bell.

Mr. Baxter mentioned that he would, if you preferred it, define a Trainload as 200 Tons.

The general agreement does not carry out the objects referred to. The privilege in favor of the lessees should be co-extensive with the duration of the leases (not exceeding 99 years), granted or to be granted to them, and Mr. Winn's privilege should extend to the future owners of his estate. The agreement mentioned Mr. Winn only, and the persons with whom agreements *have been already made.*

I return the engrossment of the general agreement, and also a draft copy of it for your use.

150. R. W. to J. H.; from Appleby Hall, 13 May 1861:

I have written Mr. Baxter by this post (and returned him the agreement) in the manner we arranged yesterday. On looking over the papers you left I found you had taken away the *letter you had written me,* however I hope I said all that was necessary. On looking over the agreement again it struck me that as there is a special clause to the effect that my Father is not to contribute to the Railway beyond finding the land it follows that if the £400 Dyson & Co. require is not paid by the Railway Companies it must be provided by Messrs. Dawes. I have therefore written them to that effect, I expect however that Mr. Baxter will pay it in all probability . . .

151. J. H. to R. W. (copy); from Brigg, 14 May 1861:

I enclose my letter to you of the 11th which I unconsciously brought away yesterday.

152. J. H. to B. R. & Co. (copy); from Brigg, 14 May 1861:

Will you have the goodness to get a copy of this [T.A.G.] Bill signed by Mr. Parker and Mr. Lister in order to signify their consent to their names appearing as subscribers and Directors, a fact requisite to be proved before the Lords' Committee.

Messrs. Dyson & Co. have requested us to remit them £400 and we have received accounts from the lithographer, and the surveyor and others. How do you consider the funds for the current expenses should be provided?

Mr. R. Winn has shown us Mr. R. D. Baxter's letter to him of the 8th May. The draft of the special agreement prepared by Mr. Lloyd and altered by you, was left with you when I called upon you in Queen Square. Your alterations were to be modified so as to stipulate for the conveyance of mineral not only to, but *along,* branches and sidings to the Trent and Ancholme, as provided for by Mr. Lloyd, and for the reconveyance of empty Waggons free of charge.

The terms were then to be embodied in the general agreement, but the special agreement was to be executed by the Company after the passing of the Bill.

153. J. H. to W. H. Dawes (at Moseley Hall, nr Birmingham); from Brigg, 18 May 1861:

Will you be good enough to let us have this [T.A.G.] Bill, signed by you, by the first post, and we shall be glad if you can give us the name of some person in London who has seen you write and can prove your signature to the Bill, if required by the House of Lords. We go before the Standing Orders Committee on *Thursday next.*

154. D. & Co. to N., H., & F.; from London, 18 May 1861:

The Proofs on Standing Orders in the Lords, will have to be given on Thursday next—please to return to us the Statement of Proofs completed.

155. J. H. to D. & Co. (copy); from Brigg, 18 May 1861:

We requested Messrs. Baxter & Co. to get a copy of this Bill signed by Mr. Parker and Mr. Lister, and to complete the proofs required as to the approval thereof by the South Yorkshire Railway and River Dun Company, and we requested Mr. Guy to procure the signatures of Mr. Chapman and Mr. W. Fenton, and to furnish proofs as regards the sanction of the M. S. & L. Railway Company.

Mr. Guy has sent us a Bill signed by Messrs. Chapman and Fenton, with the statement of proofs filled in except as to dates, and he promises that a witness shall be in attendance on the day appointed for Standing orders.

We have not heard from Baxter & Co., to whom we have written again by this post requesting them to send the proofs to you.

Mr. Rowland Winn has signed a Bill, but Mr. W. H. Dawes has not returned that which we sent to him. We will take care to have his signature in time.

Is it essential that a person who saw the parties sign or who has seen them write and can swear to their hands [*sic*] writing should attend to prove the signatures, or will a general statement by a person who has no doubt of the fact, suffice. Say by return.

It has occurred to us that under the peculiar circumstances of this Bill, it may be requisite that Mr. Chas Winn and Mr. George Dawes should sign it. Are they not persons coming under the description of "persons named in the Bill as proprietors or otherwise concerned in carrying the same into effect"?

Inform us by return.

We observe in the print of the Bill as amended, end of clause 42, the words "such compensation" to the end of the clause, have been printed by mistake. In page 20, line 14, the word "if" is an error, not intended to be inserted. In page 25—clauses are numbered 66, 67 and 68 instead of 56, 57 and 58.

156. J. H. to Mr. Josh Guy (copy); from Brigg, 18 May 1861:

The proofs on Standing Orders in the Lords will have to be given on Thursday next. Will you let Mr. Pickford be in attendance. We are not sure whether it is requisite that the signatures of Mr. Chapman and Mr. Wm. Fenton be proved by a person who saw them sign, or only a person who has seen them write and can speak to their handwriting, or whether a general statement by a person who had no doubt of the fact of their signing is sufficient. If strict proof is requisite, will you let a proper person be in attendance. Probably you can name someone in Town who can give the evidence.

157. N., H., & F. to B. R. & Co. (copy); from Brigg, 18 May 1861:

We find the proofs on Standing Orders are to be given before the Lords on Thursday next. Will you have the goodness to furnish Messrs. Dyson & Co. with the requisite proofs as regards the signatures of Mr. Parker and Mr. Lister to a copy of the Bill, and the approbation thereof by the South Yorkshire and River Dun Company.

Mr. Guy has done what is necessary as regards the signatures of Mr. Chapman and Mr. Wm. Fenton and the consent of the M. S. & L. Railway Company. We shall be glad to be favored with a reply.

158. Joseph Guy (from M. S. & L. Rly Solicitor's Office, 6 Ducie Street, Manchester) to N., H., & F.; from Manchester, 18 May 1861:

I send you herewith copy of the Bill signed by Mr. Chapman and Mr. Fenton.

I also send you statement of Proofs filled in except as to the dates of the newspapers. On hearing from you the day appointed for Standing Orders, the witness, George Pickford, shall be in attendance.

159. D. & Co. to N., H., & F.; from London, 20 May 1861:

It will not be necessary to prove the signatures to the Bills at all—the production signed is enough.

It will not be necessary for Standing Orders that the Bill should be signed by Mr. Charles Winn, and Mr. George Dawes—but by and bye it will be necessary that each of them should sign a Bill signifying their consent thereto. Mr. William Henry Dawes should do so too, besides signing the other Bill—that is the Bill for Standing Orders.

We do not understand your reference to cl. 42—we do not see the word "compensation" there at all.

160. W. H. Dawes (from Moseley Hall; printed heading "Bromford Iron Works, West Bromwich" crossed out) to N., H., & F.; 20 May 1861:

By this Post I send you the Bill signed. Mr. Baxter, of the Firm of Baxter, Rose, Norton, and Spofforth, 6 Victoria St., Westminster, or Mr. W. H. Wilson, of the same Chambers, will be able to prove my signature, or Mr. W. H. Maybury, 3 Sise Lane City.

161. R. W. to J. H.; from Appleby, 20 May 1861:

I have sent the Trent Ancholme act for my Father's signature by this post, and requested him to forward it to you, by tomorrow's post, at Dyson and Cos. I do not suppose there is the least prospect of my being wanted on standing orders, or indeed before the Bill goes into Committee. I am going to Nostell on Wednesday for about a week probably. As soon as you get to London I wish you would endeavour to get the agreement finally settled and engrossed for signature with Mr. Baxter. I think there can be no further difficulties. I have not heard from him since I wrote to him on the 14th Inst. I told him I thought something like the following should be inserted in place of the latter part of Clause 5—"For Ironstone from any part of the line between the Trent and Ancholme 6d. per ton for the whole distance in owners waggons, for any traffic belonging to the said Charles Winn his heirs and assigns coming from land between those Rivers [last six words inserted in pencil by J. H.], and the said W. H. and Geo. Dawes [inserted as before: "during the lease agreed to be made by the said Chas. Winn"] and as to any other parties for the term and to the extent of any agreements already made with them and the said Charles Winn; the empty waggons being reconveyed free of charge to the places from whence they were taken". I think it is quite essential that my Father his *heirs and assigns* should be in included or something to that effect.

162. J. H. to D. & Co. (copy); from Brigg, 20 May 1861:

We presume Mr. Rowland Winn will not be wanted on Thursday. If he is, be good enough to write to him to that effect, at Appleby Hall, Brigg, and send a copy of your letter addressed to him at Nostell Priory, Wakefield, where he might possibly go today.

One of us will go to Town on Wednesday and will call on you at 10 o'clock on Thursday morning. If you wish to see us sooner please say by return. We go to the Old Hummums.

163. J. H. to R. W. (copy); from Brigg, 20 May 1861:

Messrs. Dyson & Co. inform us that the proofs before the Standing orders Committee in the Lords are to be given on Thursday next. If you have not got the Bill signed by Mr. Winn, will you be good enough to send it today for that purpose, and request that it may be forwarded to us, by the earliest post, at Messrs. Dyson & Company's . . . I do not expect your attendance will be requisite on this occasion. If it be, I will request Dyson & Co. to write to you tomorrow.

164. J. H. to D. & Co. (copy); from Brigg, 21 May 1861:

We return by Book Post Statement of Proofs on Standing orders in the House of Lords completed so far as we are able to complete the same. We have got copies of the Bill signed by Messrs. R. Winn, W. H. Dawes, John Chapman, and Wm. Fenton. Mr. Pickford will supply the dates in his evidence, on Thursday morning.

We presume Mr. Baxter has obtained the signatures of Mr. Parker and Mr. Lister, and supplied the requisite proofs as to the So. Yorkshire Company.

In our letter of the 18th we intended to refer to the latter part of Clause *41* not *42*.

165. J. Guy for M. S. & L. Rly to N., H., & F.; from Manchester, 21 May 1861:

Mr. Pickford will go to Town tomorrow Evening and appear before the Examiner on Standing orders on Thursday as you request.

I do not apprehend that it will be necessary to prove the actual Signatures of Mr. Chapman and Mr. Fenton by a person who has actually seen them write.

166. Charles Winn to J. H.; from "Nostel", 21 May 1861:

I merely trouble you with a line to say that I forward to you by this day's post (addressed as is this letter) a Copy of the "Trent, Ancholme, and Grimsby Railway Bill" which I received from Son (Rowland) this morning as he informed me that it required my Signature before its introduction into the House of Lords and I have as you will see written my name at the foot of the last Clause of the Bill.

167. T. F. to J. H. (copy); from 124 Wood Street, E.C., 23 May 1861:

We have been before the Examiner this morning and passed Standing Orders. Mr. Baxter is not in Town and will not return until Saturday night.

I have, however, had a long interview with Mr. Dudley Baxter, and explained to him our views as to the alterations required in the Agreement. He showed me the Draft Agreement as altered by Mr. Baxter and I have taken a Copy of his proposed alterations.

At Mr. D. Baxter's request I left with him the Clause you had copied out with your suggested alterations in red Ink. I also discussed the points at issue with him and mentioned the subject of payments to Messrs. Dyson & Co., and he has promised to talk both matters over with his Father and with us next Week.

Messrs. Dyson & Co. say they have paid £225 for Fees in Commons and shall have about £90 to pay in the Lords.

They naturally ask for an early remittance.

I shall return tomorrow or at the latest on Saturday Evening. D.V.

168. R. D. Baxter to N., H., & F.; from London, 25 May 1861:
We send you a copy of the agreement between Mr. Winn and the Trent and Ancholme Company, and you will see on looking through it that it embraces all your requisitions including even the Staiths.

With such an Agreement there cannot be any use in altering the other one which is already engrossed, there being nothing between the two.

I have filled up the blank in the statement of consideration, which was unfinished when Mr. Freer was here.

[On a spare sheet in T. F.'s hand:] to Messrs. Baxter, 7 June 1861: We send you herewith Draft agreement as settled with Mr. Baxter yesterday. [And] to Mr. Edmund Winn: I beg to enclose you a Copy of the agreement as settled with Mr. Baxter yesterday.

169. R. W. to J. H.; from Nostell Priory, 28 May 1861:
I have your letter this morning. Do you anticipate from what Mr. Freer made out from Mr. D. Baxter any difficulty with Baxter Senr. about the agreements as if so I should write to him myself at once or endeavour to see him, as he may be at Doncaster. We cannot let the Bill go thro the Lords till the agreement is settled.

170. R. W. to J. H.; from Nostell, 29 May 1861:
My Brother is going up to London today or tomorrow about the Barnsley Coal line and he will do all he can to urge Mr. Baxter on about our agreements—if you have any thing to say to him a letter to the Army and Navy will find him.

I am not at all sure that it is desirable to have the Clause in the Bill authorizing the Companies to make trafic [*sic*] arrangements with my Father, because one of the last clauses says that any agreement made under authority of the Act is to be confirmed by $\frac{3}{5}$ of the proprietors present at a meeting, if I rightly recollect and I think too that the board of trade has power to revise any agreements under the act every 10 yrs.

171. D. & Co. to N., H., & F.; from London, 1 June 1861:
The Bill is we are happy to say unopposed and will be committed for Thursday next. The Proofs to be then given will be given by you, and Mr. Roseby—you will have to produce Consent Bill or Bills, signed in your presence, by Mr. Charles Winn, and the Messrs. Dawes, and Mr. Roseby will produce a Written Statement explanatory of the Level Crossings.

[Copies are included here of letters informing Charles Winn and the Dawes brothers of the need for their signatures to be obtained, and informing R. W. of the position.]

172. R. W. to J. H.; from Nostell Priory, 2 June 1861:
I send you herewith a Draft received from Mr. Baxter of the

special agreement as he proposes it should be. Will you look carefully thro and see if you think it will do, and make any additions to it, or remarks upon it you think necessary, and then write to my Brother with it at the Army and Navy, who will then see Mr. Baxter and try to get your recommendations carried out. Perhaps if you have a copy by you of Mr. Lloyds agreement you would sent [*sic*] it also to my brother to read, as he has never seen it.

The general agreement is finally settled, Mr. Baxter having consented to my alteration of the latter part of the 5th Clause, with some verbal alterations only.

173. D. & Co. to N., H., & F.; from London, 3 June 1861:

You will please to bear in mind the cheque account.

174. W. H. Dawes to N., H., & F.; (telegram); from Moseley Hall, 4 June 1861:

I will be at the Queens Hotel Birmingham about five oclock tomorrow afternoon—Say Wednesday the fifth instant.

175. G. D. to N., H., & F. (telegram); from Elsecar, 4 June 1861:

Will be at Tavistock Covent Garden Thursday morning.

176. G. D. to N., H., & F.; from M. & E. Ironworks, 4 June 1861:

I telegraphed to you today to say that I should be in London at the Tavistock at 10 on Thursday morning and could then sign the document you speak of. My brother was in Town today but suppose he has left so that if his signature is required, you must send to him at Moseley Hall.

177. J. H. to T. F.; from Brigg, 5 June 1861:

Mr. Atkinson will go to Town by the afternoon Train. Hale, Law Stationer, Covent Garden, or Waterlow, *Parliament Street,* would copy the statement as to the level crossings. Hale does not execute orders very rapidly.

178. D. & Co. to N., H., & F.; from London, 7 June 1861:

We omitted to speak to you yesterday about the cheque on account —and you said nothing about it, but we must beg that you will lose no time in letting us have it—for it is not a matter of indifference to us, seeing, that we have every week very heavy payments to make, sometimes to the tune of upwards of £2,000. You must excuse therefore our being somewhat importunate.

N., H., & F. to B. R. & Co. (copy); from ? 10 June 1861:

Messrs. Dyson & Co. have again applied to us for payment of £400 on account of the Fees etc. on this Bill. Will you be good enough to make Messrs. Dyson & Co. the payment at once? We should be glad to have a remittance on account.

[Also to D. & Co., 10 June 1861]:

After Mr. Freer saw you on Thursday he had an interview with Mr. E. Winn and Mr. Baxter, as to the payment of the Parliamentary Expenses to this Bill—and Mr. Baxter arranged that such Expenses should be paid by the M. S. & L. and the S. Yorkshire Railway Company.

Mr. Baxter gave directions for the Money to be applied for at the Board Meetings to be held on Friday and Saty last—so that by this time we have no doubt he is in a position to make you a payment of the £400 on account as we requested. We have written to him on the subject by this post.

179. John Lee to N., H., & F.; from Bishop Auckland, 9 June 1861:

Will you be good enough to inform me by return of post, if you can settle the account of Mrs. Long's for me, out of the money which I want of the owners of the Railway; as I do not know certainly whether, I can return by the time for the Court, and I do not wish to incur any additional Expense in the Case.

180. John Lee to N., H., & F.; from B. Auckland, 19 July 1861:

Is there a probability of any Payment being made for the Trent Ancholme and Grimsby Railway, for which I presented you a Bill by Mr. Winn's Instructions.

Will you be good enough to inform me and you will much oblige . . .

181. D. & Co. to N., H., & F.; from London, 20 July 1861:

This Bill [T.A.G.] will receive the Royal Assent on Monday.

182. T. F. to J. H..; from Tavistock Hotel, "Thursday" (dated on back by T. F. "July 1861"):

I have been engaged all day—and until it is nearly post time—about this matter [T.A.G.]. The Chairman of the Committee, Lord Redesdale was dead against us as to the level crossings—and only at length agreed to allow two of those which the Commons had sanctioned—viz the one near the Trent and the one on the Appleby Road. The crossing on the Turnpike he would not agree to and therefore struck it out of the Bill. I have since the Committee broke up, been with Mr. Edmund Winn to Mr. Baxters and finally settled the agreements.

I do not know whether I can get done my business here in time to return tomorrow, but shall do so if I can.

182a. W. H. Dawes to N., H., & F.; from M. & E. Works, 29 July 1861:

We are much obliged by your attention in sending us a copy of the

Trent Ancholme & Grimsby Act which by your note we are glad to find has passed and received the Royal assent.

We will look to clause No. 5 as you are good enough to point out.

183. B. R. & Co. to N., H., & F.; from London, 3 August 1861:

A Meeting of the Directors of the Trent Ancholme & Grimsby Railway Company will be held at the South Yorkshire office in Doncaster on Saturday the 10th Inst at 12 o'clock at which we hope it may be convenient to you to attend.

184. D. & Co. to N., H., & F.; from London, 13 August 1861:

We beg leave to enclose you our account in the above [T.A.G.] matter.

184a. J. R. to N., H., & F.; from Brigg, 15 August 1861:

Please to favour me per bearer with 2 copies of the T. A. & G. Railway Act and oblige . . .

185. R. W. to J. H.; from Appleby Hall, 9 September 1861:

When we were at Doncaster the other day Mr. Freer looked thro the Railway agreement which Mr. Baxter had got sealed by both the Railway Companies. There were one or two alterations but they were only trifles and both Mr. Freer and myself thought it satisfactory. Mr. Baxter left it with me to get Messrs. Dawes signature and requested me when that was done to return it him to be stamped and dated before my Fathers signature was attached. I got Messrs. Dawes signatures and then sent it to Mr. Baxter requesting him to return it within a week as my Father would then be here and would sign it. Mr. Baxter was out of England and in about 10 days I got a note from Dudley Baxter to say that in his Fathers absence my letter was sent to him, and that he would attend to the matter. I heard nothing more till Saturday when I received the enclosed. In my letter to him I remarked that I thought after the words "signed sealed" etc. he should add "the interlineations having been first made" this will explain one portion of his reply. The seal of the South Yorks^{s}. was attached before the Bill passed. What do you say to D. Baxters remarks. I don't wish to raise any difficulties if it is possible to avoid it—especially as we are to have another *traffic* agreement with the new Co. Ought I to request to be furnished with copies of the letters of the M. S. & L. secretary? It seems to me that the stamping is not very important, because if we ever had to go into Court with the document I conclude we could get it stamped any time by payment of a penalty—is it not so? I suggested to Mr. D. Baxter that the clause about the Bill being "now before Parliament" might deprive the agreement of its proper sense unless it was ante dated at a period prior to the passing of the Bill.

186. R. W. to J. H.; from Appleby Hall, 10 September 1861:

I have this morning received the agreements from London and as my groom is going over to Brigg I send it as you may like to look it thro. Perhaps you could return it by the bearer—who will be in Brigg ½ an hour—and also send me a reply to the note I wrote you by the postman yesterday.

187. John Lee to N., H., & F.; from West Auckland, 23 September 1861:

Is there any probability of a settlement in the Trent and Ancholme Railway Business—I think it high Time some thing was done, and if not attended to I must institute proceedings to enforce it.

Will you be good enough to let me know if any thing is done . . .

188. R. W. to J. H.; from Appleby Hall, 23 September 1861:

I had a note from Mr. Dudley Baxter in reply to the letter I wrote him asking for copies of the M. S. & L. Secretary's letters as to the interlineations in the Railway agreement, to say his Father would be home the middle of last week when he would name the subject to him. My Brother being in London has called to see him and writes me that Mr. Baxter says "the usual and regular way where any alteration has been made is to have the Secretary's initials attached in each case which is quite sufficient to prove that the alteration had been made previous to the sealing, and where the alteration has been made *after* the sealing as in the case of the South Yorks. the Secretary attaches the company's seal with his initials—this he considers is all that is necessary and better evidence than any letter".

What do you say to this? Will it be satisfactory if I get the initials of the Secretary of the M. S. & L.; but as regards the resealing by the Secretary of the S.Y. & Co. I should have thought that a resealing only by the Secretary would have amounted to nothing unless there was a resolution by the Board assenting to the alterations and directing the seal to be reattached. I feel very ignorant however on the subject, and should be glad if you would say what is desirable. I do not want to raise any difficulty it is possible to avoid.

188a. R. W. to J. H.; from Appleby Hall, 27 September 1861:

Will you send me by the bearer a reply to the letter I wrote you on Monday last with regard to what Mr. Baxter remarked to my Brother in London on the subject of the Railway agreement interlineations. There is a T. A. & G. Railway meeting at Doncaster tomorrow which you are no doubt aware of, and which I shall attend and when probably also the Railway agreement may be alluded to, and I therefore am anxious to hear what you say to Mr. Baxters proposals. The meeting at Doncaster is at the South Yorks. offices at 11, the train from Keadby does not get in till 11.25 but I will go direct to the South Yorks. Office on my arrival at this hour.

189. John Lee to N., H., & F.; from W. Auckland, 4 December 1861:

Can you afford me any Information as to payments of Expenses in the Business of the Trent, Ancholme & Grimsby Railway, as I think you must agree with me it is high time a Settlement was come to, as it is now near 12 months since the Work was completed . . .

190. R. W. to J. H.; from Appleby Hall, 14 December 1861:

I send you herewith a copy of the proposed new Trent Ancholme Bill—perhaps you will look it thro and see if any objection strikes you. I do not see any myself. I should be glad to have it back when you have looked it over as Mr. Dawes wishes to see it.

191. J. R. to N., H., & F.; from Brigg ?, 2 December 1862:

The enclosed was forwarded to me some days ago from Mr. Thiel. I have not any copies myself of the Plans here required. If you have any will you be kind enough to furnish him with what he requires.

[Enclosed: from T.A.G. Rly. Co. Secretary's Office, Doncaster, to J. Roseby, 14 November 1862:]

Will you oblige me with a copy of the Plans and Sections as deposited for this Line as I find I have never been supplied and occasional references are necessary. If possible let the Ordnance Map with the Line marked on it accompany the Copy.

192. T.A.G. Railway Co. Secretary's Office, Doncaster, to N., H., & F.; 23 October 1863:

I shall be much obliged if you can furnish me with a book of reference to the Plans and Sections of the Railway deposited in session 1860-1861 if you have a spare copy in your office.

I/9/7

Proposed Traffic Arrangements; the first sheet is dated 21 Nov. 1860 and the other two, probably in John Hett's writing, were bundled together with the first.

1. The South Yorkshire Company and the Manchester Sheffield & Lincolnshire Company to have the power of fixing rates for traffic carried by either of those Companies to from and over the projected Trent Ancholme & Grimsby Railway in connection with their respective districts, such rates being the same as the rates charged on their respective Railways for such traffic, and the Trent Ancholme & Grimsby Railway Company to take their mileage of such rates (less 40 per cent for working purposes inclusive of terminal and other charges) provided they receive a minimum toll of sixpence per ton on Ironstone and fourpence per ton on Coal carried on their Railway or on any portion thereof, except in cases where in the opinion of the 3 Companies, if all are interested, or of any two of them, if only 2

are interested, it is desirable for their mutual interest to make a lower exceptional rate for the time being than one halfpenny per ton per mile in which case the proportion of the T. A. & Grimsby Company to be settled in case of dispute by arbitration.

The Trent Ancholme & Grimsby Company to pay a mileage rate not exceeding one halfpenny per ton per mile for traffic carried by them to from and over the South Yorkshire or M. S. & L. Railway or any part thereof without any additional payment for terminal or other charges.

2. It is agreed that the Company shall provide and maintain a convenient Siding and Railway from the Company's Railway across lands of Charles Winn Esqre and the Highway in Frodingham to lands in Brumby belonging to Earl Beauchamp and now occupied either by himself or by one of his tenants George Chatterton Wm Bartle Moss and Poole in a situation to be agreed upon between the Company and the Earl (or to be fixed on by reference in case of their disagreement) for the conveyance and carriage along the Company's Railway of Ironstone, Coal, and other Minerals and also Corn and other agricultural produce, and other goods, wares, and merchandize, from and to the Lincolnshire Estates of the said Earl situate in Brumby, and elsewhere to and from the Company's Railway.

3. It is agreed that the Company shall provide and maintain a convenient Siding and Railway across lands of C. Winn Esqre from the Company's Railway where it passes near to the lands of the Earl of Yarborough in High Santon in the Parish of Appleby to such lands in a situation to be agreed upon between the Company and the Earl (or to be fixed upon by reference in case of their disagreement) for the conveyance and carriage along the Company's Railway of Ironstone, Coal and other minerals and also corn and other agricultural produce and other goods, wares, and merchandize from and to the estates of the said Earl situate in High Santon, Gokewell, Manby and elsewhere to and from the Company's Railway.

[In 2 and 3 the Railway referred to is the T.A.G. Railway.]

I/9/7

T.A.G.

Roads crossed on the Level Nov. 1860

1. A Public Carriage Road on the East side of the River Trent in The Township of Brumby—and Parish of Frodingham at or near the boundary between the Townships of Brumby and Gunhouse.
2. A Public Carriage Road in the Township and Parish of Frodingham and in the Village of Frodingham.
3. A Public Carriage Road in the Township and Parish of Frodingham and in the Village of Frodingham.

4. A Public Carriage Road in the Township and Parish of Frodingham leading from North-West angle of Brumby East Common to the Village of Scunthorpe and nearer the boundary between the Townships of Frodingham and Scunthorpe.
5. A Public Carriage Road at Low Santon in the Parish of Appleby at or near a Farmstead—known as the Low Santon Farm.
6. A Public Carriage Road in High Stanton and Thornham in the Parish of Appleby, at a distance of about [*sic*] chains to the South of the Appleby Steam Mill.

Crossed on a Bridge

A Public Carriage Road in the Township and Parish of Frodingham at or near the North West angle of the Brumby West Common.

Drains Crossed Nov. 1860

1. A Public drain called the Brumby sewer in the Township of Gunhouse otherwise Gunnas in the Parish of Frodingham at a point near its junction with the South site of the Warping drain of Charles Winn Esqre.
2. A Public drain called the Santon Beck dividing the Township of Scunthorpe in the Parish of Frodingham from Lower Santon in the Parish of Appleby—at a distance of about Chains south of the Township of Crosby.
3. A Public drain called the West Catchwater drain at Thornham in the Parish of Appleby at or near the Thornham Farm.
4. A Public drain called Sir Rowland Winn's drain at Thornham in the Parish of Appleby at or near a Bridge called the Thornham Bridge.
5. A Public drain called the Old River Ancholme dividing the Parishes of Appleby and Worlaby at or near the existing Bridge over the said River called the Thornham Bridge.

I/9/7

Minutes of Meeting of Ancholme Committee on Railways

At a meeting of the Committee of Commissioners of Ancholme appointed to watch such Railway Bills as may affect the lands within the level of Ancholme in the County of Lincoln under the jurisdiction of the Commissioners held at the Angel Inn in Brigg on Friday the seventh day of December 1860.

Present Mr. William Skipworth in the chair
,, Henry Grantham
,, Stephen Gibbons
,, Robert Owston

The Committee having had under consideration the proposed Trent Ancholme & Grimsby Railway with reference to the lands within the Ancholme Level.

Resolved that in the opinion of this meeting it may be injurious to the Lands in the Level if the Bill for the said Railway be allowed to pass without special provisions for preserving the jurisdiction and powers of the Commissioners including especially their right to levy Rates and to construct future works of Drainage.

Resolved that the Clerk do make application to the promoters of the said Railway to insert in their Bill clauses for the protection of the drainage under the control of the said Commissioners and that the clauses now read by the Clerk be approved of and that if any material alteration of such clauses be proposed by such promoters, such alterations be taken into consideration at a future meeting of the Committee to be convened by the Clerk.

The Committee find that in the deposited plan the Railway Bridge over the new Western Drain is specified to be of the width of 16 feet, the Bridge over Old Sir Rowlands Drain 12 feet and the Bridge over the Old River Ancholme 12 feet.

Mr. Adam Smith having stated to the Committee that the span of the first mentioned bridge ought to be 25 feet and of the other two bridges 15 feet each—Resolved that the Railway Company be required to provide bridges of those dimensions accordingly.

Wm Skipworth

Dec. 8, 1860. W. C. Atkinson's report as to the Railway Bridges over the Old Ancholme, Sir Rowland Winn's Drain, and the West Drain.

Dimensions of Bridges

Name of Drain	*Present Bridge Span*	*Railway Bridge*	*Remarks*
West Drain	26 feet	26 feet 4 inches	Partly constructed
Sir Rowland do.	8 feet	8 feet	Constructed
Old Ancholme	9 feet	14 feet	Partly constructed

N.B.—The existing Bridge over the Sir Rowland Drain is about 1½ Mile North of the line of Railway. The other Bridges are close to it.

W. C. Atkinson

I/9/7

T.A.G. Rly. Dec. 7, 1869 Minutes of Meeting of Sewers Committee on Railways.

At a meeting of the Committee of Commissioners of Sewers appointed to watch such Railway Bills as may affect the lands within the Wapentakes of Manley Corringham and Aslacoe . . . under the jurisdiction of the Commissioners held at the Angel Inn in Brigg the seventh day of December 1860.

Present Mr. William Skipworth in the chair
,, Robert Owston
,, Henry Grantham
,, John Dauber

The Committee having under consideration the proposed Trent, Ancholme & Grimsby Railway with reference to the lands within the said Wapentakes . . .

Resolved that in the opinion of this meeting it may be injurious to the lands under the jurisdiction . . . if the Bill for the said Railway be allowed to pass without the special provisions for preserving the jurisdiction and powers . . . including especially their right to levy Rates and to construct future works of drainage.

Resolved that the Clerk do make application to the promoters of the said Railway to insert in their Bill clauses for the protection of the drainage under the control of the . . . Commissioners and that the clauses now read by the Clerk be approved of and that if any material alteration of such clauses be proposed by such promoters, such alterations be taken into consideration at a future meeting of the Committee . . .

Wm Skipworth
[signature]

[Pencilled additions to the above Minute]:
Monday 2nd [186]1 [and] South Yorkshire Railway Bill (Keadby Extension) [above "Trent, Ancholme & Grimsby Railway"]

I/9/7
Session 1861 T.A.G. Rly

Petition of Manchester, Sheffield and Lincolnshire Railway Company . . .

To the Honorable the Commons of the United Kingdom . . . in Parliament Assembled.

The humble Petition . . .

Sheweth

That a Bill has been introduced into your Honorable House intituled "A Bill to authorise . . . a Railway from the Trent across the River Ancholme to the Manchester . . . Railway.

That by the said Bill it is proposed to authorise the construction of a Railway to commence on the right bank of the River Trent . . . and to terminate . . . by a Junction with your Petitioners' Railway about half-a-mile to the South West of Barnetby Station . . .

That while your Petitioners submit that the construction of the proposed Railway will be conducive to the public interests they are of opinion that sufficient provision is not made in the said Bill for protecting their Railway against the injury which may result to it during and after the construction of the proposed Junction of the intended Railway therewith nor against the interruption of the traffic thereon nor against danger arising from the proposed Junction.

That the provision of the said Bill as regards Contracting between your Petitioners and the Company proposed to be incorporated . . . with reference to the working and managing of the proposed Railway and otherwise in relation thereto are not satisfactory to your Petitioners and require amendment.

Your Petitioners therefore pray that the said Bill may not pass . . . and that they may be heard by their Counsel and Witnesses against such of the Clauses . . . as may be necessary for their protection.

I/9/4

Petition of Cary Charles Elwes against Trent Ancholme & Grimsby Railway Company Session 1861.

To the Honorable the House of Commons of the United Kingdom of Great Britain and Ireland in Parliament assembled.

The humble Petition of Cary Charles Elwes of Great Billing in the County of Northampton Esquire.

Sheweth

That your Petitioner is Tenant for life of extensive Estates in Lincolnshire and a Bill is now before your Honorable House intituled "A Bill to authorize the construction in Lincolnshire of a Railway from the River Trent across the River Ancholme to the Manchester Sheffield & Lincolnshire Railway".

That according to the deposited plans and the powers of the said Bill the intended Railway will pass through portions of your Petitioners said Estate and in such a manner as to inflict great damage on such Estates by severance and otherwise and your Petitioner is informed and believes that if the said Railway be necessary which your Petitioner is not prepared to concede it might have been laid out more advantageously and in such a way as would have been less objectionable to your Petitioner and that the line as deposited is in Engineering respects very defective and cannot be made for the amounts stated in the Estimate of expence.

That the statement in the Preamble as to the expediency of making the said Railway cannot be substantiated by Evidence and the clauses of the Bill with respect to the entering upon and purchase of lands and the construction of the Railway injuriously affect your Petitioner and no sufficient provision is made in the said Bill for the protection of his Estate.

Your Petitioner therefore humbly prays your Honorable House that the said Bill may not pass into a law as it now stands and that he may be heard by himself and by his Counsel-Agents and witnesses against the Preamble and provisions of the said Bill and in support of the allegations of this Petition and that he may have such other relief in the premises as to your Honorable House may seem meet.

Cary Charles Elwes

I/9/7

Circular from the Board of Trade as to road being crossed by the

Trent Ancholme & Grimsby Railway and Copy of Form to be filled up and returned to the Board.

As it appears that the Line of Railway passed by the Trent Ancholme & Grimsby Railway Bill, as intended to cross upon the level, the Roads specified in the enclosed Form, and as the 128th Standing Order of the House of Commons requires that the Committee on the Bill should receive from this Department a Report upon the desirableness of the proposed method of crossing the Roads in question, the Lords of the Chamber of Privy Council for Trade request that you will fill up the Form with a description of the character of the Roads proposed to be crossed on the Level, the nature and amount of the traffic upon them, stating any objections which exist to the proposed Level Crossings, and that you will return the same to them at your early convenience when filled up.

Form

Table of Public Carriage Roads proposed to be crossed on the Level by the Trent Ancholme & Grimsby Railway Bill.

Number of Road on deposited Plan	Parish	Township	Character of Road, whether metalled or un-metalled, through fields or fenced	Nature of the Traffic passing along each Road	Approximate amount of traffic passing along each Road daily and on Market Days	To state here the nature of the objection entertained, if any, . . .
7	Wrawby	Wrawby	Turnpike Metalled and fenced	Saddle Horses Horses in Waggons and Carts and in a few private Carriages and Cattle, Sheep, etc.	The Traffic produces Tolls amounting on an average to 8/6d daily except on the Market day when the average of Toll amounts to £1.7.6	

I/9/4

Letter from Railway Department of the Board of Trade to D. & Co. (copy) 11 Jan. 1861:

I am directed by the Lords of the Committee of Privy Council for Trade to call your attention to the Standing Orders of the House of Commons Nos. 127 and 128 of which the first relates to the alteration of gradients of Roads, and the other requires that all level Crossings of Railways should be reported on by an Inspecting Officer of this Department.

My Lords have appointed Colonel Yolland, R.E., Inspector of Railways, whose office is at No. 1 Whitehall, to report upon the Level Crossings contained in the Bills of the approaching Session.

Before making his report the Inspecting Officer will desire to see some persons acquainted with the Engineering details of the Plans and in some cases he may require to visit the site of the proposed altered gradients and Level Crossings, and as the time of the Inspecting Officers of this Department is already much occupied I am to request that in order to avoid the inconvenience which might be occasioned to the Committees in the several Railway Bills by these Reports not being ready you will forward to the Inspecting Officer (at as early a period as you can conveniently do so) a description of the proposed alteration of the gradients and of the proposed Level Crossings, in such of the Bills promoted by you as are intended to be proceeded with, together with a short statement of the reasons which have led to such gradients and Level Crossings being proposed.

It is desirable that you should at the same time inform the Inspecting Officer when it will be convenient for the Engineer, or some person deputed by him, to attend upon the subject of the Level Crossings.

I/9/7

Colonel Yolland's Report (to the "Secretary, Board of Trade") on Level Crossings proposed by Bill to the Board of Trade, 18 April 1861.

Sir,

In compliance with the instructions contained in your letter of the 14th January requesting [me] to report in pursuance of the 127th and 128th Standing Orders of the House of Commons on the inclinations of roads which will be rendered steeper than are allowed by the first named Standing Order and on the level crossings specified in the Trent Ancholme & Grimsby Bill of the present Session of Parliament, I have the honor to inform you that, having examined the Plans and Sections deposited in this Office, and having received an explanation from the Engineer of the line in each case submitted, I find that it is not proposed to render the inclinations of any roads interfered with steeper than are allowed by the Standing Order.

Level Crossings

Public road at 4 chains and numbered 2 in the Parish of Frodingham to be raised 5 feet 6 inches and crossed on the level.

Greatest inclination of altered road 1 in 20.

An under bridge at this spot is not practicable on account of the drainage, and an over bridge would require the road to be raised about 33 feet and involve a second bridge over the old Warping Drain.

I recommend that a level crossing be allowed, but that the road be not crossed by more than a single line of Railway while the line continues single, and by a double line when it is doubled. Also that the usual Clause be inserted respecting the standing or shunting of trains across this road, and that the meaning of the word "Lodge" be defined to mean "a residence for the gatekeeper".

Public road at 3 miles 22 chains and numbered 59 in the Parish of Frodingham to be crossed on the level—level unaltered.

The Line is on a curve at this point and the proximity of an over bridge at No. 48 in the Parish of Frodingham would obstruct the view in that direction, and render the level crossing dangerous. The Line may be lowered and an over bridge constructed at a less cost than would be involved by capitalizing the expense of the maintenance of a level crossing and gates and providing a gatekeeper etc.

I recommend that a level crossing be not allowed.

Public road at 3 miles 76 chains and numbered 84 in the Parish of Frodingham to be crossed on the level—level unaltered.

This level crossing is objectionably situated on an incline of 1 in 131 on the Railway. An over bridge can be inexpensively constructed. I recommend that a level crossing be not allowed.

Public Road at 6 miles 50 chains and numbered 23 in the Parish of Appleby to be lowered 2 feet 6 inches and crossed on the level.

Greatest inclination of altered road is 1 in 20.

This is objectionable [*sic*] level crossing situated on an incline of 1 in 97 on the Railway and on a curve with a cutting above the crossing. The road slopes down to the crossing on each side at an inclination of 1 in 20.

I recommend that the level crossing be not allowed.

Public road at 7 miles 24 chains and numbered 32 in the Parish of Appleby to be crossed on the level—level unaltered.

This level crossing also is objectionable as it is situated on an incline of the Railway of 1 in 95, while the road is on an easy slope of 1 in 42.

I recommend that the level crossing be not allowed.

Turnpike road at 11 miles 78 chains and numbered 7 in the Parish of Wrawby to be crossed on the level—level unaltered.

This is the main road between Brigg and Barton on the Humber, and the level crossing is situated at the foot of an incline on the Railway of 1 in 100. I recommend that the level crossing be not allowed.

(Signed) W. Yolland
Royal Engineers

I/9/4

Proofs as to Level Crossings [No date]

William Cook Atkinson of Brigg, Lincolnshire, Civil Engineer, will prove that he knows well the several undermentioned Roads—

As to the Level Crossing at 3 miles 76 chains numbered 84 in the Township of Frodingham. The Railway is already constructed at this point, and the crossing gates have been fixed for some time and are under the charge of a gatekeeper. Distance signals are already in use, and are about 600 yards from the crossing. The road is very little used except for agricultural purposes. There will be a station at this point.

As to the Level Crossing in Appleby, at 6 miles 50 chains, No. 23. The Line is already constructed here, and has been used for several months. This road although a Highway is scarcely ever used by the public. It is in effect little more than an occupation road to the Farm at Low Santon. It leads in a North Westwardly direction across a rabbit warren, but since Appleby and the adjoining Parishes have been enclosed, better roads have been provided.

As to the Level Crossing in Appleby at 7 miles 24 chains, No. 32. The Railway is constructed here, and has been for some time in use. There will be a Station at this road, and Distance Signals will be provided. When loaded Trains are descending the gradient, they will be upon a straight portion of the Line, and may be seen at a sufficient distance to enable them to pull up.

Rowland Winn, Esq., of Appleby, Lincolnshire, will also corroborate the evidence of Mr. Atkinson.

As to the Level Crossing in Wrawby at 11 miles 78 chains, No. 7. This Turnpike road was formerly the direct road from Hull across the Humber, to London, but since the establishment of Railways all the coaches have been discontinued, and the road is now but little used except for the conveyance of agricultural produce. Trains conveying ironstone and coal to the Port of Grimsby will change here from an ascending gradient of 1 in 616 to a gradient ascending in the same direction to 1 in 100. There will be a Station at this point, and Distance Signals.

In all the above the public would prefer that they should be on the level.

The land here belongs to Mr. Corbett (through four miles of whose property the line goes); he approves of the level Crossing. He is also Chairman of the Turnpike Trust.

John Roseby of Brigg, Lincolnshire, Mining Engineer, will corroborate the evidence given by Mr. Atkinson, and will state in addition that from his experience in the mining districts of the North of England, no inconvenience has been found to result from level crossings—Instance the Middlesborough [*sic*] and Guisborough Railway, which was constructed for the developement [*sic*] of the Cleveland Ironstone, and upon which there are several level crossings.

So also with respect to the Weir Valley Railway, the Weir and Derwent Junction Railway, and in fact with regard to the whole of the Stockton and Darlington System.

I/9/7
1861 Session T.A.G. Rly. Requisition for Warrant

To One of the Clerks of the Private Bill Office in the House of Commons.

We the undersigned being three of the directors of the Trent Ancholme & Grimsby Railway Company do hereby in pursuance of an Act passed in the ninth year of the Reign of her present Majesty . . . for providing for the custody of certain monies paid in pursuance of the Standing Orders by Subscribers to Works . . . to be effected under the authority of Parliament request that you will grant us your warrant . . . for payment into the Bank of England in the name of . . . the Accountant General of the Court of Chancery of the sum of six thousand four hundred pounds being eight per cent on the sum of eighty thousand pounds the estimated expense of the new projected Undertaking.

Dated this second day of January one thousand eighteen hundred and sixty-one.

Name	*Description*	*Place of Abode*
Rowland Winn	Esquire	Appleby Hall, Brigg
George Dawes	Iron Master	Elsecar, nr. Barnsley
Edmund John Winn	Esquire	Nostell Priory, nr. Wakefield

Signed by these three men and certified by N., H., & F., Solicitors for the Bill.

1861 Session T.A.G. Rly. Draft Declaration under Standing Orders of the House of Commons No. 40

We John Hett—one of the Solicitors for the Bill deposited in the Private Bill Office . . . , and Chas. Winn of Nostell Priory, Esqre, a responsible party promoting the said Bill do hereby declare as follows:

1. That the proposed amount of Capital of the Company is one hundred and twenty thousand pounds.
2. That the number of shares into which the proposed capital is intended to be divided is twelve hundred and the amount of each share is one hundred pounds.

3.
4. } That there are at present no shares subscribed for; nor are any provisional directors, treasurer, secretary, and other officers yet appointed.

Dated this eighteenth day of Decr 1860.

John Hett
Chas Winn

1861 Session T.A.G. Rly. Estimate of Expense (Draft)

I estimate the expense of the Undertaking and the above Bill, including the purchase of the necessary property and contingencies at eighty thousand pounds.

John Roseby Engineer
18 December 1860

Witness
Geo. Wright
Clerk to Messrs. Nicholson Hett & Freer . . .

1861 Session T.A.G. Rly. Draft of Petition for leave to bring in a Bill (Dyson & Co.)

To the Honorable the Commons . . .
The humble Petition . . .
Sheweth

That a Railway from the River Trent, near Keadby, across the River Ancholme, and joining the Manchester Sheffield and Lincolnshire Railway at Barnetby-le-Wold, would be very beneficial to the Mineral District, which it would traverse and would be of public advantage by effecting a communication between the said District and the Trent on the one hand, and the Port of Grimsby on the other hand.

That so much of the said Railway as will be between the Rivers Trent and Ancholme will be upon the land of Your Petitioner Charles Winn and great progress has been made in the construction thereof by and at the expense of Your Petitioners William Henry Dawes and George Dawes, and Your petitioners with others, are willing at their own expense to complete the construction of the Railway throughout its whole length.

That Your Petitioners have caused a Plan and Section of the Railway with a Book of Reference to the Plan to be deposited with the Clerk of the Peace for the parts of Lindsey . . .

That Your Petitioners are desirous that the South Yorkshire Railway Company with whose Undertaking the intended Railway will be connected at its western end, and the Manchester Sheffield & Lincolnshire Railway Company, whose Undertaking the intended Railway will join at its eastern end, should be authorised to enter into arrangements with respect to the working and management of the intended Railway but the purposes aforesaid cannot be accomplished without the authority of Parliament Your Petitioners have therefore caused a Bill to be prepared . . .

I/9/4

Expenses connected with T.A.G. Bill.

D. & Co. to N., H., & F.; from London, 6 May 1861:

We will thank you to let us have £400, on account of this [T.A.G.] Bill, at your early convenience.

D. & Co. to N., H., & F.; from London, 5 August 1861:
We beg leave to enclose you our account in the above [S. Yorks. Railway (Keadby Extension)] matter.

R. W. to J. H.; from Appleby Hall, 10 January 1862
Mr. Baxter has written to request that I furnish you with the amount of any expenses I may have been put to in connection with the Trent Ancholme & Co. up to the passing of the Act.

I have therefore looked into the matter and find that I was 7 times in London on the Company's business 4 times at Manchester and once at Doncaster—and that the total cost to me was £59.17.10. I was not aware till I got Mr. Baxters letter that your a/c had not been sent in but I should think the sooner you do so now the better.

Will you please return me the Trent Ancholme 1862 Bill which I asked you some time since to look thro and let me know if you see any objection to it. I think there can be none.

D. & Co. to N., H., & F.; from London, 15 January 1862:
We have no specimen Lawyers Bill of Costs, but we send you the authorized scale of charges. We have not yet been paid our account. We presume you forwarded it to the right quarter. [Refers to T.A.G. Bill].

Our charges [for S. Yorks. Railway (Keadby Extension)] herein irrespective of any payments, are £5.5.0.

R. W. to J. H.; from Appleby Hall, 13 February 1862:
I am told that in sending you the amount of my expenses in the Trent Ancholme etc. Railway I ought to have stated the number of days I was occupied. I find the number was 37 so if you happen not to have sent in your a/^{cts} yet perhaps you would state 37 d[a]ys as the time. If you have already sent in the accounts, I do not think it can be of any consequence.

I should like you at your convenience to let me know in what amount my Father is indebted to you for various matters you have done for him during some years past. I twice before named this to you and you said you had difficulty in doing it in consequence of something unsettled about the Warp land drainage. If this still exists I better [*sic*] at any rate make you a payment on a/c and we can settle the ballance [*sic*] when practicable.

Edmund J. Winn to J. H.; from Nostell Priory, 16 January 1862:
Mr. Baxter desires me to write to you respecting my Expenses on the Trent & Ancholme Railway Bill. I find I was called up to Town 8 times on this matter, viz.: 3 times during Nov. and Dec./60 and 5 times from Jany to April 1861, occupying altogether 50 or 51 days, the cost of the journeys between Yorks and London amounted to £27.13.0, my Expenses in Town I cannot tell you but I shall be quite satisfied if you will allow whatever is usual in such cases.

R. W. to J. H.; from Appleby Hall, 22 March 1862:

In sending your a/c to the T. A. & G. Co. I had rather you charged my expenses at the sum I named to you. You can call it "Mr. Winns expenses in respect of the Railway extending over so many days"—(the number I told you). What my Brother may have arranged with you about his expenses I do not know, as he told me he should call on you yesterday on his way to Yorkshire. My Brother not being a director is in a different position from myself. I had rather not take more than what I was actually out of pocket.
[At head of sheet in T. F.'s hand: "Charge for Mr. Edmund Winn £2 per day, and expenses").

John Lee to N., H., & F.; from W. Auckland, 14 January 1862:

Will you be good enough to inform me if any Settlement of the Trent Ancholme & Grimsby Railway Accounts had been made . . .

E. J. Winn to N., H., & F.; from Nostell Priory, 15 August 1862:

I think you are under a mistake as to my expences on the Trent Ancholme & Grimsby Raily. My memo. is 52 days *total* expences *including* travelling £123.15. I shall be quite satisfied with that amount.

E. J. Winn to "H. Fryer & Co."; from Nostell P., 21 August 1862:

I intended the £123.15. named in my last letter to cover *all* my expences on the T. A. & G. Railway bill, that sum is all I want from the Company.

John Lee to N., H., & F.; from W. Auckland, 20 October 1862:

I wrote to Mr. Winn last Week asking him to inform me if there was any Probability of a Settlement for the Trent Ancholme & Grimsby Railway he refers me to you, expecting that the Account with which I furnished you has been presented to the S. Yorkshire Railway Company, that being the Company to whom the line was sold, will you be good enough to inform me if that Account has been presented by you, as I do not feel inclined to wait any longer, and Mr. Winn says further in his letter that he thinks it ought to have been settled earlier.

The last Time I wrote to you Gentlemen, in the plenitude of your kindness you never so much as vouchsafed to send me a Word in reply.

E. J. Winn to J. H.; from Nostell P., 17 November 1862:

It is now a Year and a half or more since the Trent Ancholme & Grimsby Railway Bill was passed, when are Witnesses expences to be paid is it not already time they were paid.

T.A.G. Railway Co. Secretary's Office to N., H., & F.; 1 December 1862:

Mr. Baxter having mentioned that you had written him relative to your bills against this Company I may state that I will lay them before the Directors on the 20th inst. when I have no doubt a cheque for the same will be drawn. I believe expenses paid to Messrs. Winn appertain to payments made by you but I do not find and [*sic*] statement of particulars of those expenses in the bills sent me. Shall I receive them from you?

Can you oblige me with a copy of the Plans?

"Baxters & Co." to N., H., & F.; from Doncaster, 1 December 1862:

We have again mentioned your account to the Secretary.

He informs us that a cheque will be signed for the amount at the next Board meeting, and he promised to write to you himself on the subject.

9/4
Letters concerning legal charges 13 Aug. 1862—7 Jan. 1863.

Wm F. Clark to T. F.; from York, 13 Aug. 1862:

I return your paper with my remarks as to charges we make in such a business.

Our Cashier and Bill Clerk is seeing the Exhibition—he will be home in a few days when I will try to find and send you a draft Bill of Costs.

We are all well at home. I have not been very first rate lately—have had a great deal of knocking about and hard work—my partner was obliged to give up business about the middle of last month and go on the Continent and I dont expect him home for three or four weeks yet. I dont expect to get away this Season unless it be for a few days at Harrogate or Scarbro.

If we knew when you were off to Scotland and you would take York in your way for a night we shall be very glad to see you at the Mansion House.

[T. F.'s questions; W. F. Clark's answers:]

1. Is it usual or proper for a Country Solicitor employed in getting up a Railway to charge 5 Guineas a day for the time he is occupied in London—and if so does that charge include Tavern Expences or are such Expences as well as the Railway fare charged in addition?
   Time 5 Guineas per day. *Expences* in Town about 1 Guinea per day and Railway fares in addition.
2. What is the usual or proper charge per day for the Solicitor to charge for days occupied by him in the Country in taking the Reference, attending meetings journeys etc?

Some charge 5 Guineas per day—if such work as might be done by a superior Clerk then only 3 Guineas per day—we sometimes charge 4 Guineas where the day is not a very long one.

3. Is the Country Solicitor allowed any and if so what part or proportion of the Charges made by the Parliamentary Agents employed?
   Depends upon management—usually one-third of profits.
4. The Country Solicitor charges for drawing the Bill 2/- per Folio, and this seems to include *one* Copy of it, but the Parliamentary Agent also charges for a Copy. Is this correct?
   Yes.
5. The parliamentary Agent charges 25 guineas for Sessional Fee. Is not the Country Solicitor entitled to any portion of this Fee?
   In the proportion before mentioned—Country Solicitor entitled to a session fee of 25 Guineas.

C. A. Thiel (for T.A.G. Rly) to N., H., & F.; from Sec.'s office, Doncaster, 22 Dec. 1862:

Enclosed I hand you cheque value £1295.19.11 in payment of your account for professional services and also in payment of the several other accounts on the enclosed list furnished by you being payments made on expenses incurred in connection with the obtaining the Companys act. I also enclose Atkinson's Lees [*sic*], Lancaster's and Cawkwell's accounts that you may have them duly receipted and returned when paid.

R. W. to N., H., & F.; from Nostell Pry, 24 Dec. 1862:

I have found your letter here on my arrival and enclose you a receipt for the Cheque contained in it.

D. and Co. to N., H., & F.; from London, 1 Jan. 1863:

We have to acknowledge the receipt of your note of yesterday wherein you say that you presume that we shall make to you out of our charges with relation to this Bill the allowance usual in such cases.

We know of no such allowance; and we know of no reason for any such allowance; or why the parliamentary agent should not claim an allowance out of the Solicitor's Charges, as well as conceding to the Solicitor that benefit.

In fact the Charges of the agent and the Solicitor are in all respects distinct and independent, often concurrent. Both are regulated by recognized and independent scales, and established by authority. And although we have reason to believe indeed to know that there are agents who divide in some way (always surreptitiously) their Charges with their clients, we have equally good ground for knowing that this division is prejudicial to the ultimate client out of whose purse the payment must come.

Permit us to remind you that in no other case in which we have had the pleasure of acting for you have we made any allowance, or we believe been asked to do so.

D. and Co. to N., H., & F.; from London, 7 Jan. 1863:

The Acts to which we referred as having passed and to which you were Solicitors, are the Brigg Waterworks and Elwes Estate Acts. Mr. Rackham was associated with you in these matters, but neither to him nor to you did we make any allowance—nor should we had we been asked to do so. It is quite true, that there are certain Firms, but very few, who allow the Solicitor the third, but it is a practice, which by far the majority of Parliamentary agents refuse to adopt—not that they would suffer pecuniarily by doing so—for it is very easy so to make out the charges, and so to transact the business, as to secure the Agent from any loss by a division of profits—the burden falls on the Promoter or Promoters of the Bill—our charges are uniformly so made out, as not in anywise to encroach upon the Solicitors rights or functions.

I/9/4

D. & Co. to N., H., & F., from London

"An Account of Fees paid and Expences incurred in passing the Trent Ancholme & Grimsby Railway Bill".

1860					
Nov^r	9	Conferring with Mr. Hett, Mr. Winn and the Engineer upon an application to Parliament as to this Railway—advising them thereon and taking Instructions to prepare Notice Engaged 2 hours	2	2	.
		Perusing South Yorkshire Act of 1859 Examining Plan and perusing and settling Notice with special powers	2	2	.
		Fair Copy of Notice 20 folios		13	4
	10	A like conference this day on Notice—taking instructions to alter certain of the objects therein, 1 hour	1	1	.
		Finally settling Notice accordingly		10	6
	12	Perusing Letter from Messrs. Nicholson & Co. with Draft Notice—repasusing [*sic*] same and writing to them thereon		10	6
		Conferring with Mr. Baxter on this Bill and on the Claims of the South Yorkshire Company		10	6
		Writing Messrs. Nicholson & Co. fully upon this subject		5	.
	14	Perusing 2 Notes from Messrs. Nicholson & Co. and writing them in answer		5	.
		Fair Copy of Notice for the Daily News 15 folios.		10	.

	Instructions for Proof of Notice and attending at the Office of the Daily News with same		10	6
15	Fair Copy of Notice for the London Gazette 15 folios		10	.
	Instructions for Proof of Notice and attending at the Office of the London Gazette with same		10	6
16	Conferring with Mr. Roseby the Engineer and afterwards with Mr. Baxter on the arrangements required by the South Yorkshire Company, perusing notice of the arrangements with the Manchester Sheffield & Lincolnshire Company dated 8th Novr instant		10	6
	Writing to Messrs. Nicholson on these matters and with Copy of Note		5	.
	Examining and Correcting Proof of Notice for the Daily News and returning same with instructions for insertion		10	6
19	Conferring with Mr. Baxter on the necessity of the South Yorkshire Company continuing their proceedings for an extension of their Line—he requested us to write to Messrs. Nicholson & Co.		10	6
20	Writing to Messrs. Nicholson & Co. pressing for an Answer to our Letter of the 16th instant		5	.
	Preparing Instructions as to deposits to be made this month	1	1	.
	Fair Copy thereof		5	.
	Preparing Notice to Land Owners	1	1	.
	Fair Copy thereof 10 folios		6	8
	Preparing Instructions as to the service of Notices	1	1	.
	Fair Copy therof [*sic*]		5	.
	Preparing Form of special Letter to Outliers and Letter of Acknowledgement.		10	6
	Fair Copies of these Documents		5	.
	Writings [*sic*] Messrs. Nicholson Hett & Freer therewith	.	.	.
	Examining Proof of Notice Correcting same and attending at the Office of the London Gazette with instructions for insertion		10	6
28	Writing Messrs. Nicholson Hett & Freer as to preparation of Draft Bill	.	.	.
30	Attendances to procure Gazette and News-			

			£	s	d
		papers folding addressing and forwarding same		10	6
		Perusing and examining the Plans Sections and other Documents for deposit in the Private Bill Office of the House of Commons and putting up arranging and drawing out labels for same previous to Deposit. Attending to deposit same in the Private Bill Office and to have same entered	1	1	.
		Perusing and examining the Plans and other Documents for deposit in the Office of the Clerk of the Parliaments and putting up and arranging and drawing out labels for same previous to deposit attending to deposit same at the Parliament Office.	1	1	.
		Perusing and examining the Plans and other Documents for deposit at the Office of the Board of Trade, putting up arranging and drawing out labels for same previous to deposit attending to deposit same at the Board of Trade	1	1	.
Decr	5	Writing Messrs. Nicholson & Co.	.	.	.
	10	Conference with Messrs. Winn, Mr. Hett and the Engineer on the method of dealing with the Capital and Estimate: on the constitution of the Company and generally on the outline of the Bill 2 hours	2	2	.
	11	Conferring again this day determining on the method of dealing with Capital; on agreement with Messrs. Dawes and Mr. Corbett; and on the valuation of Land 1 hour	1	1	.
	12	Perusing the Agreement between Mr. Winn and Mr. Dawes and the Memm of agreement with the Manchester and Sheffield and South Yorkshire Companies and perusing and settling Draft Bill containing special Clauses as to Capital, traffic arrangements, etc.	15	15	.
	13	Perusing several Clauses prepared on behalf of Commissioners of Sewers; making alterations in same and notes thereon 9 Brief Sheets	2	2	.
		The like of Clauses prepared on behalf of Commissioners for River Ancholme 12 Brief Sheets	3	3	.

		£	s	d
	Writing to Messrs. Nicholson, Hett & Freer with Bill and on Clauses		5	.
	Fair Copy and Draft Bill for Messrs. Nicholson & Co. 222 folios	7	8	.
	Perusing and settling Petition for Bill	1	1	.
	Fair Copy thereof 8 folios		5	4
	Drawing Estimate of Expense		10	6
	Fair Copy thereof		2	6
	Drawing Declaration under 40th Standing Order		13	4
	Fair Copy thereof		5	.
	Writing fully to Messrs. Nicholson & Co. thereon		5	.
	Preparing Instructions as to the several Documents to be prepared and deposited on or before the 31st December		13	4
	Fair Copy thereof		5	.
	Drawing Form for separate List of Owners			
	The like for Lessees			
	The like for Occupiers		13	4
	Fair Copy thereof		2	6
14	Making Fair Copy of Draft Bill for Printer 222 folios	7	8	.
	Attending him therewith and instructing him with reference thereto		10	6
17	Perusing Proof of Bill sent by Mr. Hett, subsequently conferring with him thereon settling Drainage Clauses with him and additional Clause as to Mr. Winn's Warping Drain and settling Bill for Press with the exception of the Estimate three hours	3	3	.
	Attending Printer with Bill and with instructions for revise		10	6
18	Perusing revise of Bill and Proof of Drainage Clauses 41 Pages	1	11	6
	Conferring with Mr. Hett thereon and settling same for Press excepting Estimate and Capital		10	6
19	Conferring with Mr. Hett on the Declaration under the 40th Standing Order and on the omission of the Township of Gunhouse		10	6
21	Conferring with Mr. Roseby on the Estimate of past and future Expenditure		10	6
	Settling Bill for Press	1	1	.
	Writing to Messrs. Nicholson on this subject and in answer to their Letter		5	.
	Drawing arrangement of Clauses and Copy		10	.

	Attending the Printer with Bill and with Instructions for Copies		10	6
22	Drawing Agent's Declaration and Copies	1	1	.
	Putting up Bill Petition and Declaration and arranging same for Deposit. Putting up Bills for deposit therewith		10	6
	Attending at the House of Commons to deposit the petition and Bill etc. and to enter same on list	1	1	.
	Attending to deposit Bill at the Parliament Office		10	6
	The like at the Board of Trade		10	6
	Preparing Bill for Lord Redesdale and his Counsel and attending at the House with same		10	6
27	Writing Messrs. Nicholson & Co. in answer to . . . their Letter on the Declaration under Standing Order 40		5	.
	Making Fair Copy of Estimate of Expence for the Printer		2	6
	Attending him therewith and instructing him as to Proofs		10	6
28	Examining Proof and returning same for Copies		10	6
	Fair Copy Declaration for Printer		5	.
	Attending him therewith and with Instructions for Proofs		10	6
	Examining and Correcting Proof of Declaration and returning same to Printer for Copies		10	6
29	Preparing Draft Requisition to Private Bill Office Clerk for Warrant to pay money into Bank		10	6
	Fair Copy thereof		5	.
	Writing Messrs. Nicholson & Co. therewith and instructing them with respect to the mode and time of making the Deposit		5	.
31	Perusing Letter from Messrs. Nicholson & Co. and advising them as to a mistake in the name of a particular Owner		5	.
	Perusing and Examining the Lists Estimate and Declaration and printed Copies of the two latter and Putting up and arranging same for deposit in the Private Bill Office		10	6
	Perusing and Examining the Lists and Estimate and Printed Copies of the latter and Putting up and arranging same for deposit in the Office of the Clerk of the Parliaments		10	6

			£	s	d
		Attending to deposit Lists of Owners etc. at the Private Bill Office		10	6
		The like at the Parliament Office		10	6
		Attending to deposit Documents at the Vote Office		10	6
1861					
Jan^y^	9	Drawing Warrant for deposit of money in Bank and making Fair Copy	1	1	.
		Attending at the Private Bill Office to get same executed		10	6
		Preparing Affidavit verifying signature and making Fair Copy	1	1	.
		Clerk attending to be sworn and afterwards to lodge these Documents at the Accountant Generals to bespeak his directions		10	6
	10	Settling Statement of Proofs of compliance with the Standing Orders (Lords and Commons)	3	3	.
		Fair Copy 50 folios	1	13	4
		Settling Affidavit as to deposit of Plans with Clerk of the Peace		10	.
		The like with Parish Clerks		10	.
		The like as to application to Owners etc.		10	.
		Fair Copy of these Affidavits		7	6
		Drawing Memo of Instructions as to the mode of giving Proofs		10	6
		Fair Copy thereof		2	6
		Writing Messrs. Nicholson & Co. therewith	.	.	.
	11	Attending at the Office of the Accountant General when we obtained his directions		10	6
	12	Writing Mr. Winn acknowledging receipt of money	.	.	.
	15	Conferring with Mr. Roseby on the cause of delay in the deposit; recommending that if possible the money should be paid in tomorrow and that Mr. Winn and Mr. Hett should meet here to confer on the matter		10	6
	16	Conferring with Mr. Hett and Mr. Winn on the neglect of Mr. Dawes to provide his share of the deposit—on the effect of this neglect upon the agreement between Mr. Dawes and Mr. Winn and upon the Bill, 3 hours	2	2	.
		Conferring with Mr. Baxter upon the same subject; he offered to provide the money for the deposit upon certain conditions		10	6
	17	Conferring with Mr. Winn and subsequently with him and Mr. Baxter as to the advance			

	of the money. Ultimately Mr. Baxter agreed to lend £6200 upon condition that we should undertake to withdraw the Bill at his request if the money is not paid by the 5th February. Drawing and signing Undertaking accordingly	1	1	.
	Preparing new Warrant for the deposit being made by Mr. Rowland Winn and Mr. Edmund John Winn and attending at the Private Bill Office to get same executed		10	6
	Attending at the Office of the Accountant General when he amended his directions		10	6
	Attending at Messrs. Glyns and at the Bank of England to complete the deposit	1	1	.
18	Writing to inform Messrs. Nicholson & Co. of the day this Bill would be before the Examiner	.	.	.
19	Attending at the Office of the Accountant General to file the Bank receipt and to bespeak his Certificate		10	6
	Making fair copy of Letter received from Board of Trade as to Level Crossing for Messrs. Nicholson & Co.		5	.
	Writing them therewith	.	.	.
	Conferring with Mr. Beale on behalf of certain Lessees of Minerals under Mr. Winn as to provisions to be made both in the Leases and in the Bill		10	6
23	Conferring with Messrs. Winn, Mr. Dixon and Mr. Roseby on the means of securing the carriage of Minerals and on the proposed arrangements with the South Yorkshire and Sheffield Companies. $1\frac{1}{4}$ hour	1	1	.
24	Conferring with Mr. Dixon on the Agreement come to this day for the contribution of one-third of the Capital by the South Yorkshire Railway Company one-third by the Manchester Sheffield & Lincolnshire Railway Company and the remaining third by Mr. Winn and his Lessees and the intimation that the Bill would be in Mr. Baxter's hands		10	6
25	Attending at the Office of the Accountant-General when we obtained his Certificate		10	6
30	Writing Messrs. Nicholson & Co. as to names of members to bring in Bill	.	.	.

	31	Making 3 Fair Copies statement of Proofs for use before the Examiner 50 folios each	5	.	.
		Attending Mr. Freer going throught [*sic*] and settling statement of Proofs		10	6
Febry	1	Attending Examiner Standing Orders complied with the exception of late deposit of money	2	2	.
		Clerk attending as a Witness		10	6
		Conferring with Mr. Baxter in Victoria Street on the arrangements made with the South Yorkshire and Sheffield Companies as to this Line and the mode of treating the Mineral Lessees	1	1	.
	5	Attending Chairman of Ways and Means by appointment with respect to the division of the Bills between the two Houses when it was provisionally determined that certain of the Scotch Bills the Irish Bills, Gas and Water Bills, and the Metropolitan Railway's Bills should begin in the House of Lords and therefore that no Petition for any such Bills should be presented to the House of Commons tomorrow	1	1	.
	6	Attending at the House to get Petition for Bill presented and referred to the Select Committee on Standing Orders	1	1	.
	7	Attending to order and procure Office Copy of Examiners Report		10	6
		Fair Copy thereof		2	6
		Attending Meeting of Chairman of Ways and Means as to course to be pursued with reference to this Bill beginning in the Lords or Commons. Subsequent attendance upon Lord Redesdale when it was determined that Bill should commence in the Commons	1	1	.
	8	Conferring with Mr. Baxter on the alteration of the Bill 1 By giving to the South Yorkshire and Sheffield Companies power to subscribe 2 To alter the Works by substituting Cutting for Tunnel and altering Gradients—recommending that the first proposition should be adopted by Petition for additional provision but that the second should not be attempted		10	6
	12	Attending the first Meeting of the Committee of Selection and handing in Copy of the Bill as required by the Standing Orders	.	.	.

		£	s	d
14	Attending Committee of Selection same adjourned until tomorrow 15 Attending Committee of Selection Chairman's Panel appointed	1	1	.
	Perusing letter from Messrs. Nicholson & Co. as to statement for Standing Order Committee and writing to them in reply		5	.
16	Conferring with Mr. Baxter on the Letter from Messrs. Nicholson and on the future conduct of the Bill.		10	6
	Perusing Examiners Report and preparing Statement in answer thereto	1	1	.
	Fair Copy of Statement		5	.
18	Perusing Letter from Messrs. Nicholson and the Correspondence attached to it. Reperusing Examiner's Report and redrawing Statement for the Standing Orders Committee	2	2	.
	Fair Copy of Statement for Messrs. Baxter Rose & Co.		5	.
	The like for Colonel Wilson Patten		5	.
	Attending at his Residence to deliver same to him		10	6
	Two Fair Copies for the Standing Orders Committee		10	.
19	Attending Standing Orders Committee who (after oral explanations) dispensed with Standing Orders	2	2	.
	Attending at the House to get Report from Standing Order Committee made and leave given to bring in Bill	1	1	.
	Drawing Motion for leave and Fair Copy		10	6
	Attending the Printer with instructions as to printing Bill for 1st Reading		10	6
	Putting up Bill and Papers in Parliamentary form and endorsing titles	2	2	.
20	Attending at House to get Bill read a 1st time	1	1	.
21	Attending general Committee of Railways and Canals—Bills grouped—this made part of group 6 Committee to meet on Tuesday March 5. Doncaster & Wakefield Bill to be taken first and Writing Messrs. Nicholson & Co. thereon	1	1	.
25	Making 2 Copies of Statement for the Lords Standing Order Committee		10	.

			£	s	d
		Attending at the Parliament Office to deposit same		10	6
		Attending at House to get Bill read 2°	1	1	.
	26	Attending Standing Orders Committee of the Lords in support of Bill. Bill allowed to proceed	2	2	.
	27	Attendances to order and procure Office Copy Petition of Manchester Sheffield & Lincolnshire Railway Company		10	6
		Fair Copy thereof for Messrs. Nicholson & Co.		5	.
		The like for Messrs. Baxter Rose & Co.		5	.
	28	Conferring with Mr. Winn and Mr. Hett on the Agreement with the two Railway Companies and on the insertion of a Clause as to the Tolls 1 hour	1	1	.
Mar.	1	Conferring with Mr. Winn and Mr. Hett on the means of securing the Carriage of minerals Drawing Clause for that purpose and making note of certain other amendments in the Bill 1 hour	1	1	.
		Conferring with Mr. Baxter on the Draft Clause which he declined but suggested a certain other process for the security of Mr. Winn and his Tenants		10	6
		Writing Messrs. Nicholson & Co. thereon		5	.
	5	Attending to order and obtain Office Copy Petition of C. C. Elwes against		10	6
		Fair Copy thereof		5	.
	16	Conferring with Mr. Watkin on the means of securing Mr. Winn as to his Covenant with his Lessees—he suggested a Toll of 4½d.		10	6
	18	Conferring with Mr. Winn and with Mr. Watkin on the means of securing the covenant with the Lessees		10	6
	19	Conferring with Mr. Baxter and Mr. Watkin in Victoria Street they ultimately consented to take powers to agree with Mr. Winn and to make Agreement securing the carriage of minerals at 6d. per Ton	1	1	.
	22	Perusing Lord Redesdale's Remarks on Bill and making Notes thereon and Writing Messrs. Nicholson & Co. and Messrs. Baxter Rose & Co. with Copies		10	6
		Fair Copy of Lord Redesdale's remarks on Bill for Messrs. Nicholson & Co.		7	6

			£	s	d
		The like for Messrs. Baxter Rose & Co.		7	6
		The like for own use		7	6
April	1	Setting Clause authorizing Agreement with Mr. Winn		10	6
		Fair Copy thereof		2	6
		Preparing outline and Agreement between Mr. Winn and others as to conveyance of minerals	2	2	.
		Fair Copy thereof 14 folios		9	4
		Writing to Messrs. Nicholson & Co. with and on the foregoing matters		5	.
	2	Fair Copy of Clause for Mr. Baxter		2	6
		Fair Copy outline of Agreement for Mr. Baxter		9	4
		Writing to Messrs. Nicholson with reference to Mr. Rowland Winn's letter of the 2nd March		5	.
		Writing to Mr. Baxter at Doncaster with Draft Clause and outline of Agreement and on the Bill		5	.
	4	Writing to Messrs Nicholson & Co. in answer to their letter		5	.
		Conferring with Mr. Watkin on the securing the transit of Minerals on spots intermediate between the Trent and the Ancholme		10	6
	5	Perusing Petition of Mr. Elwes and the Manchester Sheffield & Lincolnshire Railway Company and making Notes thereof [*sic*]	1	1	.
	8	Attending Mr. Speakers Counsel upon this Bill and taking Notes of his Observations thereon	1	1	.
		Conferring with Mr. Hett upon the Draft Agreement and upon Mr. Winn's Notes thereon 1 and ½ hours	1	11	6
		Re-settling Agreement previously to its being submitted to Mr. Bullar		10	6
		Fair Copy suggestions for agreement and Clause as to resettled [*sic*] for Mr. Hett 16 folios		10	8
		The like for our own use		10	8
	10	Conferring with Mr. Hett on result of his Conference with Mr. Lloyd on the Clause and Agreement Conferring also on the Evidence and on Mr. Elwes Petition		10	6
		Conferring with Lord Redesdale on Bill and taking Notes of his observations	1	1	.

	Conferring with Mr. Hett on Lord Redesdales observations		10	6
12	Conferring with Mr. Hett on the statements made with respect to Mr. Winns Mineral Field in the opening of the Barnsley Coal Case		10	6
13	Conferring with Mr. Baxter and subsequently with Mr. Watkin on the Agreement with Mr. Winn which they undertook to settle		10	6
	Subsequently conferring with Mr. Winn and Mr. Edmund Winn on the arrangements with the two Companies on Lord Redesdale's objections etc.	1	1	.
15	Attending Committee on Group Bill fixed for Thursday	1	1	.
16	Long conference with Mr. Hett on agreements		10	6
	Writing Messrs. Hett & Co. with Copy of Letter received from Colonel Yolland and Copy		5	.
18	Attending the Solicitor and one of the Directors (Mr. Gamble) of the Manchester Sheffield & Lincolnshire Railway Company as to withdrawal of their Company Petition and arranging same		10	6
	Attending Committee—neither of the Petitions being appeared upon Bill was referred to the Chairman of Ways and Means	1	1	.
19	Making Copy of Colonel Yollands Report for Mr. Hett 10 folios		6	8
20	Conferring with Mr. Baxter in Victoria Street on this Bill—especially on the Directors and the Drainage Clauses—subsequent conference with Messrs. Winn and Mr. Hett conferring on the Conditions of the Agreement and settling the Bill so far as we now could 4 hours	5	5	.
23	Attending Committee adjourning Bill to Thursday next	1	1	.
24	Conferring with Mr. Hett and Mr. Atkinson and afterwards with Mr. Winn on amendments in Bill and on Evidence especially as to Level Crossings 1 and ½ hour	1	11	6
	Settling Bill with reference to Board of Trade			
	Report Lord Redesdales and Mr. Rickard's remarks and suggestions of Mr. Baxter 1 and ½ hour	1	11	6

	25	Settling Report from Committee		13	4
		Fair Copy thereof		5	.
		Conferring with Mr. Baxter on the amendments in the Bill and settling Bill finally with him		10	6
		Making Fair Copy of amended Bill and Clauses for Lord Redesdale 30 folios	1	.	.
		The like for his Counsel	1	.	.
		Making Copy thereof for Messrs. Nicholson and Company	1	.	.
		The like for Messrs. Baxter Rose & Co.	1	.	.
		The like for the Chairman of Ways and Means and the Speakers Counsel	2	.	.
		Making 3 Copies for Committee	3	.	.
		Attending Committee Bill passed excepting Level Crossings	2	2	.
		Attending Lord Redesdale by appointments [*sic*] on Bill after waiting four hours Bill abjourned [*sic*]	2	2	.
	29	Attending Lord Redesdale on this Bill and making Notes of his observations	1	1	.
		Re-settling the Report		10	6
		Two Fair Copies thereof		10	.
May	1	In consequence of suggestions from Mr. Baxter, Mr. Saunders, Mr. Seymour Clarke and Mr. Stewart as to Lord Redesdale's striking out from Bills the authority for Terminal charges attending Lord Redesdale to fix appointment for conference with Deputation from Railway Companies	1	1	.
	2	Attending Lord Redesdale accordingly Mr. Coates and Mr. Baxter stated the Case in favor of the Terminal charges—Lord Shelburne Mr. Walpole and Honble Mr. Egerton supported it. Lord Redesdale stated himself to be ready to consider any words authorizing the charge within due limits	1	1	.
		Making copy of alterations made in Committee in the Chairmans Copy of Bill		5	.
		Attending Committee on Bill—Level Crossings allowed—Bill passed	2	2	.
	3	Making Copy of Bill as passed for Report	1	.	.
		Attending to get the Bill reported	1	1	.
	6	Settling Statement of Proofs for the Lords	1	1	.
		Writing Messrs. Nicholson & Co. advising them as to signing Bill		5	.

		£	s	d
	Conferring with Mr. Baxter on the Level Crossings allowed and on the Agreement with Mr. Winn		10	6
	Conferring with Mr. Baxter and settling with him form of Clause for Terminals		10	6
	Attending with him at the House of Commons conferring with Mr. Walpole Mr. Beale and Mr. Packe thereon—they approved of the Clause	1	1	.
7	Conferring with Mr. Stewart, Mr. Smithells, Mr. Allport Mr. Saunders and Mr. Pritt thereon form of Clause was ultimately settled	1	1	.
	Making Copy of further Proofs for the Lords for Messrs. Nicholson & Co. 12 folios		8	.
	Writing them therewith	.	.	.
10	Attending to get Bill considered	1	1	.
14	Attending to get Bill read 3rd time	1	1	.
	Attendances to give the requisite Notices of the several stages of the Bill in the House of Commons Attendances to deposit Copies of the Bill with the Door-keepers and at other Public Offices in that House—Attendances upon the Chairman of Ways and Means and the Speakers Counsel and Secretary not before specified Formal Attendances at the various Offices of the House of Commons and other attendances and Correspondence not before specified or charge [*sic*] for	13	13	.
14	Attending the printer with Bill instructing him as to striking off copies for the Lords		10	6
16	Attending to get Bill carried to the Lords read 1st and refferred [*sic*] to the Examiners	1	1	.
18	Writing Messrs. Nicholson Hett & Freer as to the proofs before the Examiner on Thursday	.	.	.
20	Writing Messrs. Nicholson & Co. as to contents to [*sic*] Bill		5	.
22	Writing Messrs. Baxter Rose & Co. advising them as to the Proofs required as regards the South Yorkshire Company		5	.
23	Attending Mr. Freer going through and completing the Statement of proofs		10	6
	Making 3 fair Copies Statement of proofs for use before the Examiner—12 folios each	1	4	.
	Attending Examiner proofs given Standing Orders complied with	2	2	.
	Clerk attending to give evidence		10	6

	27	Conferring with Mr. Baxter on a case submitted by him to Mr. Phipson and on the opinion settling with him form of Clause as to terminals		10	6
	28	Attending Lord Redesdales secretary to fix appointment and subsequently attending Lord Redesdale with Mr. Baxter. His Lordship disapproved of the Clause and of any recognition of terminals in Railway Bills	1	1	.
		Conferring with Mr. Wickham and others on this result determining to have a deputation to the Chairman of Railway groups	1	1	.
	30	Attending Mr. Ingham asking for an appointment to meet Chairman and subsequently attending Committee of Chairmen when they desired that an appointment should be made with Lord Redesdale	1	1	.
		Attending Lord Redesdale, his Lordship stated his willingness to meet the Committee of Chairmen any day next week which they would appoint except Wednesday		10	6
June	1	Preparing Proofs and evidence to be given in the Lords in support of the Bill	1	1	.
		Writing Messrs. Nicholson Hett & Freer advising them with reference thereto		5	.
	3	Making Copy of proofs for Mr. Birch		2	6
		Attending at House to get Bill read 2nd [*sic*] and committed for Thursday	1	1	.
	5	Making 4 Copies of Bill for use in Lords Committee		5	.
	6	Attending Mr. Freer and Mr. Atkinson going through the evidence and particularly as to the level crossings—perusing Coll Yollands report and settling Statement	1	1	.
		Fair Copy of Statement as to level crossings		5	.
		Attending Committee Bill passed with amendments subject to terminal Clause	2	2	.
	7	Four Copies of Bill as passed Lords Committee for report The like for Chairman of Ways and Means The like for Speakers Counsel The like for the Board of Trade		5	.
	11	Writing Messrs. Baxter Rose & Co.	.	.	.
	14	Attending printer with Bill as passed and with Instructions for proofs		10	6
	17	Attending to get Bill reported	1	1	.

	18	Repeated attendances during the month by appointments with Lord Redesdale; with the General Committee on Railway and Canal Bills with Mr. Baxter, and with the Managers and Secretaries of Railways and at General meetings of Directors of Railway Companies. The form of a Clause authorizing terminal charges was this day finally agreed on in conference with Lord Redesdale, Mr. Ingham, Mr. Baxter and Mr. Coates	3	3	.
	21	Attending to get Bill read 3rd time and amendments made	1	1	.
		Fair Copies terminal clause for insertion in Bill		5	.
	25	Attending the Speaker with and on the Lords Amendments to which he assented		10	6
		The like attendance on Chairman of Ways and Means		10	6
		Preparing amended Bill for these parties		10	.
		Fair Copies clauses and papers of amendments and clauses in extension for the printer of the votes 24 folios		16	.
	28	Attending at the House to get the consideration of Lords Amendments postponed sine die in consequence of further difficulties raised by the authority as to the terminals clause	1	1	.
July	5	Conferring with Mr. Baxter, Mr. Swift, Mr. Smithells and Mr. Harrison on the case to be made against the Coal Owners today—subsequently attending the Committee of Chairman [*sic*] and Lord Redesdale—Mr. Parkes opened and after discussion room was cleared and parties informed that the new clause would not be inserted but that the words in the London & North Western Act (9 & 10 Vict. cap. 204. sec. 63) would be inserted in the Bill, engaged from 11 till 5	3	3	.
	6	Settling the amendments to be made in the Commons to the Lords Amendments		10	6
	8	Lord Redesdale having inserted additional words in clause definning [*sic*] terminal stations, conferring with Mr. Baxter, and afterwards with him and Mr. Ingham and Mr. Stone thereon, and with Mr. Pritt and Mr. Graham subsequent interviews with Lord Redesdale, he adhered to the addition 4 hours	3	3	.

10	Attending the General Committee of Railway and Canal Bills, further discussion of the terminal Clause it was ultimately determined to leave clause as last settled		10	6
11	Attending to get Lords Amendments agreed to with Amendments	1	1	.
	Preparing amended Bill as passed the Commons and lodging same at the Lords to get their agreement thereto		10	6
12	Attending at the House of Lords to get the Commons Amendments to the Lords Amendments agreed to	1	1	.
20	Writing Messrs. Nicholson, Hett & Freer as to royal assent on Monday	.	.	.
22	Attending at the House when the royal assent was given by Commission	1	1	.
23	Preparing Bill for press as it received the Royal assent and attending the Printer therewith instructing him as to copies		10	6
	Attendances to give the requisite notices of the several stages of the Bill in the House of Lords			
	Attendances to deposit copies of the Act with the Door keepers and other Officers of that House			
	Attendances upon Lord Redesdale's Counsel and Secretary and correspondence not before specified or charged for sessional fee, etc.	12	12	.
	Paid House in fees in the Commons	224	2	6
	,, Copying and Inspection fees		13	6
	,, House fees for the Lords	116	10	.
	,, Orders on Bill, Committee Clerks fees	26	18	6
	,, Amending the record	1	1	.
	,, Inserting notice in Daily News	15	4	6
	,, Inserting notice in London Gazette	4	18	6
	,, Printing Bill and Act	115	9	.
	,, Declaration estimate and amendments	14	17	6
	,, Letters and other small miscellaneous expences	4	12	8
		£794	7	4

I/9/6

In Parliament Session 1861

1. Messrs. Nicholson, Hett & Freer's Charges for preparing and passing the Trent Ancholme & Grimsby Railway Bill.

			£	s	d
1860					
Oct.	26	Attending Mr. Roseby the Engineer as to the Railway proposed to be made from the Eastern terminus of the Trent and Ancholme Railway to Barnetby and on his informing us that Mr. Rowland Winn would see us this morning on the subject and afterwards attending Mr. R. Winn and Mr. Roseby thereon and as to the appointment Mr. Winn had made to meet Mr. Hutton at Mr. Corbetts on the business on Tuesday next when we informed Mr. Winn that Mr. Corbett was going to Town next week and he wished us to endeavour to see Mr. Corbett at Elsham tomorrow on the business and endeavour to get an early day fixed for a meeting with him		13	4
		Attending Mr. Stephen Gibbons (Lord Yarborough's Agent) thereon with reference to the land of his Lordship which would be affected by the proposed line when he expressed himself favorable to the project so far as he could at present judge of it.		6	8
			£1	0	0

			£	s	d
2. 1860					
Oct.	27	Journey to Elsham to see Mr. Corbett when we ascertained he was from home but would return in the evening, and journey again to Elsham in the evening and explaining to Mr. Corbett the nature of the project when he promised to consider the matter and to meet Mr. Winn and Mr. Hutton on his return from London at our office on Thursday next	2	2	0
		Horsehire		10	6
		Letter informing Mr. R. Winn the result of the interview with Mr. Corbett		5	0
	29	Long attendance on Mr. R. Winn and also upon Mr. Roseby and Mr. W. C. Atkinson the Surveyor this morning on the same subject examining plans and conferring as to the line of country it was desirable to cross between the Ancholme and the Junction at Barnetby-le-Wold having regard to the			

			£	s	d
		owners whose land would be interfered with and other considerations when Mr. Atkinson was instructed to make the Parliamentary Plans and Sections for that portion of the line	1	1	0
	31	Attending Mr. Corbett examining with him the Ordnance Map with reference to the route proposed to be taken in forming the line of Railway from the Ancholme to Barnetby, and	4	18	6
3.		conferring with him as to the supposed advantages which the Railway would afford, when he said he must take time to consider the matter.		6	8
		Attending Mr. Elwes and explaining the matter to him when he said he would consult with Mr. Barnard on the subject		6	8
Nov.	1	Long attendance on Mr. Corbett, Mr. Hutton and Mr. R. Winn respecting the proposed Railway, on Mr. Corbett wishing to have the project fully explained in order that he might be able to judge of the propriety of allowing the line to cross his lands in Worlaby, Elsham and Wrawby when on the understanding that he should have a station in Elsham and Sidings for his Brickyard and also for his Ironstone bed if it should be found worth while to work it, provided at the Company's expense Mr. Corbett's objections appeared to be removed, but he wished to have the line pointed out on the ground and arranged to go over the line with Mr. Hett and Mr. Atkinson tomorrow.	1	1	0
	2	Journey to Elsham accordingly and going over the ground with Mr. Corbett and Mr. Atkinson.	2	2	0
		Attending Mr. R. Winn on his return from Manchester after attending a meeting of the Directors of the Manchester	8	14	10
4.		Sheffield & Lincolnshire Railway Company there, and arranging with them the terms upon which they would consent to the proposed Railway running into their line between Wrawby and Barnetby.		6	8
	3	Attending Mr. R. Winn after his having seen Mr. Corbett today and communicated to him the alteration proposed to be made in			

			£	s	d
		the course of the line stipulated for by the Manchester Sheffield & Lincolnshire Railway Company to which he assented and also having called upon Mr. Elwes and Mr. Barnard who he found would not oppose.		6	8
	5	Attending Mr. Corbett on his calling to inspect on the map the course now fixed upon for the Line in Elsham and also attending with him at Mr. Atkinsons for that purpose when he appeared satisfied understanding that he was to have the same accommodation as to Station and Sidings as before agreed upon		13	4
	6	Attending Mr. Atkinson and Mr. Roseby on the subject of the Plans and explaining what information we required in preparing the Notices and as to the tracings we should want before we could prepare the Books of Reference and on other matters		6	8
			£10	8	2
5.		Having received a letter from Mr. R. Winn as to meeting him in London on Thursday, letter in reply and requesting him to take a sketch of the Line with him		5	0
		Preparing description of the course of the Line from the Trent to Barnetby and Copy		10	0
		Preparing list of Parishes, townships, and places through which the line is proposed to pass and copy		10	0
	8	In consequence of a Telegram received from Mr. R. Winn Journey to London to meet him and Mr. Roseby and long conference with Mr. Coates of the Firm of Messrs. Dyson & Co. Parliamentary Agents on the peculiarities of the case and the mode of dealing with the same when it was determined to apply to Parliament for power to form a Company and to transfer to them the Railway now in course of construction by Mr. Winn and to authorise them to form an extension to the Manchester Sheffield & Lincolnshire Railway near Barnetby Station 3 days	15	15	0
		Railway fare and expences	3	18	0
		Drawing Notice for the Gazette folios 20	2	0	0

			£	s	d
		Fair Draft Copy thereof for Parliamentary Agents		13	4
			£33	19	6
6.		Mr. Coates having sent us the Draft Notice with alterations perusing and considering same when Notice appeared to us to require further alteration and altering same accordingly		13	4
		Making Copy of the Draft as altered folios 14		9	4
	11	Letter to Messrs. Dyson with and returning Notice for reconsideration		5	0
	12	Making Copy letter received this morning from Mr. Corbett for Mr. R. Winn and letter to him therewith		6	0
		Letter to Mr. Corbett in reply		5	0
	13	Attending Mr. Atkinson for information required to enable us to complete the Notice and as to the position of the junction with the Manchester Sheffield & Lincolnshire Railway		6	8
		Making Copy of the Notice as settled by Parliamentary Agents folios 14		9	4
		Letter to them forthwith			
		Fair copy Notice for insertion in the Stamford Mercury		9	4
		Clerks journey to Stamford and attending at the Office of the Mercury with same and examining and correcting proof	2	2	0
		Railway fare and expences	1	7	8
		Fair copy Notice for insertion in the Doncaster Gazette		9	4
		Clerks journey to Doncaster and attending at the Office of the Gazette with same and examining and correcting proof	2	2	0
		Railway fare and expences		16	6
			£44	1	0
7.		Fair copy Notice for the Barton News		9	4
		Letter to the Publisher therewith and re-requesting to have proof for examination		5	0
		Examining and correcting proof of Notice and letter to the Publisher returning same with instructions for insertion		10	6
		Having received a letter from Messrs. Dyson & Co. respecting a threatened opposition by Mr. Baxter on behalf of the South Yorkshire			

		Railway Company, attending Mr. R. Winn on the subject when we found Mr. Winn had seen Mr. Watkin the Manager of the Manchester Sheffield & Lincolnshire Railway Company and had agreed upon an arrangement with him as to the rates for running over the new line with Ironstone and Coal which Mr. Watkin anticipated would be satisfactory to Mr. Baxter whom he undertook to see on the subject		6	8
		Writing to Messrs. Dyson & Co. in reply to their letter		5	0
		The Revd. C. J. Barnard having called upon us this afternoon on the subject of the objectionable character of the Railway as regards the Estate of Mr. Elwes, long conference with him on the subject when he informed us that he thought it would be his duty as a Trustee of Mr. Elwes' Settlements to oppose the Bill, and afterwards attending Mr. Roseby on the subject		13	4
			£46	10	10
8.		Writing letter to Mr. R. Winn thereon		5	0
	14	Fair copy Notice to the Manchester Guardian		9	4
		Clerks journey to Manchester attending at the office of the Guardian with same and examining and correcting proof	3	3	0
		Railway fare and expences	1	15	7
		Attending Mr. R. Winn and Mr. Roseby this day as to Mr. Elwes' threatened opposition when it was determined that we should look over the proposed line across Mr. Elwes' Estate tomorrow in order to ascertain whether any slight alteration could be made with a view to a less objectionable mode of crossing the Estate and also conferring as to the arrangement with Mr. Watkin (which Mr. R. Winn had authorised that Gentleman to make on Mr. Winn's behalf with Mr. Baxter also) when it was settled that Mr. Roseby should go to Town tonight to see Mr. Watson [*sic*] and if necessary to telegraph for Mr. R. Winn tomorrow		13	4
		Letter to Messrs. Dyson & Co. with 6 copies of the Parliamentary Notice as inserted in the Doncaster Gazette	.	.	.

15 Attending Mr. Adam Smith the Engineer of
the Ancholme Commissioners, Mr. R. Winn
and Mr. Atkinson with respect to the height
and span of the Bridge to be carried over
9. the River Ancholme and the adjoining Drain
when it was decided that the same headway
should be left under the new Bridge as was
given in the Railway Bridge over the new
cut in Scawby Parish and that the span
should embrace the River and the Cess of
12 feet on each side thereof 13 4

16 Attending Mr. R. Winn and Mr. Atkinson on the subject of the preparation of the Plan and Section of the line east of the Ancholme in consequence of Mr. Lee not having yet furnished Mr. Atkinson with the necessary particulars with regard to the datum and level at the Trent and the Ancholme to enable Mr. Atkinson to proceed with his Section, and afterwards attending Mr. Lee and Mr. Atkinson and conferring when we found that Mr. Lee was now in possession of the necessary information for proceeding with the Section 13 4

17 Attending Mr. Lee as to his progress with
the Plan between the Trent and Ancholme
and examining a portion thereof and making
suggestions as to numbering the same etc
when he said he could have a portion ready
for the Lithographer on Monday, and also
attending Mr. Atkinson as to the Eastern
portion and examining his Plan, when
10. 1861 he said the whole of that portion would be £54 3 9
[*sic*] ready for the Lithographer on Monday 6 8

Messrs. Dyson & Co. having sent us Copy of Note of arrangements made with the Manchester Sheffield & Lincolnshire Railway Company dated 8th Novr inst and intimated that Mr. Baxter would be satisfied with the same terms perusing and considering the Memorandum and making alterations therein 6 8

Fair copy Memorandum with alterations for Mr. R. Winn's consideration 2 6

Attending Mr. Roseby and conferring with him as to the terms proposed, and the alterations which we considered desirable 6 8

		£	s	d
	Attending upon Mr. Roseby in the evening after he had submitted the Memorandum to Mr. R. Winn and conferring on the subject		6	8
	Attending Mr. Atkinson on his bringing us a tracing of the line from the Ancholme to Barnetby Station and examining same when there appeared a question whether the Road leading across the Manchester Sheffield & Lincolnshire Railway in the parish of Bigby to the Brigg Turnpike was a public Road or an occupation road merely		13	4
	Journey to Kettleby and attending Mr. Hobson on the subject when he informed			
11. 1861 [*sic*]	us that the Road in question was an occupation road only with a public footpath along	£56	6	3
	it, and Horse hire	1	5	0
	Letter to Mr. Lancaster informing him we should send a Messenger over to York on Monday evening with a portion of the Plan and Section to be lithographed and requesting him to be prepared to proceed immediately with the Plans	.	.	.
19	Journey to Frodingham and thence down the Railway to the River Trent and taking reference in Brumby and Frodingham	5	5	0
	Horsehire and expences		11	6
	Attending Mr. Atkinson and examining with him the tracing for the Lithographer of the Plan and Section of a portion of the line from the Ancholme to Barnetby	1	1	0
	Clerks journey to York therewith and to instruct the Lithographer thereon	2	2	0
	Railway fare and expences	1	11	4
20	Attending Mr. Sherwood (Mr. Winns Agent) at the Town hall in Brigg and going through the Plans of the line of Railway from the Trent to the Ancholme and completing the references for the parishes in that district, engaged all day	5	5	0
	Attending Mr. Corbett and producing to him the tracings of the intended line for his inspection and arranging for			
12. 1861 [*sic*]	his Agent Mr. Dodds to give us information	£73	7	1
	as to the present Occupiers of his Estate at Elsham etc.		6	8
	Attending Mr. R. Winn and Mr. Roseby and conference [last two words inserted in pencil]			

			£	s	d
		as to the terms of arrangement to be made with the South Yorkshire and the Manchester Sheffield & Lincolnshire Railway Companies, Mr. Roseby being about to proceed to London to confer with Mr. Beale and Mr. Watkin thereon		6 [crossed out and 13	8 4 inserted in pencil]
		Making 3 fair copies of the Memorandum of proposed arrangements to be sent to Mr. Roseby in town		7	6
	21	Journey to Worlaby Elsham Wrawby Bigby and Barnetby and taking the reference of the lands to be affected in these parishes by the intended line	5	5	0
		Paid Horsehire and expences and for Assistant	1	0	6
		Having received a letter from Messrs. Dyson & Co. as to the terms of the arrangements proposed to be made with Mr. Baxter on behalf of the South Yorkshire Railway Company Writing them in reply		5	0
		Letter to Mr. Lancaster with further part of the Plan to be lithographed.	.	.	.
	22	Attending Mr. Mundey of Wrawby and obtaining from him the names of the Lessees of the Farm occupied by him under Clare Hall College, Cambridge		6	8
13.	1860 [*sic*]		£81	5	1
		Attending Mr. Abraham of Worlaby and obtaining from him the names of the present occupiers of the Carr pasture and other lands in Worlaby		6	8
		Attending Mr. Joseph Dodds and going through and completing particulars for Book of Reference as to the estate of Mr. Corbett in Elsham and Wrawby		13	4
Novr	23	Attending Mr. R. Winn prior to his going over to Manchester this morning to meet Mr. Watkin on the subject of the proposed arrangement between the Companies and also attending him and Mr. Roseby in the evening on the terms which had been finally agreed to		6	8
		Examining and correcting proof Sheets of lithographed Plans of portions of the line	1	1	0
		Letter to Mr. Lancaster with same returned and with further portion of the Plans to be lithographed	.	.	.

	24	Letter to Mr. Lancaster with the remainder of the Plan	.	.	.
		Examining and correcting further proof Sheets	1	1	0
		Attending Mr. Atkinson and arranging to accompany him to York on Monday next to have the Plans and Sections examined and completed there		6	8
		Letter to Mr. Lancaster informing him	.	.	.
	26	Journey to York with Mr. Atkinson and attendance with him upon the Lithographers and examining and correcting the plans 2 days	10	10	0
			£95	10	5
14.	1860	Railway fare and expences	2	4	6
		Attending Mr. James Dawson and obtaining from him the names of the Occupiers of the Road No. 10 in the parish of Wrawby and the occupiers of the fields Nos 20 and 36 in Bigby		6	8
		Attending Mr. Roseby and Mr. Lee and conferring as to altering the gradient in the Tunnel with a view to dispense with the embankment in Frodingham Village when they decided to go over to York to consult with Mr. Atkinson on the subject		6	8
		Writing letter to Mr. Freer informing him at York		5	0
	28	Attending Mr. Sherwood and obtaining from him the names of the occupiers of the additional numbers which had been inserted in the Plans at York		6	8
		Attending Mr. John Nelson of Wrawby and obtaining information from him to enable us to complete the reference for that parish		6	8
		Drawing Book of Reference folios 81	8	2	0
		Making 7 fair copies thereof	28	7	0
		Attending at the Townhall and examining and comparing Plans Sections and Books of Reference with Mr Roseby Mr. Atkinson and Mr. Lee, Mr. Freer and 5 Clerks engaged 3 hours each	7	7	0
	29	Letter to Messrs. Dyson informing them			
			£143	2	7

			£	s	d
15.		that Mr. Freer would be in town tonight to make the Deposit tomorrow	.	.	.
		Journey to London with Plans Books of Reference and other documents to be deposited at the Parliamentary Offices and the Board of Trade and attending with Mr. Roseby at Messrs. Dyson & Co. to examine and complete the documents and afterwards to make the necessary deposits 3 days	15	15	0
		Paid Railway fare and expences	6	0	0
		Examining Book of Reference and Gazette Notice and also Plans and Sections for deposit with the Clerk of the Peace at Spilsby		13	4
		Clerks journey to Spilsby to deposit the several documents with the Clerk of the Peace	2	2	0
		Railway fare and expences	1	1	6
		Paid Clerk of the Peace's fee and Post Office Order	3	3	6
		Endorsing title on the plans and Sections to be deposited with the several Parish Clerks		13	4
		Examining Books of Reference and Notices and Plans and affixing cross sections to Plans previous to depositing same with the several Parish Clerks	1	1	0
	30	Clerks journey to Frodingham and Appleby to deposit the Documents with the Parish Clerks there	2	2	0
		Gighire and expenses		8	0
			£176	2	3
16.		Clerks journey to Wrawby Worlaby Elsham Barnetby and Brigg for the like purpose	2	2	0
		Gighire and expenses		9	7
	Decr	Preparing alphabetical list of the Owners Lessees and Occupiers of land on the line and fair copy 41 folios	4	2	0
	5	Having received a letter from Mr. R. Winn requesting us to be prepared to meet him and Mr. Dawes in London on Monday and to write to Messrs. Dyson for an appointment on that day Writing letter in reply and as to several matters that Messrs. Dyson should be made acquainted with		5	0
		Letter to Messrs. Dyson & Co. for an appointment accordingly	.	.	.

		Attending Surveyor ~~with Plans~~ and Sections and instructing him to mark on each number on the line the height of the embankment and depth of cutting to enable us to fill up the Notices to owners and occupiers [inserted between lines: "and obtaining from him particulars of the embankments and cuttings"]	6 8 [struck out and 1 1 0 inserted]
		Instructions for Bill	2 2 0
		Drawing Bill folios 222 [number in pencil]	22 4 0 [in pencil]
		Fair copy thereof for perusal of Parliamentary Agents	7 8 0 [in pencil]
		Instructions for Clauses to be introduced into the Bill on behalf of the Ancholme Commissioners for the protection of the Ancholme level	1 1 0
		Drawing same folios 70	7 7 0
17.	1861 [*sic*]	Writing 7 letters to the Committee of the Ancholme Commissioners appointed to watch such Railway Bills as might affect the Ancholme level informing them of meeting to be held on Friday next to consider the Clauses [added in pencil:] for their protection inserted in the Bill	1 4 6 17 6 [latter sum struck out]
		Writing to Mr. Smith the Engineer to the Ancholme Commissioners requesting his attendance at the meeting	5 0
	7	Attending Meeting of the Committee reading over the Clauses and settling same and taking instructions to apply to have same inserted in the Bill	1 1 0
		Fair Copy of the Clauses for Parliamentary Agents	2 6 8
		Letter to them therewith	. . .
		Instructions for clauses to be introduced into the Bill on behalf of the Commissioners of Sewers for the protection of the levels within their jurisdiction	13 4
		Drawing same folios 51	5 2 0
		Writing 7 letters to the Committee of the Commissioners of Sewers appointed to watch the Railway Bills as might affect the Sewers District informing them of meeting on Friday to consider the clauses	17 6

		Attending the meeting reading over the clauses and taking instructions to apply to have same inserted in the Bill	1	1	0
		Fair copy Clauses for Parliamentary Agent	1	14	0
		Letter to them therewith	.	.	.
18.	1861 [*sic*]	Drawing Notice to Owners on land on the line with Schedules annexed and examining same with Plans and Book of reference and with each other (88 Notices)	22	0	0
		The like charge for Notices to Lessees (15 Notices)	3	15	0
		The like charge for Notices to Occupiers (160 Notices)	40	0	0
		Postage stamps affixed to forms of assent etc.		9	0
	10	Writing to Mr. W. Sowerby to enquire the Christian name and residence of Mr. Parkinson the owner of a field in Brumby occupied by James Benson		5	0
		In consequence of a letter from Mr. R. Winn Journey to London to confer with Mr. Coates as to the form of the Bill under the special circumstances of this case and respecting the provisions with reference to the land provided by Mr. Winn and the expenditure by Messrs. Dawes upon the works constructed or in course of construction and as to the principal [*sic*] upon which the capital of the Company should be estimated, and the sums to be deposited in the Court of Chancery calculated 3 days	15	15	0
		Railway fare and Hotel expences	3	19	3
		Examining and directing Notices to distant Owners and Occupiers engaged all day	3	3	0
		Making list of names and addresses of the distant Owners to whom Notices were intended to be sent by post and copy		10	6
19.	1861 [*sic*]				
	11	Journey to Lincoln and attending at the Post Office with Notices comparing same with the list and obtaining the Postmaster's receipt for same	3	3	0
		Railway fare and expences		17	6
		Paid Postages and for registering letters		14	0
	12	Journey to Brumby Frodingham Scunthorpe and Gunhouse and serving Notices in those places	2	2	0

		Horseshire and expences		9	6
		Journey to Appleby to serve Notices there	1	1	0
		Horsehire etc.		5	0
	13	Attending serving the Rev. C. J. Barnard with Notice		6	8
		Serving Notices at Brigg		6	8
		Letter informing Mr. R. Winn we had received the Draft Bill from Messrs. Dyson & Co.		5	0
	14	Journey to Bonby Worlaby Elsham and Wrawby and serving Notices there	2	2	0
		Gighire and expences		11	2
		Journey to Lewisham and thence to Gloucester to serve Notices on Mr. Chambers and the Revd [blank] Balfour 3 days	6	6	0
		Railway fare and expences	5	0	10
		Journey to Scarborough to serve Notices there	2	2	0
		Railway fare and expences	1	10	9
20.	1861 [*sic*]	Attending Mr. Roseby and Mr. Atkinson on the subject of the estimate and the principle upon which it was to be made and urging their early attention to the matter		6	8
	15	Journey to Fenton to serve Notice on Mr. G. W. Cole	2	2	0
		Railway fare and expences		9	7
		Journey to Elsham Carrs and Wrawby Moor Kettlebythorpe and Newstead to serve Notices	2	2	0
		Horsehire and expences		6	7
		Instructions for Declaration by Mr. Winn and Mr. Hett as to the capital of the proposed Company		6	8
		Drawing same and ingrossing for signature		8	0
		Perusing first print of the Bill and making several corrections and alterations therein	2	2	0
		Journey to Appleby to confer with Mr. R. Winn and take his directions as to some of the provisions of the Bill, when we left with him for signature the Declaration as to capital, etc.	2	2	0
		Gighire and expences		6	6
		Attending Mr. Atkinson and obtaining from him particulars of the several level crossings which required to be noticed in the Bill and inserting same therein		6	8

			£	s	d
	17	Instructions for Clauses as to Warping to be inserted in the Bill			
		Drawing same folios 6			
		[All the above from the 29th November has a vertical drawn through it.]			
		Journey to London to confer with			
21.		Parliamentary Agents as to several of the provisions of the Bill and with them finally settling same, and also to peruse and correct revised Proof of the Bill 3 days	15	15	0
		Railway fare and expences	4	0	4
		Drawing Petition for Bill	1	1	0
		Ingrossing for signature folios 8		8	0
		Paid for parchment		2	0
		Writing to Mr. Winn therewith for signature		5	0
		Also writing to Messrs. Dawes informing them that the Petition would be sent to them by Mr. Winn for their signature		5	0
		Journey to Frodingham and perusing the Inclosure Award to ascertain whether the boundaries of the Township of Gunhouse had been set out by the Commissioners when we found that the Award contained no mention of such boundaries and attending examining Witnesses on the subject when we found that there was a Hamlet of Gunhouse in the Parish of Frodingham and that the Township of Gunhouse was in the parish of West Halton	3	3	0
			2	2	0
			[latter sum crossed out]		
		Horsehire		6	0
	19	Attending at Mr. Roseby's Office and also upon Mr. Atkinson as to the estimate when we found that it could not be completed in time for the evening's post		6	8
		Letter to Messrs. Dyson & Co.	.	.	.
22.	1861 [*sic*]	Having received a letter from Mr. R. Winn informing us that Mr. C. [initial inserted in pencil] Winn had hesitated to sign the Declaration as to capital [last three words inserted in pencil] we had forwarded for his signature Writing an explanatory letter to Mr. Winn on the subject		5	0
		Making copy of such letter and writing to Mr. R. Winn therewith		6	0

	20	Having received a letter from Mr. George Dawes saying he had received the Petition for the Bill Letter informing Mr. Winn		5	0
		Mr. George Dawes having sent us the printed letter assenting to the Bill letter to Mr. W. H. Dawes requesting him to return the one sent to him		5	0
		Writing to Messrs. Dyson & Co. informing them that the Declaration had been signed by Mr. Winn and the petition signed by Mr. Geo. Dawes and forwarded to his Brother for his signature	.	.	.
	24	Letter to Mr. R. Winn informing him of the amounts of capital inserted by Mr. Coates in the Bill and the amount of deposit which would have to be paid before the 15th Jan^{ry}			
		Three fair copies of Estimate of expence for Mr. Roseby's signature and attending him on signing same		9	8
	26	Letter to Messrs. Dyson & Co. with estimates and Declaration	.	.	.
23.	1861 [*sic*]	[Vertical line drawn through all items from here to half way through entries of 13 Jan.]			
		Drawing out list of Owners on the line		5	0
		Two fair copies thereof		5	0
		The like list of Lessees		2	6
		Two fair copies thereof		2	6
		The like list of Occupiers		10	0
		Two fair copies thereof		10	0
		Perusing and considering Copy of the South Yorkshire Railway (Keadby extension) Bill for the purpose of ascertaining how it affected Mr. Winn's property on this line when it appeared to us that the provisions of the Bill upon certain points were very objectionable		13	4
		Writing letter to Mr. R. Winn fully thereon		5	0
	27	Attending him in consequence and conferring upon the Bill and as to the most advisable course to be taken by Mr. Winn with respect to answering the Parliamentary notice to Mr. Winn as a landowner affected by the South Yorkshire Bill		6	8
	28	Writing letter to Mr. R. Winn on the subject		5	0
		Writing to Messrs. Dyson with lists of Owners etc.	.	.	.

		Writing letter to Mr. Roseby informing him that the deposit (£6,400) upon the Bill must be in the hands of Messrs. Dyson & Co. on Monday morning the 14th January, and requesting him to inform Mr. Winn and Messrs. Dawes what sum was to be paid by each and also arrange for the money to be paid at the time stated	5	0
24.	1861	Writing letter to Mr. R. Winn thereon	5	0
	[*sic*] 29	Writing letter to Mr. R. Winn in reply to a letter of enquiry from him as to the Assents received from the Occupiers on the line	5	0
	1861			
	Jany 3	Fair copy Requisition to Private Bill Office Clerk for Warrant to pay money into the Bank	3	0
		Attending Mr. R. Winn on signing same and attesting his signature	6	8
		Writing to Mr. E. J. Winn therewith for signature	5	0
		The like to Messrs. Dawes	5	0
	8	Having received Requisition signed Letter to Messrs. Dyson therewith	.	. .
		Letter informing Mr. R. Winn	.	. .
	12	Writing to Messrs. Dyson in reply to a letter from them as to payment of the deposit	5	0
	13	Attending Mr. Roseby in consequence of his having this morning received a letter from Mr. Geo Dawes stating his inability to provide the deposit of £6160 by tomorrow (Monday) as arranged and enquiring whether some arrangement could be made for obtaining the amount and long conference thereon	6	8
		Attending Mr. Roseby again after his having seen Mr. R. Winn and long consultation with him when it was settled that he should request Mr. Winn to meet [Vertical drawn through items ends here]		
25.		here on Tuesday by which time we should have heard from Messrs. Dyson & Co. as to the payment of the deposit after the day fixed by the Standing Orders for the payment thereof	6	8
		Writing letter to Messrs. Dyson & Co. on the subject	5	0
	15	In consequence of a Telegram received from Mr. Roseby in London after an interview		

			£	s	d
		with Mr. Coates journey to London with reference to arrangements to be made for paying in the deposit by means of funds to be raised independently of Messrs. Dawes 3 days	15	15	0
		Railway fare and expences	4	8	3
	19	Fair copy letter from the Railway Department of the Board of Trade as to the level crossings upon the line		5	0
		Writing to Mr. Roseby therewith and thereon		5	0
		Making copy for Mr. R. Winn		5	0
		Letter to him therewith		5	0
		Drawing statement of Proofs of Compliance with Standing Orders (Lords and Commons) folios 50	3	6	8
	22	Writing letter to Messrs. Dyson & Co. as to the witnesses whose attendance would be required before the Examiner	.	.	.
	28	Attending Mr. Roseby and Mr. Atkinson as to the evidence they could give before the Examiner on Standing Orders and making minutes thereof		13	4
		At the request of Mr. Roseby making copy Statement of proofs to be made by himself and Mr. Atkinson for his use 3 Brief Sheets	1	0	0
		Drawing Affidavit by Mr. Geo. Wright as to service of Notices on Owners and Occupiers and fair copy for signature		10	0
26.		Fair copy list of persons served to annex and writing two exhibits on forms of Notice and list		4	6
		Attending before a Magistrate to be sworn thereto		6	8
		Justice Clerk's fees for oath and 2 exhibits		3	0
		Drawing Affidavit by Mr. W. H. Tinkler as to service of Notices and fair copy for signature		10	0
		Fair copy list of persons served to annex and 2 exhibits		4	6
		Attending to be sworn thereto		6	8
		Justice's [*sic*] Clerk's fee for Oaths and Exhibits		3	0
		Drawing Affidavit by Mr. S. Upton and fair copy for signature		10	0
		Copy list of persons served and 2 exhibits		3	0
		Attending to be sworn thereto		6	8
		Justices Clerks [*sic*] fee for Oath and Exhibits		3	0

		Drawing Affidavit by Mr. J. R. Hett and fair copy for signature		10	0
		Copy list of persons served and 2 exhibits		3	0
		Attending to be sworn thereto		6	8
		Justice [*sic*] Clerk's fees for Oath and Exhibits		3	0
		Drawing Affidavit by Mr. Geo. Wright as to deposit of Plans and Sections, etc., with the Clerk of the Peace and fair copy for signature		10	0
		Attending to be sworn thereto		6	8
		Justice Clerk's fee for Oath		1	0
		Drawing Affidavit by Mr. Thos Wilson as to deposit of Plans and reference with the parish Clerks and fair copy for signature		10	0
27.		Making list of Parishes to annex and exhibit [Above line partly pencilled through]		2	0
		Attending to be sworn thereto		6	8
		Justice Clerk's fee for Oath and Exhibit		2	0
		Drawing Affidavit by Mr. J. R. Hett as to deposit of Plans, etc., with Parish Clerks and fair copy for signature		10	0
		Making list of parishes to annex and exhibit		2	0
		Attending to be sworn thereto		6	8
		Justices Clerks [*sic*] fee for Oath and Exhibit		2	0
		Drawing Affidavit by Mr. Freer as to service of Notice on the Revd C. J. Barnard and fair copy for signature		10	0
		Attending to be sworn thereto		6	8
		Justice Clerk's fee for Oath and Exhibit		2	0
		Drawing Affidavit by Mr. Freer as to Notices sent by post and fair copy for signature		10	0
		Fair copy list of addresses to annex and 2 exhibits		4	0
		Attending before Magistrate to be sworn		6	8
		Paid for Oath and Exhibit		2	0
		Fair copy list of Owners Occupiers and Lessees for Mr. Freer's use before Examiner		9	0
		The like of acknowledgments received		5	0
		Having received a letter from Mr. Winn enquiring whether Mr. Rosebys attendance in London on Friday could be dispensed with Letter in reply		5	0
28.	Jany 31	Perusing and examining the Affidavits Notices lists and papers and arranging same for production before the Examiner in London	1	1	0
		Journey to London with Mr. Roseby and Mr. Atkinson and attending before Examiner			

to prove compliance with Standing Orders 3 days 15 15 0

Railway fare and expences 4 14 0

Feby 4 The Board of Trade having sent a form to be filled up relative to the contemplated crossing of the Turnpike Road by the Railway attending Mr. Owston one of the Trustees of the Road [last three words inserted in pencil] therewith and conferring thereon 6 8

Filling up the Form and obtaining the signature of the Clerk to the Turnpike Trustees thereto 6 8

Fair copy thereof to keep 2 0

Writing to the Secretary of the Railway Department therewith 5 0 [inserted in pencil]

13 Attending Mr. R. Winn on his return from London and long conference as to the proposed Deed of Arrangements between the Manchester Sheffield and Lincolnshire and South Yorkshire Railway Companies and Mr. Winn and Messrs. Dawes prepared by Mr. Baxter prescribing how those Companies and Messrs. Dawes and Mr. Winn should be respectively interested in this line and the traffic arrangements proposed to made when the matter stood over for further consideration until Mr. R. Winn should have heard again from Mr. Baxter 13 4

29. Feby 14 Letter to Messrs. Baxter with a Copy of the deposited Plans and Sections of this line as required by them . . .

16 Fair copy of our letter to Mr. Geo Dawes of the 3rd Janry last informing him the amount of deposit and the time of payment and of his reply and also of Mr. Dawes' letter to Mr. Roseby received on the 13th Janry 3 0

Writing to Messrs. Dyson & Co. therewith and thereon 5 0

18 Fair copy of the letter sent by Mr. Roseby to Mr. Geo Dawes on the 12th Janry 1 0

Letter to Messrs. Dyson therewith and inclosing them the original letter from Mr. Dawes on the same date 5 0

19 Perusing the Bill of the proposed South Yorkshire Railway with reference to its

			£	s	d
		connection with the Trent Ancholme & Grimsby Railway	1	11	0
				[in pencil instead of] 13	4
		Writing letter to Mr. R. Winn thereon		5	0
	21	Attending Mr. R. Winn as to the precautions necessary to be taken by Mr. Winn with regard to some of the powers sought to be embodied by the South Yorkshire Company in the Keadby Extension Bill, and as to his reserving power to carry a Warping Drain under that Railway etc.		6	8
	23	Writing to Messrs. Dyson & Co. on the subject of some of the powers conferred by the South Yorkshire Railway Bill		5	0
30.	24	Writing to Messrs. Baxter to enquire whether they would undertake to insert into their South Yorkshire Bill a Clause for affording Mr. Winn facilities for Warping etc.		5	0
	25	Perusing Draft Agreement prepared by Messrs. Baxter between the Manchester Sheffield & Lincolnshire Railway Company the South Yorkshire Railway Company and Mr. Winn and Messrs. Dawes with respect to the construction and management of the proposed Railway by the 3 parties and the traffic arrangements with regard to Ironstone and Coal		6	8
		Attending Mr. Winn thereon and taking instructions to consult Counsel as to the legal effect of the Agreement in the absence of any confirmation in the Bill for this Railway		6	8
		Drawing instructions for Mr. Bullar to settle the Draft on Mr. Winns behalf and to advise and fair copy folios 8		13	4
		Making fair copy Draft Arrangement to accompany same folios 11		7	4
		Letter to Agents therewith and thereon		5	0
		Agents attending Mr. Bullar with papers		6	8
		Paid him fee and Clerk	3	5	6
		Agents letters, etc.		7	6
		Paid for Telegram to Mr. Dickson		2	3
		Perusing Opinion of Mr. Bullar		6	8
	27	Journey to Doncaster with Mr. R. Winn to meet Mr. Dickson and conferring with him			

31.	respecting the engagements Mr. Winn was under to his Lessees as to the Conveyance of their Ironstone to the Trent and Ancholme and journey thence to London to confer with Mr. Baxter and Mr. Watkin as to the arrangements to be made for Mr. Winn's indemnification by the Trent Ancholme & Grimsby Company in respect of his engagement to the Lessees and for the conveyance of the Ironstone from his Estates between the Trent and Ancholme to those rivers and also to confer with Mr. Coates as to the means of obtaining a sufficient Indemnity from the Company and as to the form of Clause which it was desirable to be introduced into the Bill for Mr. Winn's security 3 days	15 15 0
	Railway fare and expences	4 13 10
March 2	Having received a letter from Mr. Coates in consequence of his having had an interview with Mr. Baxter as to the proposed clause who objected to its introduction, and proposed another clause	6 0
	making copy of the letter for Mr. R. Winn writing him therewith and thereon	
4	Writing letter to Mr. R. Winn in reply to one from him as to the stipulation for the delivery of Ironstone being extended to the whole of Mr. Winn's estate between the Trent and Ancholme whether at present in lease or not	5 0
32. Feby [*sic*] 9	Writing letter to Mr. Coates as to the proposed clause to be inserted in the Bill	5 0
12	Writing to [deleted and "Correspondence with" inserted] Messrs. Dyson & Co. as to the evidence to be got up in support of the Bill when it was expected to come before the Committee, etc.	13 4 [in pencil]
15	Writing again to them thereon	. . .
19	Writing another letter on the same subject [both these entries pencilled through]	. . .
20	Fair copy of our letter of the 9th inst to Mr. Coates for Mr. R. Winn and letter to him therewith	6 0
	Having received letter from Mr. R. Winn with an extract from a letter he had received	

			£	s	d
		from Mr. E. Winn respecting an interview he had had with Mr. Coates and Mr. Watkin as to the clauses which it was desirable to have in the Bill, writing to Mr. E. Winn on the subject		5	0
		Fair copy of our letter to Mr. Coates of the 9th to accompany		1	0
		Writing to Mr. R. Winn in reply to his letter		5	0
	23	Writing to Mr. R. Winn with the Draft Agreement and instructions laid before Mr. Bullar with his remarks and opinion thereon and informing him we had received a letter from Mr. E. Winn stating that it was doubtful whether arrangements with the Manchester Sheffield & Lincolnshire Railway Company would be come to		5	0
33.	April 2	Having received draft clause from Mr. Coates to enable the Company to enter into Contracts with Mr. Winn for the carriage of minerals to and from his estate and also draft heads of an agreement to be made in pursuance of such power Perusing and considering same		6	8
		Writing letter to Mr. R. Winn therewith and thereon		5	0
	3	At the request of Mr. R. Winn writing to Messrs. Buck and Dickson solicitors Preston for a copy of the Clause in the Lease from Mr. Winn to Messrs. Dawes as to the carriage of Ironstone etc. by the Lessees and also copy of the stipulation made with Mr. Beale		5	0
		Letter to Messrs. Dyson informing them we proposed going to Town on Friday and would call on them on Saturday with a view to arranging for proceeding with the Bill	.	.	.
	5	Journey to Winterton to meet Mr. R. Winn and conferring with him as to the clause and heads of Agreement after his conference with Mr. Beale and Mr. Dawes yesterday	2	2	0
		Gighire, etc.		10	6
		Letter to Messrs. Dyson & Co. proposing to call on them on Monday	.	.	.
	6	Attending Mr. Atkinson as to the evidence he could give with regard to the advantages in point of cost and convenience of the proposed			
34.		line over a line on the north side of Mr. Elwes'			

	preserves as at first projected and as to taking levels of the latter line if found necessary in case Mr. Elwes' opposition should be proceeded with and also as to evidence to be given in support of the estimate of the cost of the Railway	6 8
7 to 26	Journey to London attending with and conferring with Messrs. Dyson & Co. upon the Draft Agreement between this Company and the Manchester Sheffield & Lincolnshire Railway and South Yorkshire Companies and Mr. Winn and Messrs. Dawes and the alterations suggested therein by them prior to our laying the same before Counsel many attendances upon Messrs. Dyson & Co., Mr. Baxter Mr. R. Winn and Mr. Watkin on the subject of the arrangements and	89 5 0
	also as to the Drainage and Warping Clauses and the evidence to be given in support of the Bill especially as to the level crossings, and attending before the Committee of the House of Commons on the Bill when the same was passed except as to the level crossings 17 days	
	Railway and Hotel expences	17 6 6
	Instructions for agreement between Mr. Winn and Messrs. Dawes and the promoters of the Railway as to the carriage of minerals, etc.	6 8
	Drawing same and fair copy thereof folios 27	[blank]
	Drawing instructions to Mr. Lloyd to peruse same and fair copy thereof	1 0 0
35.	Copy Clause and heads of agreement received from Mr. Coates to accompany same folios 15	10 0
	Attending him therewith and to appoint conference thereon	6 8
	Attending conference	1 1 0
	Paid Mr. Lloyd's fees for conference settling Draft Agreement and Clause and for his opinion	10 1 6
	Making 2 fair copies of the Agreement and Clause as settled by Mr. Lloyd for Messrs. Baxter & Co. and Mr. R. Winn folios 27 each	1 16 0
	Perusing Draft Agreement received from Messrs. Baxter & Co.	6 8
	Making 2 fair copies thereof folios 12 each	16 0

		£	s	d
	Drawing Statement of proofs to be given in support of the level crossings authorised by the Bill and making fair copy thereof folios 12	1	4	0
[May?] 13	Journey to Appleby to see Mr. R. Winn and confer with him as to the pending arrangements as to the conveyance of Ironstone, etc.	2	2	0
	Horsehire etc.		7	0
	Preparing further statement of Proofs for the Lords folios 12	1	4	0
	[Vertical line drawn through all items from 27th Feb. to here]			
15	Fair copy of the Proofs as regards the South Yorkshire and River Dun Company to be obtained by Messrs. Baxter & Co. folios 5		3	4
	Letter to them thereon and with Copy Bill for signature by Mr. Parker and Mr. Lister		5	0
36.	The like as to the Manchester Sheffield & Lincolnshire Railway Company folios 5		3	4
	Writing to Mr. Guy thereon and with Copy Bill for signature by Mr. Chapman and Mr. Fenton		5	0
21	Letter to Messrs. Dyson & Co. with Statement of proofs on Standing Orders in the Lords and names of Witnesses etc.		5	0
23	Journey to London and attending before Examiners of the House of Lords to prove compliance with Standing Orders 3 days	15	15	0
	Railway fare and expences	4	12	6
31	Having received a letter from Mr. R. Winn for our opinion as to the effects of the Clauses 66, 67 and 68 in the Bill, Perusing and considering same		6	8
	Writing him thereon		5	0
	Writing to Mr. R. Winn as to the completion of the Agreements between the Companies and Mr. Winn		5	0
June [*sic*]	Messrs. Dyson & Co having informed us that the Bill would be in Committee on Thursday next and that it would be necessary for us to procure the consents of Mr. Winn and Messrs. Dawes to a copy of the Bill signed in our presence and for Mr. Roseby to attend and give evidence relative to the level crossings, letter to Mr. Winn informing him we should be at Nostell			

			£	s	d
37.		on Monday next with a Copy of the Bill for his signature		5	0
		The like to Mr. W. H. Dawes		5	0
		Attending at Mr. Roseby's house when we found that he was in Paris and arranged for a Telegram to be sent to him requesting his attendance before the Committee in London on Thursday		6	8
	3	Journey to Nostell and attending and obtaining Mr. Winn's signature to a copy of the Bill	3	3	0
		Railway fare and expences	1	10	6
		Perusing and altering Draft Agreement sent by us to Mr. R. Winn		5	0
		Attending Mr. R. Winn therewith and conferring thereon		6	8
	5	Mr. Roseby not having returned home attending Mr. Atkinson and arranging for him to attend in London tomorrow to give evidence before the Committee		6	8
		Journey to Birmingham to meet Mr. W. H. Dawes and obtain his signature to a consent to the Bill and thence to London to obtain Mr. George Dawes' signature and attending to give evidence before the Committee of the House of Lords 3 days	15	15	0
		Railway fare and expences	5	15	6
	7	Attending with Mr. E. Winn upon Mr. Baxter and discussing and finally settling the terms of the special Agreement between Mr. Winn and his Lessees and the Trent Ancholme & Grimsby Railway Company		13	4
		[Vertical line through last 16 lines]			
38.		Examining and correcting Copy Agreement as finally settled		5	0
		Letter to Messrs. Baxter & Co. with the Draft Agreement as settled		5	0
		Letter to Mr. E. Winn with the Copy Agreement for Mr. Winn's use		5	0
	28	Letter to Messrs. Dawes with Copy of the Act as passed		5	0
		The like to Mr. R. Winn		5	0
Aug^t	8	Having received a letter from Messrs. Baxter informing us of a meeting of Directors at Doncaster on Saturday and requesting our attendance Letter in reply		5	0

			£	s.	d.
	10	Journey to Doncaster to attend the first meeting of the Directors when there being only one Director present no legal meeting could take place but arrangements were made for the works now in progress at the Frodingham Hill to be carried on under the direction of Mr. Bartholomew the Engineer of the South Yorkshire Company	3	3	0
		Railway fare and expences	1	2	0
Septr	10	In consequence of a letter received from Mr. R. Winn respecting the Agreement between the Manchester Sheffield & Lincolnshire Railway and the South Yorkshire Railway Companies and Mr. Winn and Messrs. Dawes and the execution thereof by the Companies Perusing and considering the Agreement with reference to Mr. Winn's letter		6	8
		Writing to him in reply		5	0
39.		Making fair copy of the Agreement as signed folios 15		10	0
	26	Having received a letter from Mr. R. Winn as to some alterations made in the Agreement Writing him in reply		5	0
	27	Attending Mr. Winn on his informing us that he had been summoned to attend a meeting of the Directors to be held at Doncaster tomorrow and conferring thereon when as we had received no notice of the meeting it was arranged that Mr. Winn should send a telegram to Messrs. Baxter & Co. stating that if our attendance should be required they must telegraph to us this evening		6	8
		Attending at the Railway Station to send Telegram to Messrs. Baxter		3	4
		Paid for Message		1	6

[In pencil:] Town Hall
[Numbers on the left indicate the order of folios]

1/9/6

Summary of Expenses: T.A.G. Railway	£	s.	d.
Expenses of applying for, obtaining, and passing the Act			
Nicholson Hett & Freer, Solicitors' Bill	710	2	0
Messrs. Dyson & Co. "Parliamentary Agents' Bill"	794	7	4

[The above line is crossed out and at the side in red ink: "paid by B.R.N. & Co."]

Mr. W. C. Atkinson, Engineer's and Surveyor's Bill	211	19	0
Mr. John Lee, Surveyor's Bill	93	4	8
Mr. L. W. Lancaster, Lithographer's Bill	65	10	0
Mr. William Cressey, Printer's and Advertising Bill	23	6	10
Messrs. Brook & Co. Advertising Bill	5	1	7
Rowland Winn Esq. for Expenses in respect of this Railway extending over 37 days	59	17	10
Edmund Winn Esq. for time and expenses attending in London, 52 days	123	15	0
J. Cawkwells Bill for use of Townhall at Brigg and attendance	3	3	0
	£2090	7	3

[Crossed out]
£1295 19 11
Add^{n} correct
NW[?]

I/7/36

Correspondence on terms of agreement between R.W. and the railway companies (M.S.L. and S.Y.)—copies made by R.W.
R.W. to R. Baxter, 14 Feb. 1861

. . . .

4. You must please bear in mind . . . that I do not consent to any agreement which is not *legally* binding on the New Co and on the M.S. & L. and S.Y. Companies in perpetuity, and I think it will be necessary that the agreement should be submitted to Counsel on our behalf. I say this as I am ignorant on such matters myself but I have always been under the impression that such agreements are easily repudiated by Railway Companies tho they cannot be in the case of private individuals.

. . . .

R. Baxter to R.W., 14 Feb. 1861

. . . .

As to the last clause of your letter there is no objection of course to your taking any opinion you think necessary, but Mr. Watkin's remark upon your former letter will be increased by this that you seem to forget that the Companies are coming to your assistance, and make stipulations as if you were assisting them, and not they assisting you.

. . . .

R.W. to R. Baxter, 16 Feb. 1861

. . . .

As regards the last clause you must recollect that it is a matter of great importance to us, and I think you cannot reasonably find fault with my being cautious on the subject. We have a binding agreement with Messrs. Dawes to deliver the stone for 6d. If we forgo that and have not a binding agreement with the Railways instead, what security have we? and is it possible to forsee [*sic*] what liabilities we may [?] hereafter incur from the existing obligations with other lessees for the delivery of stone at 6d. I want nothing more than proper security to which you cannot in reason object.

I/7/36
Agreement between T.A.G. Rly, Charles Winn, and W. H. & G. Dawes. "Dated 2nd August 1861"
This Indenture made . . .

Between the Manchester Sheffield & Lincolnshire Railway Company hereafter called The Sheffield Company of the 1st part The South Yorkshire Railway and River Dun Company hereafter called the South Yorkshire Company of the 2nd part and Charles Winn of Nostell Priory in the County of York Esq and William Henry Dawes and George Dawes of Elsecar in the County of York Iron Masters hereinafter called Owners and Lessees of the 3rd part, Witnesseth that each of the said companies and the said Owners and Lessees do hereby consent and agree with and to the others and other of them as follows

1. The Bill for the Trent Ancholme and Grimsby Railway hitherto promoted by the said Owners and Lessees shall be henceforth promoted by all the said parties hereto conjointly each of the said Companies having power to nominate two Gentlemen to represent them and the said Owners and Lessees appointing two others all matters to be determined by a majority. The deposit in respect of the same Bill has as to £240 been paid by the said Chas Winn and as to the residue been paid in equal moieties by the said Sheffield and South Yorkshire Companies.

2. That the Capital required for the construction of the Line shall be found in equal third parts by the said parties hereto of the 1st 2nd and 3rd parts the said companies having power any time hereafter to buy up the shares representing the Owners and Lessees' Capital by payment of 10 Per Cent premium upon the amount.

3. That the land required for the construction of the Line between the Rivers Trent and Ancholme the property of the said Charles Winn shall be conveyed by him to the Company at the price of £110 per acre including compensation for minerals but with liberty at Mr. Winn's cost to have made by the Railway Company roads under or over the Railway not being on the level for the working of minerals on his estate lying between the Rivers Trent and Ancholme and that the works and materials already executed and found by the said Wm Hy Dawes and Geo Dawes shall be valued by the Company's Engineer Chas Bartholomew, and Messrs. Dawes Engineer Mr. John Roseby and in case of dispute shall be settled between the parties by Jno Fowler as umpire and the amount placed to their credit in their

contribution of Capital to the undertaking it being understood that as between the said Charles Winn and Wm Henry Dawes and George Dawes but not as between such 3 parties and the Company the amount to be paid for land shall be the Capital found by the said Charles Winn and the remaining capital to make up the full one-third shall be furnished by the said Wm Hy Dawes and Geo Dawes.

4. That provision shall be made if practicable in the present Bill to enable the two Companies to subscribe their two thirds and if not practicable in the present Session Parliamentary powers shall be obtained as soon as can be.

5. The following rates exclusive of pontage on the Trent shall be taken in respect of all Coal and Ironstone traffic passing for consumption on the Trent and Ancholme Local Line or passing from the Local Line and carried in Owners Waggons and in Train Loads that is to say for all such traffic to and from the Districts of the South Yorkshire Coal field loading both ways in Owners Waggons one halfpenny per ton per mile when only loaded in one-way three farthings per ton per mile for all Ironstone traffic from the Local District into Staffordshire or other foreign Station as to which the foreign Company may agree to accept their proportion of such rates one half penny per ton per mile. For Ironstone from any part of the Line between the Trent and the Ancholme in Train loads either to the sidings near the River Trent or to the sidings near the River Ancholme Sixpence per ton for the whole distance in the owners waggons for any traffic belonging to the said Chas Winn or his lineal descendants the Owners for the time being of the Appleby and Frodingham Estate and as to any other parties for the term and to the extent of any agreement already made but not further the empty waggons being brought back without charge.

6. The Bill so far as practicable to be so framed as to dispense with the Viaduct and Tunnel by adopting the gradient of 1 in 60 and the owners and lessees to give their consent to the Line being so constructed.

7. That each of the said Sheffield and South Yorks Companies shall have power to work over the Line paying in respect of such working sixty per cent of the mileage receipts (after deducting terminal charges) on all traffic worked by them.

8. That provision be made in the Bill for the management of the Line by a Joint Committee of Six of which two members shall be appointed by the Sheffield Company two members by the South Yorkshire Company and two members by the Owners and Lessees so long as the latter hold shares in the Company.

9. That the arrangement as to Tolls shall rest in the Agreement of the parties and not be inserted in the Bill.

10. A more full Agreement to be made hereafter drawn up between the parties to be settled in case of difference by J. H. Lloyd.

INDEX OF PERSONS AND PLACES